SMOKE-FILLED ROOMS

W. KIP VISCUSI

SMOKE-FILLED ROOMS

A POSTMORTEM ON THE TOBACCO DEAL

WITHDRAWN

THE UNIVERSITY OF CHICAGO PRESS
CHICAGO AND LONDON

W. Kip Viscusi is the John F. Cogan Jr. Professor of
Law and Economics and director of the Program on
Empirical Legal Studies at Harvard Law School.

The University of Chicago Press, Chicago 60637
The University of Chicago Press, Ltd., London
© 2002 by The University of Chicago
All rights reserved. Published 2002
Printed in the United States of America

11 10 09 08 07 06 05 04 03 02   1 2 3 4 5

ISBN: 0-226-85747-6 (cloth)

Library of Congress Cataloging-in-Publication Data

Viscusi, W. Kip.
   Smoke-filled rooms : a postmortem on the tobacco
deal / W. Kip Viscusi.
       p.   cm. — (Studies in law and economics)
   Includes bibliographical references and index.
   ISBN 0-226-85747-6 (alk. paper)
       1. Tobacco industry—Government policy—
   United States.   2. Cigarette industry—United
   States.   3. Cigarette smoke—Health aspects—
   United States.   4. Advertising—Cigarettes—
   Government policy—United States.   5. Tobacco
   industry—Law and legislation—United States.
   6. Smoking—Law and legislation—United States.
   I. Title.   II. Series.

   HD9136 .V57   2002
   362.29'65—dc21

                                    2002018012

♾ The paper used in this publication meets the
minimum requirements of the American National
Standard for Information Sciences—Permanence
of Paper for Printed Library Materials,
ANSI Z39.48-1992.

CONTENTS

Acknowledgments   vii

I Introduction   1

II The Proposed Federal Settlement   15

III The Settlement of the State Lawsuits   33

IV The Financial Costs of Smoking to Society   60

V The Financial Costs to the States and the Federal Government   79

VI Environmental Tobacco Smoke   101

VII Risk Beliefs and Addiction   136

VIII Youth Smoking: Beyond Joe Camel   176

IX Promoting Safer Cigarettes   194

X Lessons from the Tobacco Deal   215

Notes   223

References   243

Index   253

ACKNOWLEDGMENTS

This book is the outgrowth of more than a decade of research on smoking-related issues. During the course of this work I received funding from the National Bureau of Economic Research, the Sheldon Seevak Research Fund, the Olin Center for Law, Economics and Business at Harvard Law School, and summer research grants from Harvard Law School.

I have also served as an expert witness on behalf of the cigarette industry in a variety of venues. These efforts have focused almost exclusively on issues pertaining to risk awareness. The theme of this testimony, which is based on my extensive analysis of survey data, is simple. The health risks of smoking are considerable but are known to the public. Most of the topics addressed in this book, such as my assessment of the social costs of smoking, have not been the subject of my appearances as an expert. Neither the writing of this book nor any of the underlying statistical work was supported through any funds from either the tobacco industry or law firms representing them. Although most of the book relies on publicly available data, three smoking risk belief surveys discussed in chapter 7 were administered by nationally recognized survey research firms that were funded by the law firms representing the tobacco industry. The 1985 survey provides the basic structure that was carried over in successive versions of the survey. This survey has been the subject of my previous peer-reviewed publications, and I have published the text of the survey questions should any other researchers wish to replicate the survey. In addition, I will make available to any interested researcher the entire set of survey data for the 1985, 1997, and 1998 surveys that are discussed in the book.

This book could not have been completed without the assistance of two individuals. Neda Jury sifted through the mountain of tobacco-related materials that I had accumulated over the years and also tracked down an endless series of loose ends using her expertise in the public health field. Regina Roberts was responsible for all phases of manuscript production, as she cheerfully tackled the endless series of revisions in the draft book. Joni Hersch provided suggestions for sharpening the economic and statistical arguments. In addition, Jahn Hakes, Robert Scharff, Brett Conner, and DeYett Law assisted with statistical analyses and presentation of the statistical results.

I am especially grateful to the University of Chicago Press for their superb handling of this book project. Kathryn Krug provided excellent editing, and Geoffrey Huck and Mark Ramseyer provided enthusiastic support of the book throughout its development.

Portions of the book draw on empirical work, and some material has appeared previously in the *Journal of Law and Economics, Regulation,* the *Cumberland Law Review, Duke Law Journal, Brookings Review, Journal of Behavioral Decision Making,* and the *Tax Policy and the Economy* series published by MIT Press for the National Bureau of Economic Research.

INTRODUCTION

Cigarettes in a Market Economy

Cigarettes are the most dangerous consumer product used on a mass scale. The risks associated with smoking are extreme, including outcomes such as lung cancer, cardiovascular disease, and emphysema. Indeed, official estimates suggest that over 400,000 smokers die prematurely every year because of their smoking behavior—a figure representing more deaths than are attributed to any other product and roughly ten times the number of people killed every year in automobile accidents. Smoking is also addictive; it is hard to quit.

These risks of smoking are well known. Indeed, surveys show that people now consistently overestimate how risky smoking actually is. This awareness that smoking is dangerous is not a new development. The potential hazards of cigarettes have been well known for decades and perhaps centuries.[1]

The extent to which people who smoke are aware of the risks, together with the fact that smoking arises from market transactions by the smokers themselves, provides the context of both cigarette litigation and the smoking policy debate. Cigarettes are sold in the marketplace to consumers who choose to make these purchases. Enjoyment of smoking is not an idiosyncratic taste: smoking was once the norm among the U.S. adult population. Even now, over one in five American adults still smoke. Comparable statistics exist throughout the world.

The fundamental principle of a market economy is that consumer choices should be respected. Freedom to make such choices enables people to select those goods that best advance their welfare. If we limit these choices because we believe that people's decisions are not good for themselves or are harmful to others, then consumers will be worse off in terms of how they perceive their well-being. As a general rule, we should interfere with these private decisions only if people are making misinformed choices or if there is a pressing overriding societal concern.

In light, then, of the respect usually accorded to private consumption decisions, why is it that smokers themselves should be compensated considerable sums of money because of their smoking-related illnesses? How could a legally sold product have given rise to such a diverse assault on legal and regulatory fronts?

In the case of cigarettes, there is not only substantial knowledge in the public domain, but also the first formal warnings program that ever emerged for any consumer product other than prescription drugs. Warnings are now commonplace. While we now take warnings on dangerous products for granted, it was cigarettes that were the first among mass-marketed consumer products to bear on-product warnings, almost four decades ago. The only products with earlier warnings were those that posed acute hazards, such as rat poison and sulfuric acid, not general consumer products. Moreover, unlike the acute hazards that merited legally mandated warnings before cigarettes, the threats posed by cigarettes are not immediate or certain. Furthermore, Congress did not simply indicate a general need for cigarette warnings. It completely specified the text, format, and placement of the warnings. Public health officials have also fostered smoking risk communication efforts for decades.

In spite of these efforts to publicize the hazards of smoking, paternalism often intrudes on smoking debates in the form of claims that consumers still have not gotten the message. Such claims are not supported by empirical evidence but rather seem to be the conjecture of nonsmokers who are puzzled by people's decision to smoke despite overwhelming evidence of risks of staggering magnitude. Surely people would not smoke if they really knew the risks. Inferences along these lines, however, are contradicted by extensive survey data on smoking risk beliefs. The idea that nonsmokers have been privy to information not known to smokers simply lacks any foundation.

A second paternalistic approach is to deny the rationality of choices even if they are informed. This line of reasoning suggests that smokers are addicted and are acting in an irrational manner. Quitting smoking is certainly very difficult for many smokers, and the influence of such difficulties will be explored in this book.

When assessing such irrational-choice hypotheses, it is important to distinguish what, in fact, is really driving the paternalistic concern. Is it that smokers are making erroneous decisions given the character of their preferences and their own valuation of the smoking experience? Or is it that given our preferences as nonsmokers, we believe that they should not smoke? If people are smoking cigarettes, then surely they must be irrational. As a policy matter, extremely strong justification should be required whenever paternalistic preferences are imposed on others, because any such intervention will necessarily reduce the perceived well-being, in their own eyes, of those who are being regulated.[2]

The most extreme antismoking advocates would support a complete ban on cigarettes. However, the experience with the alcohol bans during Prohibition suggests that a ban is not feasible and will simply spur considerable illegal activity. More fundamentally, the economic basis for a ban, even if it were feasible, seems problematic. Once we have restricted smoking to the adult population and have undertaken a vigorous risk communication effort that adequately conveys the risks of smoking, then any further limitation on smoking behavior has the character of an intrusive form of paternalism. If there is harm to others in terms of medical costs or effects of secondhand smoke, these can be addressed by targeted policies short of a ban on cigarette sales.

Cigarette Litigation

Understanding the recent tobacco litigation first requires an understanding of the legal environment. Whereas personal injury cases were formerly a small-stakes legal backwater, over the past two decades there has been a tremendous change in the character of personal injury litigation. Beginning in the mid-1980s there was a substantial explosion in product liability litigation in the United States. Multimillion-dollar lawsuits, such as those for asbestos, often involve mass toxic torts with thousands of claimants. Such large-scale suits boosted the stakes involved in litigation, offering unprecedented payoffs for the plaintiffs and unprecedented losses for the defending companies.

Even within the realm of high-stakes litigation, cigarette litigation has a *Guinness Book of Records* quality. For years the industry fought off lawsuits filed by individual smokers. Despite a continuing wave of individual plaintiff lawsuits, the tobacco industry had an unblemished record of courtroom success that was possibly unrivaled by any other litigation effort. Though some plaintiffs attribute this success to "scorched earth litigation tactics," the basic fact is that when cases reached the jury, the jurors consistently concluded that the risks of cigarettes were well known and voluntarily incurred.[3]

This unbroken string of industry successes came to a halt with the state attorney general suits that began in the mid-1990s. This litigation was based on a completely untested legal concept, the validity of which many continue to question. Did states have a legal right to be reimbursed for the health-related costs that state programs incurred due to cigarettes? These lawsuits were not about health status and individual smokers' well-being at all, so there would be no emotional appeal to jurors. Rather, the lawsuits were strictly an accounting exercise, albeit a quite expensive one. What financial costs did cigarettes impose on the states? Without ever suffering an adverse jury verdict, the cigarette industry settled these suits in separate deals with four states and a Master Settlement Agreement with the remaining states. The combined price tag was $243 billion—setting a record for any damages payment. The industry's payoff of billions of dollars in plaintiffs' attorneys' fees also set records for lucrative paydays. Some observers pegged the fee amounts to be in the thousands of dollars per hour actually worked, or $18 billion to $38 billion overall.[4] The exact totals have not been made public. However, the Freedom of Information Act request by the U.S. Chamber of Commerce yielded data on twenty-one states, indicating legal fees totaling $11 billion.[5]

This turn of fortune did little to enhance the tobacco industry's image or its future prospects in court. The press labeled the industry "the new evil empire."[6] One governor justified possible ethical lapses in his antitobacco efforts as being warranted, "because I was fighting the powers of darkness."[7] When tobacco is the target, usual legal and ethical standards need not apply. The industry appeared likely to sweep all possible adverse comparisons: "Now, the tobacco industry has little more support in Congress than the Mafia, and being on the wrong side of the smoking issue would be like being on the wrong side of communism."[8]

The enormous payoff of tobacco and other large-scale suits also has profound implications for the character of the plaintiff's bar and personal injury litigation. Lawyers in such cases often work out of small firms, with modest resources to muster on behalf of their clients. The outcome of most of these suits is not a million-dollar payday, but rather coverage of the injured person's medical expenses and lost earnings.

There is also a different class of tort litigation. This is the world of high-stakes litigation, often involving class-action suits that result from the mass nature of product-related disease cases such as asbestos. One such high-stakes attorney is Texas lawyer John O'Quinn. O'Quinn and his partner, John Laminack, have been featured on the cover of *Fortune* magazine for its story on "Lawyers from Hell," or as Mr. O'Quinn likes to rephrase it, "lawyers who give them hell."[9] For these lawyers, cigarettes is just another high-stakes pit stop after reaping major rewards from the asbestos and breast implant litigation.

O'Quinn was not the only high-profile lawyer engaged in the tobacco litigation. In the tobacco litigation, I have also been deposed by a prominent Louisiana attorney, Daniel E. Becnel Jr.[10] Notwithstanding his homespun manners, Mr. Becnel is a shrewd, talented, and highly successful plaintiffs' attorney. As are many of the cigarette lawyers, he is a successful veteran of the asbestos litigation. In the year 2000, he was simultaneously juggling his involvement in large-scale suits involving cigarettes, the diet drug combination phentermine-fenfluramine, and Firestone tires. The cost of this frenzy of activity is that he is unable to spend time at his vacation home in Aspen, where he keeps a spare Mercedes for guests. However, there appear to have been offsetting financial rewards, as he claims to now own Jetway, the Mercedes-Benz dealership in Paris, and what he described to me as perhaps the world's most extensive collection of Nazi memorabilia, including Hitler's uniform.

John O'Quinn and Daniel Becnel Jr. are not the only high fliers among the cigarette case attorneys. Richard (Dickie) Scruggs, who represented Mississippi and other states, reaped roughly a billion dollars from the state tobacco settlement, and others are not far behind.[11] Indeed, ten of the top-earning lawyers profiled in the 2001 *Forbes* magazine cover story on "Killer Lawyers" were veterans of the tobacco litigation. Some, such as South Carolina attorney Joseph F. Rice, have not had the high media profile of attorneys such as John O'Quinn and Dickie Scruggs, but have nevertheless scored big in the tobacco settlement.[12] Joseph Rice brought back $2 billion in legal fees to his firm as a result of the tobacco settlement. Not wishing to be left out of the tobacco feeding frenzy, O. J. Simpson attorney Johnnie Cochran launched a cigarette class action in 2001.[13]

These successful plaintiffs' attorneys do not cash in their winnings and retire to a world of golf, though some such as Dickie Scruggs have purchased private jets to ferry them to various cases. Rather, they use these payoffs to bankroll subsequent litigation, such as Firestone tires and HMOs. The ultimate impact of the tobacco settlement will consequently go well beyond the initial price tag, as it provides the financial backing for additional suits against cigarette companies and other products, altering the tort liability landscape.

The battle against the cigarette industry had an additional element as well—consumers against Big Tobacco. Populism and the desire to transfer money from corporations to individuals remains a prominent force. The lucrative nature of high-stakes personal injury litigation seems somewhat at odds with this populist approach. In this book I will explore how these suits arose, what issues were at stake, and how a catastrophic error in judgment by the tobacco industry led to a dramatic decline in its fortunes and that of other similarly situated companies.

Information, Regulation, and Smoking Policy

Both antismoking regulations and litigation against the cigarette industry can be traced back to issues of information. Do smokers, in fact, understand the risks consequent upon their smoking decision? If people are embarking on smoking behavior with full knowledge of the consequences, their decisions should be respected. Alleged wrongful conduct by the industry is of legal concern almost exclusively to the extent that it may lead people to make mistaken decisions to smoke. As I hope to demonstrate, there is widespread understanding of the potential adverse health consequences of cigarettes as well as the difficulties of quitting smoking.

This result does not imply that there is no additional role for government policy. More can and should be done to promote market competition on the basis of the comparative safety of various cigarettes. There needs to be a better comparative risk rating scheme so that people can better understand the risks associated with particular brand choices. Safety information will promote competition among cigarette companies in developing safer cigarette designs, ultimately promoting smokers' health and well-being.

There is also a need for more financial information on which to base public policy. We often hear claims that smokers cost society a dollar a pack, perhaps even two dollars a pack. Where do such estimates come from? Shouldn't cost estimates of this magnitude play a key role in driving smoking policy? The first task is to determine whether such claims are in fact true, and we can then determine how these costs can be addressed. Do cigarettes, in fact, impose substantial costs on society, and, if so, what are these costs?

Then, too, environmental tobacco smoke has generated its own scientific debate and policy remedies. Surely cigarette smoke is a smelly annoyance. But will environmental tobacco smoke also kill you? Is secondhand tobacco smoke in fact a serious health threat? Is it as great a threat as people believe it to be? What is the most sensible basis for a regulatory policy given the effects of smoking in public places on others?

Fashioning responsible risk policies in these areas requires an accurate and honest assessment of the real consequences of smoking. Too often these debates are dominated by claims of risk of unspecified magnitude. Misrepresenting the risk to the public is not acceptable whether it is by antismoking advocates trying to stop smoking or by tobacco companies trying to encourage smoking. Policies must be based on an honest assessment of the risks, not worst-case scenarios or hopeful best-case possibilities.

Given the public's general tendency to respond in an alarmist fashion to dimly understood risks that are given substantial public attention, there is also danger for overreaction. The policy task is to convey risks of true consequence, not create alarm about minor risks. Risks that cigarettes pose to smokers are enormous, but the damages to others are not. These differences in risk do not imply that there should be no policy for minor risks, but rather that any policy that is adopted should be based on a legitimate scientific assessment of the merits of such efforts.

Unfortunately, tobacco policy is not being shaped within usual policy arenas. The most recent wave of cigarette regulations was not the result of conventional regulatory channels, but the result of the cigarette industry's backroom deal with the state attorneys general to settle their litigation. The Master Settlement Agreement with the states imposed a wide range of regulatory restrictions on the cigarette industry, including the formal retirement of Joe Camel, extensive restrictions on advertising, and public education efforts. Some of the hastily drafted policies that emerged are sensible, but others have complex repercussions including adverse anticompetitive effects on an already highly concentrated industry.

Unlike officials in regulatory agencies, these deal cutters had no legislative mandate guiding their regulatory efforts. Nor did the regulations receive scrutiny by the experts within a regulatory agency. There was no evaluation of the merits of that regulatory approach or competing alternatives. Contrary to the standard practice with federal regulatory policy, there was also no review by the U.S. Office of Management and Budget. Nor was there any public comment period so that diverse points of view and information from a wide variety of sources could be incorporated in the regulatory design. Rather, the regulatory policy emerged as the result of a secret deal cut between the tobacco industry and the state attorneys general. This agreement received no public scrutiny whatsoever. The process by which these regulations were imposed is itself objectionable in that it short-circuits the usual political processes and public input on such matters. Moreover, as I will detail below, the policies that emerged fell short in a variety of measurable ways.

The tobacco settlement also was distinctive in that it was not a damages payment in any conventional sense. Rather, it was an unprecedented imposition of an excise tax on cigarettes that was sold to the public as a damages award paid by the companies. If there are financial costs that cigarettes or other products impose on the government, the solution is simple. Legislatures can levy additional taxes to reflect these harms.

Using litigation to impose taxes usurps the traditional governmental responsibility for fiscal matters. The tobacco industry accepted the deal because it escaped litigation at a cost that would not bankrupt the industry. States embraced the deal because of the enormous financial gains—far more than could be squeezed out of the companies in any one-time damages payment. The losers in this litigation tax were the smokers, who will actually pay almost all of the tax.

These issues are of much broader significance than tobacco alone. The same kinds of suits waged against the tobacco industry could also be filed against many other risky products. Armed with their tobacco winnings, plaintiffs' lawyers have already filed similar suits against HMOs, the gun industry, and manufacturers of lead paint. Producers of alcoholic beverages and other products with a health-cost linkage may not be far behind.[14]

The harmful policy consequences of the tobacco deal and extensions of this approach to other products might have been avoided if the efforts had gone through conventional channels. The legitimate forum for regulatory policies is through regulatory efforts sanctioned with legislatively determined legal mandates. Responsibility for taxation and regulation lies with the U.S. Congress and the federal regulatory agencies. Fiscal policies such as those involving taxes receive extensive analyses by the U.S. Office of Management and Budget, the Congressional Budget Office, and the legislative committees. For regulatory efforts, agencies are required to follow a formal rulemaking process. What the tobacco litigators and their successors have done is to use litigation as the financial lever to force tax and regulatory changes. But these changes do not reflect the diverse public and institutional input that the established governmental processes incorporate. Indeed, litigation deals may even seek to overturn past legislative action. For example, the original draft Proposed Resolution of the settlement with the states would have supplanted the long-standing cigarette warnings effort with new warnings devised as part of the backroom deal. Congress, however, balked at approving this package of disguised taxes and complex regulations.

While relying on litigation makes for bad regulatory and fiscal policy, could it nevertheless have been useful in getting money to the states to defray the health-care costs of smoking? Whether there are in fact net financial costs depends on what gets counted and how the counting is done. Moreover, much of this money has not gone into health efforts. As I will document, states have used their tobacco payments to finance programs that bear little relation to the actual health costs of smoking. States did not allocate the funds to shore up Medicaid or even to launch vigorous antismoking campaigns. Rather, programs such as public works projects, highway construction, juvenile detention centers, legal fees for policemen accused of brutality, and sidewalk repair often head the list of uses.

Even if one questions the accounting of the overall level of cigarette-related health costs, there is the additional discrepancy that the share of the settlement each state reaped was not driven by their cigarette health cost share. The ultimate settlement was a political document, not a damages award. States with especially strong bargaining power, such as the state of Washington, whose attorney general brokered the deal, garnered a disproportionate share of the payoff.

Private attorneys representing the states also reaped windfall gains, with individual plaintiff attorneys getting payments in the hundreds of millions of dollars. This lucrative payday was out of line with any reasonable justification based on effort and highlights the need for establishing future reimbursement guidelines. With such enormous stakes, there is the potential for cutting sweetheart deals with political allies rather than establishing a competitive process in which lawyers are reimbursed fairly for their efforts. The way in which attorneys are recruited and reimbursed for such cases should be the focus of a serious reform effort so that payments will be fair, will elicit appropriate legal assistance, and will not be a reward to politically connected attorneys.

Putting hundreds of billions of dollars on the table did not prove to be a settlement for the industry in any meaningful sense. Other potential plaintiffs eyed the multibillion-dollar payoffs that occurred without ever going to a verdict, and saw an easy road to riches. After the state suits ended, the federal government and a whole range of other entities, ranging from labor unions and asbestos trust funds to foreign governments, sought a similar payoff. The billions in attorneys' fees also provided the financial base enabling the tobacco plaintiffs' attorneys to launch new suits against the tobacco industry and other risky products as well.

The success of the states in negotiating the settlement with the industry led to an improvement in the fortunes of individual plaintiff cases. After decades of failures, plaintiffs now started to win a few cases. A noteworthy plaintiff victory involved Patricia Henley, a lifelong smoker who contracted lung cancer and who in 1999 received a judgment of $51 million from the industry.[15] In her suit against Philip Morris, her lawyer asked for $15 million in damages. The jury topped that amount, awarding $51.5 million in damages. Subsequently, a judge reduced the damages award to $25 million, which has since been appealed. Even though such verdicts often get reduced on appeal, investors took note of this award in an individual case. Philip Morris stock dropped $12 billion in value right after the verdict.[16] The loss far exceeded the damages award in the Henley case because it increased investor expectations of losses in similar smoking cases.

Shortly thereafter, a jury in Oregon awarded $81 million to the family of Jesse Williams. Like Patricia Henley, Jesse Williams was a Marlboro smoker. Each of these awards set a record as the largest ever received in an individual lawsuit against the cigarette industry. The magnitude of the awards raised fundamental issues regarding the broader question of whether juries are able to successfully map their liability concerns onto dollar amounts in damages, which is a failing that has received substantial documentation in the law and economics literature.[17] However, even if the damages are substantially reduced on appeal, with hundreds of thousands of smokers dying every year from smoking, the scale of the potential plaintiff pool coupled with even modest damages awards could bankrupt the industry.

While these few plaintiff successes have been highly publicized, for the most part the cigarette industry has continued to win such lawsuits. These industry successes do not receive the national media coverage of the plaintiff victories. A typical example is the case of Bonnie Apostolou, a Brooklyn woman who died of lung cancer attributable to her smoking. In this 2001 Brooklyn case in which I testified for the industry on the general public knowledge regarding smoking risks, the plaintiff's attorney maintained that Bonnie Apostolou had never noticed that there were warnings on cigarette packs.[18] Moreover, even though her mother banned smoking in the house after contracting emphysema, there purportedly was never any discussion with the daughter of the link between smoking and health. The jury resoundingly rejected these claims as implausible.

Another individual case that went to trial in 2001, which seemed to fit the same profile, was that of a Los Angeles smoker who claimed to have been somehow excluded from the onslaught of smoking information. In his deposition for his case against the industry, the plaintiff, Richard Boeken, claimed to have not paid attention to the warnings on the packs of cigarettes.[19] Personal knowledge seems to have had little effect, either. His mother, who smoked two packs a day, died of lung cancer. Nevertheless, this knowledge did not influence his assessment of the risks of smoking. Mr. Boeken's background as a self-described former heroin addict with an extensive criminal record also did not seem to make him the ideal plaintiff. Shortly before I testified in this case, Michael Piuze, the attorney representing the plaintiff, remarked that he could easily sign up hundreds of such individual smoker cases, but he wanted to be selective. What was attractive about Mr. Boeken, although his personal profile seemed less than ideal, is that his case would be brought in one of the most impoverished and least well educated sections of Los Angeles. The lack of juror sophistication introduces a significant random element, which combines with the anticorporate attitude of many disaffected members of society. Some plaintiffs' attorneys hopefully refer to such juries as "slot machines."

The jury in this case paid off in record-breaking fashion—$5.5 million in compensatory damages and $3 billion in punitive damages.[20] While the appeals process has already reduced the punitive amount to $100 million, this case reflects jurors' inability to map their outrage onto dollar values in a sound way. The potential for losing big stakes in individual smoker cases was becoming an increasingly real threat.

The state settlement also may have led some jurors to view the formerly futile lawsuits by plaintiffs more favorably. Jurors might reason that surely the industry must be guilty of record-setting harms if, in fact, they paid out record-setting amounts in the hundreds of billions of dollars to settle the state attorney general cases. It is unlikely that the public will appreciate the reality of actual litigation in which firms often settle prospectively costly and uncertain litigation even in situations in which they do not believe that they will or should be found liable.

The state settlement established a high dollar anchor for future awards. Perhaps not coincidentally, the Master Settlement Agreement for over $200 billion was followed by the largest punitive damages award by a jury in U.S. history, as a Florida jury awarded $145 billion in punitive damages in a cigarette class action in the summer of 2000.[21] Although the industry may eventually succeed in its appeal of the Florida verdict, it has already paid out $709 million into a nonrefundable escrow account to eliminate the uncertainties arising from laws capping the bond amount that companies are required to post.[22] These record-setting payoffs in turn provide anchors for juries in individual cases, which have involved very large awards by any standard, such as the $51 million judgment for Patricia Henley, the $81 million judgment for the family of Jesse Williams, and the $3 billion for Richard Boeken.[23] Many observers believe the $4.9 billion award against General Motors in a rear-impact burn case also was the result of the cigarette settlement anchor, as jurors now began to think in terms of billions rather than millions.[24] The prospect of such high awards will provide additional incentives for litigation by other smokers. Consequently, rather than resolving litigation with a settlement as industry officials hoped to do, the settlement only fueled an additional wave of lawsuits against the industry.

From a societal standpoint, these private suits raise a fundamental question. Do we want to provide a bounty for people to engage in hazardous activity such as smoking cigarettes? Suppose people are aware of a risk and choose to take it. If the health outcome lottery turns out to be unfavorable, should people be rewarded with a multimillion-dollar pay-off? Future smokers, in effect, will pay for this lottery ticket at the time when they make their cigarette purchases. Companies cannot, however, recoup litigation payout costs attributable to past smoking. Past smokers who are able to claim the court payoff consequently will not pay for the lottery ticket in advance, leading to net gains for them and losses for the company.

The tobacco litigation also shapes future public policy with regard to smoking. The question is not whether the regulation of cigarettes should be more vigorous, but how cigarettes should be regulated. While the U.S. Supreme Court struck down the Food and Drug Administration's (FDA) effort to regulate cigarettes as a drug, future legislation could establish a basis for additional regulation. As I will show in this book, there is a real role for constructive cigarette regulation.

What form should such regulation take? Should the sale of ciga-rettes be discouraged through additional taxes? Should we increase the penalties on retail establishments that sell cigarettes to minors? As I will demonstrate, neither of these remedies that head the usual policy agenda should be at the top of our list. The purchase of cigarettes is al-ready discouraged more than adequately through excise taxes and the tax equivalent of the cigarette settlement payment. Prohibiting sales to minors is a worthy objective that should merit continued vigilance. However, improvements in this area will yield little additional progress in our well-founded efforts to reduce youth smoking.

The centerpiece of my cigarette policy proposal is an information effort in which the FDA rates cigarettes on the basis of their relative safety. The government should then foster competition in marketing of cigarettes along this safety dimension. It should promote technological advances in cigarette safety design just as it has fostered technological improvements in other regulatory contexts, such as the environment.

Why hasn't such an effort already happened? Indeed, why has the government often seemed to have done the opposite, by discouraging ad-vances in cigarette safety, while in every other area of government safety policy the focus has been on technological solutions to safety problems?

This gap in the smoking policy area can be traced to an overly nar-row framing of smoking policy. Government efforts have been driven by a genuine, but exclusive, concern with individual health. No form of tobacco use is completely free of risk. Stopping smoking altogether is surely safer than smoking even the safest cigarette and, as a result, the only acceptable choice in the view of public health officials is not to smoke at all.

This all-or-nothing approach misconstrues the legitimate policy mission. The appropriate policy objective is not minimizing risks to public health. Rather, it is to promote individual welfare, however that can best be done. As part of such an effort, we must also recognize that people are generally free to choose activities with some risk. Policymakers often fall prey to the zero-risk mentality. We cannot eliminate all risks from our lives. More importantly, we will harm people's welfare levels if we prohibit them from taking risks which they fully understand.

Requiring that such choices be risk-free makes not smoking at all the only permissible choice. However, so long as tobacco products are not banned, many people will continue to take risks. Taking risks is not unique to cigarette smokers. We take risks every day, whether in our jobs, our transportation decisions, or our recreational activities. The risks posed by cigarettes are not unique, but they are real and considerable. We want these tobacco risk choices to be as sensible and informed as possible, allowing people to select from a broad spectrum of risk options so that they can strike the balance between safety and product taste that best matches their own preferences. Making policies as if people will not choose to smoke neglects an important policy dimension within which we could foster safer decisions. Recognizing that some people will in fact continue to smoke, what can we do from a policy standpoint to improve their welfare?

The public health establishment also has framed its smoking position in anti-industry terms of a holy war against the evil tobacco empire. A preferable approach would be to shift the focus to advancing consumer welfare. Current policies have sacrificed a potentially powerful mechanism for promoting smokers' well-being. Once the government's task is reframed as promoting individual well-being, not waging war against the cigarette industry, there will be greater opportunity to consider policy measures that may not end smoking but will promote the health of smokers.

This informational effort might appear to be less concrete than regulatory restrictions such as advertising bans or former FDA commissioner David Kessler's proposal "to dismantle the industry" by having the government take over companies' tobacco sales.[25] However, the reliance on the informational strategy that has been a hallmark of cigarette policy is not unwarranted. Information, not regulation, has produced the greatest shift in smoking behavior. Public awareness of smoking risks is now universal. There has been a dramatic shift to filtered cigarettes and low-tar cigarettes as consumers have sought to reduce their risk. Whether current risk ratings are adequate remains a matter of much debate. What is needed is a governmental safety rating system that is recognized as being valid, enabling consumers to better match their safety concerns with their product choice. More fundamentally, the task for cigarette policy is to become pro–consumer welfare rather than simply anti-smoking.

THE PROPOSED FEDERAL SETTLEMENT

For decades the cigarette industry had maintained a record of unblemished success in the courtroom. Withstanding a steady onslaught of lawsuits, the industry succeeded in avoiding any payoffs either in out-of-court settlements or in court-awarded damages. The dangers of settlement or unfavorable verdicts were enormous; with hundreds of thousands of smokers dying annually (a figure based on the surgeon general's estimates), a successful individual suit could trigger a wave of litigation.

By 1997, however, most states had joined in this litigation effort, in a flurry of over forty lawsuits. Cigarette policy was also an active topic for the U.S. Congress, as there continued to be support for a major increase in cigarette excise taxes. It was in this atmosphere that the cigarette industry took a surprising gamble on June 20, 1997, by offering a $368.5 billion package over twenty-five years to settle the state suits seeking reimbursement for Medicaid costs attributable to smoking. After decades of avoiding any payouts, the cigarette industry was offering to make the largest payoff in the history of the U.S. civil liability system. This effort, known as the "Proposed Resolution," was intended to be the basis for federal regulation, but Congress never adopted it.[1] Why should a policy proposal that was never even adopted be of significant interest? Because for the first time, the cigarette industry displayed a willingness to pay off in litigation. The scale of the proposed payoff in the hundreds of billions of dollars was surely a landmark event in the history of cigarette litigation and civil liability more generally. The issue was no longer whether the industry would pay off, or even whether the size of the payoff would be enormous, but what exactly the final deal would be. The Proposed Resolution also established the framework for the final state settlement of the litigation. This proposal proved to be a catastrophic error in judgment on the part of the industry and, with less dire consequences, on the part of various political actors as well. How this resolution worked, why it failed, and what implications it had for the industry will be explored in this chapter.

Before considering the proposed settlement, it is useful to inquire whether there is any validity to the state suits at all. The foundation for any such suit must be some tortious conduct. How do cigarettes fare under the usual product liability criteria?[2]

As dozens of unsuccessful private suits against the industry have indicated, almost all juries conclude that the usual assumption-of-risk defense is pertinent. Smokers know that cigarettes are dangerous. The hazards of cigarettes are public knowledge and have been well known for decades, if not centuries.

Because of this knowledge, plaintiffs have often framed their cases in retrospective terms. Did the cigarette industry, for example, withhold risk information from the public back in the 1950s? Linking current smoking behavior to alleged transgressions in dimly remembered time periods often proves to be a formidable task for plaintiffs. But perhaps the warnings are inadequate? This claim is difficult to make, as Congress has specified the warnings language, format, and placement since the mid-1960s. Warnings legislation has given the industry substantial protections against warnings-based suits for the post-1969 period.

Could one instead base liability on a product defect? Cigarettes are surely very risky. However, this risk does not arise from manufacturing defects. Moreover, for there to be a design defect, the industry must have failed to adopt a safer design that does not compromise other benefits of the product. Safer cigarettes do exist and have been test-marketed, but these cigarettes provide less taste and a less enjoyable smoking experience.

If there is no basis for individual claims, then industry defenses would travel with such claims if the states undertook subrogation-like actions on behalf of the individuals. Alternatively, could the states seek reimbursement for costs they incur due to alleged tortious conduct by the industry? Public entities do not generally have the right to sue companies for such losses. Economic loss alone is not sufficient to justify such suits, according to previous court rulings.[3]

The tenuous nature of these suits is reflected in the only state supreme court ruling on the litigation. In 1998 the Iowa Supreme Court threw out the suit by the state of Iowa against the cigarette companies.[4] Despite this favorable ruling and the fact that no state case ever reached a jury verdict, the industry sought and eventually obtained a record-breaking settlement of the litigation, including a payoff to the state of Iowa. This settlement is the subject of this and the following chapter.

Fundamental Components

The Proposed Resolution was not a voluntary agreement between the cigarette industry and all the state attorneys general, as was the final outcome to be discussed in chapter 3. Rather, it was a blueprint for federal legislation that would have to be passed by Congress and signed into law by the president. That is, it was a political document subject to the subsequent political process. The parties who drafted the settlement included industry representatives and some key representatives of the states' interests, such as Mississippi attorney general Mike Moore, Republican Senate majority leader Trent Lott's brother-in-law,[5] and the increasingly well publicized brother of Hillary Rodham Clinton, Hugh Rodham.[6] Thus, there was a semblance of bipartisan participation as well as possible bipartisan sharing in the spoils of the litigation. Missing were any legislators or representatives of the public health community, although they would eventually surface in the debate over the proposal. Also absent was any real effort to develop broad political support in the development of the proposal.

Public understanding of the settlement may not have extended much beyond a single number—the widely publicized $368.5 billion face value of the first twenty-five years of cigarette industry payments. The first payment, $10 billion up front, would be followed by annual payments rising from $8.5 billion the first year to $15 billion in five years. The payments would not end after twenty-five years, but would continue in perpetuity so that focusing only on the first twenty-five years understates the long-run implications of the settlement. Payments to lawyers would be in addition to this amount but would be funded separately by the cigarette industry. Side deals to compensate the attorneys would, of course, reduce the amount the states could negotiate, but the existence of a trade-off would not be as apparent. Instead, there would be the illusion that it is only the industry bearing the costs. Keeping the legal fees separate and hidden from public scrutiny would presumably boost the payoff to plaintiffs' lawyers, who might otherwise have their share diminished if there was a perceived trade-off between the payment to the state government and the payment to the lawyers. Publicizing exorbitant lawyer fees also might lead to public pressures that could kill the agreement altogether.

The timing of the payments was not inconsequential. Although payment amounts would be adjusted upward over time to reflect price increases (by 3 percent annually or the percentage increase in the consumer price index, whichever is greater), the settlement price tag of $368.5 billion was not discounted to reflect its present value. If we were to discount the settlement payments using a 3 percent real rate of interest, the present value of the first twenty-five years of payments would be $255.6 billion, with a present value in perpetuity of $494.4 billion. Because of possible disagreements about the rate of discount, the focus of the press was on the total undiscounted package value. Not discounting also gives payments a larger and more impressive price tag.

The more important complication was that the value of the payments would vary proportionately with the unit sales volume of tobacco products. If cigarette consumption were to drop by one-fourth, the settlement payments would fall similarly. Because of the sales volume linkage, the best way to think about the proposal is in terms of the cost per pack: the payment was equivalent to an additional $0.62 per pack tax. The cigarette industry in effect agreed to an additional tax amount of $0.62 in return for reduced liability. Marketing the settlement as a damages payment by the companies rather than a tax ultimately borne almost entirely by smokers clearly boosted the public salability of the effort.[7] State and federal taxes already totaled $0.56 a pack for an annual total of more than $13 billion. The new levy would have brought the total state and federal tax per pack to $1.18.

The Role of Taxes

A lawsuit that results in a tax rather than a damages payment in itself is a noteworthy event. What is the practical economic consequence of the settlement being tantamount to a tax? Taxes have a variety of functions, from raising money for the government, to penalizing behavior some may view as immoral, to helping align private and social incentives. While this $0.62 per pack tax increase figure nominally was related to health-care costs, in fact it had little to do with these expenses. As the calculations in chapter 5 will indicate, the gross medical cost of smoking to the states is less than a tenth of this amount for every state other than New York. Net costs of course are far less.

Although the cost of the tax would be shared by consumers and firms (for firms will lose profits as sales drop), in fact almost all of that cost would be borne by consumers. Tobacco industry payments could have been structured differently—for example, as a lump sum tax on companies rather than as a per unit tax. If the tax did not vary with cigarette sales, then from an economic standpoint the tax would be borne solely by tobacco producers. But such a tax would do nothing to discourage smoking or to align private and social incentives, which also was an objective of the settlement.

Spreading the payments out over time enabled the states to receive a higher total payoff. If the states had insisted on an immediate lump sum damages payment, the affected firms could reorganize under bankruptcy laws, thus limiting their liability. Firms likewise benefited by paying off the damages through the mechanism of a tax, thus shifting most of the costs to smokers. The main losers from this proposed deal consequently would be smokers themselves.

Antismoking critics of the Proposed Resolution wanted to have it both ways. They liked per unit taxes borne by smokers because such taxes would discourage consumption and reduce societal smoking rates. But they also wanted companies to suffer and to bear all the tax, and they wanted payments to the government to remain the same even as sales declined with high per pack tax levies. The form a tax takes will affect whether it primarily decreases consumption or it decreases firm profitability alone. From the standpoint of social efficiency, it makes the most sense to link the tax to cigarette consumption if our intent is to make product purchasers recognize the social costs of their smoking decision, assuming of course that the penalty is in fact based on social costs, not simply on what the traffic will bear in the negotiations between the industry and the attorneys general litigants.

The differential effects of the tax are of particular interest. The general range of empirical estimates suggests that a 10 percent jump in cigarette prices would cause a 4–7 percent drop in smoking overall. Suppose that younger smokers tend to be more responsive to cigarette prices than are older smokers. Some estimates suggest that a 10 percent price increase could cause smoking by teenagers to fall 12–14 percent. If such estimates are in fact true, the tax may be particularly effective in discouraging youth smoking. Many other studies fail to show a differential effect for younger smokers, so that tax penalties may affect all smokers symmetrically, in which case the youth smoking deterrence argument is less compelling. But even if there is no differential effect on youths, higher taxes will reduce smoking overall.

Another noteworthy distributional aspect of the taxes is that cigarette smokers tend to be poorer and more likely to be blue-collar workers than the average American. Indeed, cigarette taxes are regressive not only in terms of the percentage of income going toward the tax, but also in absolute terms. Those in lower income groups pay more in terms of the total dollars of cigarette taxes than the very affluent. Such concerns may have led to the failure to enact a cigarette tax as part of the mid-1990s health insurance proposals.

Viewed in political terms, what was at stake? Even in the absence of this Proposed Resolution, there was considerable pressure in the U.S.

Congress for a major tax increase on cigarettes. If taxes would rise anyway, why not get something in return? Through this agreement the industry was proposing to trade off a $0.62 per pack tax increase against protection from much of the pending litigation. If this disguised tax increase dampened legislative enthusiasm for other excise tax proposals, then the cigarette industry would have obtained partial relief from litigation costs in return for some tax increases that it expected to incur independently of the Proposed Resolution.

Nonprice Components of the Proposal

Although the settlement's impressive price tag captured most public attention, the agreement would also have led to sweeping nonprice regulatory measures. The Food and Drug Administration would have taken on broad authority to regulate cigarettes. The marketing and advertising of cigarettes would have changed dramatically. The settlement was not a "settlement" in any usual sense, but a comprehensive and complex regulatory and tax package, a major public policy initiative.

The significance of the proposed policy changes was enormous. The Proposed Resolution would have given the FDA authority to regulate cigarettes as a drug. This issue has since been the subject of a major line of litigation in which the tobacco industry prevailed. After a series of appeals, the Supreme Court ruled in 2000 in favor of the industry.[8] If the FDA had obtained regulatory authority, the prospect of regulating nicotine levels and other cigarette characteristics would be quite real.[9]

Whether the FDA could regulate cigarettes as a drug was a difficult legal issue. Justice Stephen Breyer and prominent legal scholars such as Cass Sunstein (1998) observed that the medical designation of nicotine in cigarettes had changed over time, from a habituating substance to an addictive drug. As a result, in their view, it now was within the purview of FDA drug regulation. A four-judge majority of the Supreme Court led by Justice Sandra Day O'Connor concurred with scholars such as Richard Merrill (1998) who maintained that if Congress had wished to include cigarettes in the FDA mandate, it would have done so.

Regulation through litigation rather than agency rulemaking is not a satisfactory outcome. Cigarette regulations would be emerging not through a rulemaking process, in which the merits of regulations are properly assessed, but as the result of negotiations between the state attorneys general and the industry.

A superior outcome from the standpoint of sound public policy would be for Congress to broaden the FDA's authority in an explicit manner if it believes that the scope of its regulation of cigarettes should be greater. Subject to these legislative constraints, the FDA can establish regulations that conform to its legislative guidelines and which reflect the diverse input by the public and the Executive Office of the President, which are key components of the rulemaking process. In that regard, the FDA's attempt to venture into the cigarette regulation area had far more legitimacy than would a privately negotiated settlement with the states.

If, however, the FDA had the authority to regulate cigarettes as a drug, the consequences for cigarettes as a product might have been dire. All drugs must meet requirements of safety and efficacy. Because cigarettes are inherently unsafe, it is difficult to see how the agency could have done anything except ban cigarettes altogether.

Under the terms of the Proposed Resolution, cigarette packages would have a new series of nine rotating warnings, all intended to be bolder than those used now. The principal change was not in terms of signaling risk levels, but in conveying more succinct and diverse messages than those now included on cigarettes. The new set of rotating warnings would have been the following:

- "WARNING: Cigarettes are addictive."
- "WARNING: Tobacco smoke can harm your children."
- "WARNING: Cigarettes cause fatal lung disease."
- "WARNING: Cigarettes cause cancer."
- "WARNING: Cigarettes cause strokes and heart disease."
- "WARNING: Smoking during pregnancy can harm your baby."
- "WARNING: Smoking can kill you."
- "WARNING: Tobacco smoke causes fatal lung disease in non-smokers."
- "WARNING: Quitting now greatly reduces serious risks to your health."

At first glance, such warnings might seem to be innocuous and possibly even desirable. But do those new warnings make sense? Do they fill any actual gaps in consumer knowledge and foster more accurate risk beliefs? Cigarette warnings would have emerged from a process in which lawyers huddled around a conference table and drafted what they thought was appropriate language rather than finding out from consumers what they need to be told to be better informed. In this case, the secret negotiations of plaintiff and defense attorneys led to the proposed warnings list without any input from the public or responsible regulatory agencies.

How should warnings be devised? Over the past two decades I undertook a series of efforts for the U.S. Environmental Protection Agency to establish guidelines for hazard warning designs.[10] First, the government should identify informational gaps. What is it about the risks of smoking that people don't already know? A salient informational gap for which there is actual evidence is that concerning the comparative risks of different cigarette brands. As I will outline in the chapter 9, the government can take a much more aggressive role in fostering an understanding of the hazards of different cigarette brands.

Second, warnings that simply serve as reminders and tell people what they already know have no significant effect on behavior. Does the general public really believe that smoking does not boost mortality risks? Many of the proposed warnings either assume a stark level of ignorance, or, in effect, attempt to browbeat consumers into changing their behavior rather than providing new knowledge. The experience with such reminder warnings has been so dismal that some former U.S. Consumer Product Safety Commission officials concluded that such warnings are not a workable policy option.[11] A prominent example is the "Buckle Up for Safety" campaign, which yielded few demonstrable increases in seatbelt usage. Wasting valuable warning space on smoking information that is well known has a real opportunity cost. Reminder warnings decrease the frequency with which more effective warnings can be provided and read. They also needlessly distract consumers' limited attention, and make consumers more resistant to warnings by giving them practice in ignoring them.

Third, the processing of warnings is subject to a variety of cognitive limitations. Information content, structure, and format have a substantial effect on how the warning is processed. Does it matter that the warnings in the Proposed Resolution are not from the U.S. surgeon general? There is no source at all indicated in the warnings specified by the Proposed Resolution. Does the change in the wording of the warnings lead people to form different and more accurate risk beliefs than they otherwise would?

These and other issues should be the subject of field testing for which the objective is to ascertain what warnings language will foster more accurate consumer risk beliefs, which is different from simply creating antismoking attitudes. The task is to inform choice, not to discourage choice if it happens to be a prosmoking choice. If we believe that those who smoke are doing so in error, we should explore what it is that people need to be told to give them the informational base to make sound decisions that avoid these purported errors.

Credible warnings efforts ultimately hinge on whether consumers believe the effort to be honest and objective. By leaving consideration of consumer knowledge and warnings processing out of the warnings design effort, the drafters of the Proposed Resolution failed to exploit the insights of what is now a substantial scientific literature on hazard warnings design.

The Proposed Resolution would have banned outdoor advertising of cigarettes, and have restricted advertising to prohibit the use of cartoon characters, such as Joe Camel, and human figures, such as the Marlboro man. Except in adults-only facilities and publications, cigarette companies would be restricted to black text advertising. The federal government would launch a $500 million annual antismoking advertising campaign, as well as a variety of other antismoking efforts, such as federal restrictions on smoking in public.

The Proposed Resolution would also have restricted tobacco sales in a variety of ways. In addition to restrictions such as a minimum age of eighteen for the purchase of tobacco products, the proposal sought to ban all cigarette sales through vending machines as well as all self-service tobacco displays except in adults-only facilities. The proposed legislation would also have established a licensing system for tobacco sellers, coupled with a monitoring system. There would be penalties for violations such as selling to underage smokers as well as the prospect of suspension or revocation of licenses.

A potentially innovative reform in the Proposed Resolution called for the establishment of explicit policies for lower-risk cigarettes. Whether this effort would have institutionalized current barriers to disseminating information about lower-risk cigarettes or promoted such information dissemination depends on its implementation, which was not specified. Some provisions would discourage or regulate claims such as "low tar" and "light" unless the product could be proven to "significantly reduce the risk to health." No details were provided as to how this would be done. A manufacturer could demonstrate that a product had lower tar levels, but would that suffice in proving a significantly lower health risk? Whether this aspect of the proposal would promote diversity in cigarette risk choices, as I propose in chapter 9, or be used to discourage such efforts is unclear.

If the company devised safer cigarettes, there would be some opportunity to market cigarettes with safety claims. Under the proposal, the FDA could "permit scientifically-based specific health claims" and even "mandate the introduction of 'less hazardous tobacco products' that are technologically feasible." As a consequence, the FDA might be in the position of fostering safer cigarette designs. This quite sensible policy approach would in fact have been a marked departure from the current policy emphasis.

Both the nonprice regulatory provisions and the financial costs associated with the proposal would have lowered cigarette consumption. As sales declined, so too would the amounts paid by the tobacco industry as part of the settlement. Industry critics bemoaned the decrease in revenues that necessarily will accompany reduced consumption achieved through higher cigarette prices. However, setting taxes and penalties that reflect the costs of cigarettes should discourage smoking.

As indicated above, the Proposed Resolution included a wide variety of measures targeted at reducing underage smoking. In addition to setting a minimum age of eighteen to purchase tobacco products, it would have required photo identification of anyone under age twenty-seven, banned the sale of tobacco products through vending machines, banned self-service displays of tobacco products except in adults-only facilities, licensed retail tobacco product sellers and required conformance with the terms of the license as a condition for holding it, imposed penalties for violations, and decreased payments to states that do not meet the "no sales to minors" performance targets. Such stringent, carefully structured efforts are well suited to addressing a problem restricted to a segment of the smoking population.

The Proposed Resolution would have established a series of targets for reducing smoking by youths: a 30 percent decline in underage use of cigarette products within five years, a 50 percent decline within seven years, and a 60 percent decline within ten years. If these targets were not met, additional "look-back" provisions would have increased the penalties by up to $2 billion per year. Penalizing firms for such failures to meet youth smoking targets is problematic unless tobacco firms exerted more control than they currently do over young people's access to cigarettes.

Much of the impetus for proposals that the tax be raised by $1.50 per pack was that a $0.62 tax alone will not discourage consumption sufficiently to meet the stated youth smoking targets. The estimates of the effect of the $0.62 tax, however, neglected the role of the nonprice measures as well as the markup that will occur on the taxes before they reach the retail level.

A more basic concern about using price as the principal policy lever for discouraging youth smoking is that underage smokers are but a small fraction of the total cigarette market. As will be discussed in chapter 8, the best available estimates indicate that roughly 95–97 percent of all cigarettes are consumed by those over eighteen years of age. Increasing prices for all consumers is thus a blunt policy instrument for discouraging youth smoking. Doing so will impose substantial costs on people who are of legal smoking age and too often are relatively poor. Policies specifically targeted at reducing underage smoking can foster this objective more equitably.

What Tobacco Firms Would Get

Not all the provisions in the proposed legislation favored the states. Others, pertaining primarily to civil liability, were favorable to the financial health of the cigarette industry, thus making the deal attractive to both sides.

Most important, the legislation would have ended all present and future actions by state attorneys general. Cigarette companies would escape the potential liability they could face because of an unfavorable ruling about which costs count or because of an unpredictable jury.

The settlement would also have precluded all future addiction or dependence claims, all class actions, and all claims for punitive damages. Individuals, however, could still sue for past conduct, so that in the long run the industry would not be free of the current set of liability concerns. However, an overwhelming amount of the current high-stakes litigation would have disappeared. Thus, the Florida class action verdict for $145 billion would have been precluded because it was for a class action and consisted almost entirely of punitive damages.

The value of these restrictions on liability is hard to assess. Certainly the tobacco company payments stipulated by the legislation greatly exceeded any liability sum that would be estimated on the basis of past success rates in litigation. But the stakes involved are enormous, with the outcomes being highly correlated. Additional amounts imposed by suits similar to the Florida class action could boost these costs even further. Losing one state suit, for example, greatly increases the likelihood of losing others. Addiction claims likewise could snowball if the cigarette industry developed a losing track record. A global settlement would give the industry a safe harbor from the vagaries of the tort system and the randomness of jury awards.

The Proposed Resolution would not have provided for compensation of the plaintiffs' lawyers, but parallel agreements would have led to such payouts. Total fees to lawyers would be in the billions. At the time the Proposed Resolution was being debated, the private lawyers retained by Florida sought contingency fee payments of $2.8 billion, or 25 percent of the total settlement. This amount dwarfs their actual legal expenses, much of which were incurred after the national settlement was proposed, making compensation likely.[12] Thus, the lawyers in this case were not gambling their time for the hopes of a contingency fee payoff. In its initial review, the court rejected this legal fee claim, noting that "$2.8 *billion* simply shocks the conscience of the court."[13] Shocking or not, the multibillion-dollar payday was not far off.

How the Proposed Resolution Failed

This Proposed Resolution of the summer of 1997 was the landmark event in the history of the cigarette litigation. It marked a dramatic shift in the balance of power between the cigarette industry and plaintiffs against the industry. For the first time, it was clear that the cigarette industry was willing to make enormous payments in the hundreds of billions of dollars to settle litigation against it. The Proposed Resolution initially received broad support when the announcement was forwarded to Capitol Hill, but neither house of Congress ever enacted legislation on that matter.

Missing from the political effort was an endorsement of the Proposed Resolution by President Bill Clinton. He withheld his endorsement, waiting to see the reaction of the public health community. That contingent, which included people such as former FDA commissioner David Kessler, believed that if the cigarette industry could afford $0.62 a pack, that they could be squeezed for much more. Thus, the task was not to find a penalty amount that bore a relationship to what the parties had agreed to or any measure of the costs of cigarettes. Rather, they set out to find the highest tax that the traffic would bear so as to discourage cigarette smoking.

In September 1997, President Clinton lent some public support to the $1.50 hike in a pack of cigarettes sought by public health advocates.[14] What is noteworthy is that President Clinton also never endorsed the Proposed Resolution or advanced a proposal of his own. Put somewhat differently, he never became actively engaged in the legislative resolution of the controversy. Without such presidential support, there was not sufficient backing for any legislative solution. Whether this lack of support was the fault of the Clinton administration, the failure of the negotiators of the Proposed Resolution to engage the administration earlier, or the pressures exerted by the more extreme public health officials and antitobacco forces is unclear.

Clinton did attempt to have the federal government share in the payoff. Clinton suggested that the federal government was entitled to a share of the tobacco money from the state settlement to pay for Medicaid-related recoveries.[15] Thus, rather than filing a separate claim for damages, as became the federal strategy announced in 1999, in 1997 Clinton simply sought a share of the payment to the states to be designated for the federal government. His efforts were resisted by the states, which viewed the federal encroachment on the settlement as taking funds that were rightfully theirs. While it is true that the states initiated the litigation, the basis for the claims in the litigation was that cigarettes increased the total cost of Medicaid, including the federal costs. In preparing their calculations of the dollar losses to the states, the universal practice in the state lawsuits was to include not only the state costs of Medicaid, but also the federal share. Thus, Clinton's attempt to obtain part of the settlement for the federal government was entirely consistent with how the states calculated the damages for which they should be compensated. It was not an unwarranted money grab, as the states characterized it.

In the fall of 1997, lawmakers began to hold hearings on the Proposed Resolution and to prepare alternative versions of the tobacco legislation. In November 1997, Senator Ted Kennedy introduced legislation to increase the cost of the proposed tobacco agreement by raising federal excise taxes on each pack of cigarettes by $1.50 over the next three years.[16] Whereas the cost of the proposed settlement of the litigation was $368.5 billion over twenty-five years, the cost of the Kennedy bill to the industry was pegged at $600 billion over that same period.[17] Moreover, in addition to hammering the industry with substantial financial penalties, the Kennedy bill would have taken out of the Proposed Resolution all the various protective provisions granting the tobacco industry immunity from some kinds of litigation. From the industry's standpoint, the agreement was all costs and no benefits.

Because Clinton had backed off of attempting to reap a portion of the state settlement for the federal government, in January 1998 he proposed a $0.50–$0.60 a pack federal price increase in the fiscal 1999 budget. His proposal had the political hook of being an antitobacco measure; in addition, he designated these funds for a series of new programs including a $21.7 billion child care program. Linking children's health and smoking would be an ongoing theme used in attempting to broaden the political appeal of his initiative.[18]

Although President Clinton included some funds from the prospective tobacco litigation as part of his 1999 budget, for the most part he remained on the sidelines well into the tobacco bill debates. Even long before the negotiations unraveled, the dangers of presidential inaction were apparent to Senate majority leader Trent Lott, who observed that the Proposed Resolution was "dead in the water" unless President Clinton showed more initiative: "He's got to put his fingerprints on it, and he's got to lead . . . now he's spending the money."[19] Similarly, Representative Tom Bliley (R-VA) noted Clinton's expressed concern with teen smoking, but also indicated a need for White House action to assist in this process. More specifically, he observed: "If reducing teenage smoking is the White House's bottom line, as it is mine, calling for action is not enough. The president must take action, exert leadership and work with Congress to resolve the problem. We've yet to see a legislative proposal from the White House."[20]

As the terms of the initial Proposed Resolution continued to spin out of control, at the end of January 1998 representatives for the tobacco industry appeared before the House Commerce Committee to reexamine the addictiveness of nicotine and to boost support for the $368.5 billion settlement they had negotiated.[21] This effort did not prove to be successful in making the Proposed Resolution the focal point for legislation. Various alternative bills began to proliferate. Senator James Jeffords of Vermont offered legislation to give the FDA authority to regulate tobacco products, and Senator Kent Conrad of North Dakota also developed a proposed bill.[22] At that point the issue was not simply the exorbitant cost of the proposed bills, but also the issue of immunity. Whereas the initial proposal was for a $0.62 per pack cost increase for which the tobacco industry would receive the benefit of legal immunity in various contexts, the industry was now losing on both fronts. The increased cost per pack in some bills had risen as high as $1.50, and the immunity provisions were gone. The terms of the original bargain began to become quite unfavorable to the industry, which threatened a walkout of their support if the Clinton administration did not commit on the immunity issue.[23]

Notwithstanding these protestations that the deal would fall apart if there were not some immunity provisions, other bills continued to emerge that were highly unfavorable to the industry. On March 28, 1998, Republican Senator John McCain of Arizona, who was chair of the Senate Commerce Committee, introduced a bipartisan bill that would have been much tougher on the industry than was the Proposed Resolution.[24] The bill provided for a $1.10 per pack cost increase over the next five years, which was roughly double what the Proposed Resolution had set as the levy. Moreover, the bill would have denied the industry almost all the provisions for legal relief that were included in the Proposed Resolution.[25] In the industry's view, the support of the White House for the McCain bill, which did not include immunity provisions, was a reversal of the president's previous position. He had indicated on February 5, 1998, that he would accept reasonable limitations on civil liability of the tobacco industry in return for appropriate restrictions and regulation of the industry.[26]

After hearing that McCain's Senate bill would not include protections for industry, the company reaction was swift and direct. As British American Tobacco Limited Industries chief executive Martin Broughton responded to this prospective bill: "If that's all that's on the table, forget it. Not interested. End of story."[27]

The prospects for immunity for the tobacco industry with respect to lawsuits against it faded as more comprehensive pieces of legislation were rejected by the Senate. Ultimately, immunity provisions were off the table altogether. In April 1998, the Senate voted 79 to 19 to oppose granting the tobacco industry immunity against lawsuits as part of any package.[28]

The industry announced its opposition to the McCain bill almost immediately.[29] RJR chief executive officer, Steven F. Goldstone, held a highly publicized press conference in which he vowed to devote all of his company's resources to defeating the McCain bill. Whereas the industry had supported the Proposed Resolution which had a substantial cost of $368.5 billion, he observed that the industry's funds were not unlimited: "The industry is not a Brinks truck overturned in the middle of the highway." Goldstone commented, "Washington has rushed to collect more tobacco revenues while playing the politics of punishment."[30]

It was only after the industry withdrew its support for the legislation and indicated that it would aggressively oppose such legislation that President Clinton became a truly visible figure in the debate, calling the industry's position "a big mistake" and indicating "We're going to get this done. Now they can be part of it, or they can fight it." This saber-rattling by President Clinton proved to be largely symbolic, as it was too late to have any effect.[31]

As the debate over cigarettes evolved, one problem that was never solved even by the ultimate resolution of the settlement with the voluntary bargains with the states was the limitation on the fees for the attorneys for the states. There was little public support for these attorney fees, which surpassed even generous lottery winnings and dwarfed the payoffs on the *Who Wants to Be a Millionaire?* TV show. As Senator John McCain observed: "There is a lot of ill will out there over the prospect of these attorneys becoming billionaires."[32] The allusion to "billionaires" was not hyperbole—this in itself was a telling indication of the unprecedented magnitude of the stakes.

To bolster political support for the effort, the youth smoking political hook became increasingly prominent as the last stages of the tobacco legislative debate unfolded. Some Republicans used the youth smoking issue as the rationale for breaking with industry in supporting prospective legislation. House Speaker Newt Gingrich appearing on *Larry King Live* observed: "I thought that the documents that came out that proved that tobacco companies had tried to addict 14-year-olds and that proved they have been lying to us for the past 40 years totally left the tobacco companies without any defense."[33]

The youth smoking rationale for marketing tobacco legislation was exemplified in the statement by spokeswomen Linda Ricci for the U.S. Office of Management and Budget, who made the following comments on behalf of the McCain bill: "We believe that the bill is supported by Democrats and Republicans because it will curb youth smoking in a sensible way without putting anyone out of business."[34] However, the overwhelming share of the costs would not be borne by underage smokers. Moreover, the youth smoking regulatory provisions could stand on their own without a broader cigarette tax.

As the debate over the tobacco bill became increasingly undisciplined, the Senate included a marriage penalty tax cut as part of the bill on June 10, 1998, and then on June 11, 1998, rejected an amendment to the bill that would have limited attorneys' fees arising from the tobacco settlement. By June 17, 1998, the Senate had killed the tobacco bill altogether.[35]

The White House eventually attacked the industry opposition and indicated that it would attach tobacco legislation to "every piece of legislation that comes down the pike."[36] However, this pledge occurred after the White House had been relatively silent for almost a year after the announcement of the Proposed Resolution. Notwithstanding this bravado, tobacco legislation faded from view until the following January when President Clinton made allusions to proposing a new tobacco excise tax as a late addition to his 1999 State of the Union Address. This tax increase proposal disappeared without a trace.

Senator McCain blamed uncompromising public health officials for the failure of his legislation: "We were driven by [former surgeon general C. Everett] Koop and [former Food and Drug commissioner David A.] Kessler and organizations that said we couldn't give up on anything. It's a lesson I've learned for campaign finance reform: You can't let the perfect be the enemy of the good."[37]

The Significance of the Proposed Resolution

The Proposed Resolution was the watershed event in the history of tobacco litigation. For the first time, the tobacco industry not only did not vigorously resist efforts to provide compensation in a cigarette-related matter, but in fact offered to provide for hundreds of billions of dollars in compensation to the states. Had this gambit succeeded, the tobacco industry would have greatly restricted its liability and put an end to the state cigarette cases in return for a $0.62 per pack increase in the cigarette tax. Rather than a conventional damages payment borne by the industry, the payoff would be an excise tax borne largely by smokers. Because there were already pressures in Congress to boost the excise tax, to the extent that this effective tax increase dampened those pressures, the net cost would have been far less than $0.62 per pack. For example, if there had been a $0.55 per pack federal tax increase along the lines suggested in 1999 by President Clinton, then the net excise tax boost would only be $0.07 per pack above this amount.

This bold gamble on the part of the cigarette industry proved to be a catastrophic error. Rather than resolving the cigarette litigation, this venture simply set the stage for the subsequent payoff to the states without the accompanying restriction on liability. Armed with the proceeds of the billions of dollars of legal fees derived from the state settlements, plaintiffs' lawyers would soon be mounting an attack on a wide variety of fronts against the cigarette industry and other potentially lucrative industry targets. The net effect was that rather than putting an end to the litigation, the failure of the Proposed Resolution sparked an enormous wave of high-stakes multibillion-dollar cases that continue to threaten the viability of the entire industry.

The representatives of the public health community also did not fare particularly well. By insisting on a draconian tax increase of $1.50 per pack without any reduction in cigarette company liability, the health-care establishment overplayed its hand. While there was widespread public support for serious reform, it did not provide sufficient political impetus for the kinds of restrictive measures that would impose costs on the tobacco industry with no apparent benefits. The public at large was potentially a principal loser, because Congress could have used this opportunity to enact appropriate regulatory reforms based on a thorough legislative review of regulatory options.

The broad scope of the Proposed Resolution was also much more comprehensive than the ultimate outcome resulting from negotiations with the various state attorneys general. There were many attractive features in some of the policy proposals included in the Proposed Resolution. However, the context in which these proposals were developed was certainly not ideal for developing a responsible cigarette policy. The principal players were state attorneys general and representatives of the industry. Representatives of executive-branch agencies with ongoing authority over cigarette-related matters had no central role in the negotiations. This lack of political input on what would ultimately be a legislative proposal in the U.S. Congress contributed to its failure.

Neither the industry nor the public health representatives should be taken to task for protecting the interests of their respective groups. The agreement failed in part because of a lack of political support from President Clinton. After the Proposed Resolution was announced, there was no endorsement by the White House. More tellingly, there was not even an alternative proposal advanced by the White House that could serve as the focal point for the public debate. Unfortunately, the extreme positions of the public health community may have discouraged more active presidential involvement. The most prominent piece of legislation that did emerge was the bill proposed by Republican Senator John McCain. However, this bill always lacked any industry support, at the same time that it was viewed as insufficiently stringent by the most prominent public health advocates, and as a consequence went down to defeat. The Proposed Resolution did, however, provide the basis for a negotiated settlement that would soon follow.

THE SETTLEMENT OF THE STATE LAWSUITS

The settlement of the suits brought by the state attorneys general against the cigarette industry for $206 billion in 1998 resolved the impasse over the Proposed Resolution. The financial stakes dwarfed even the largest tort liability judgments and punitive damages awards in U.S. history. Moreover, the party paying the costs was the cigarette industry, which to date had been almost unscathed after decades of litigation involving the hazards of smoking.

Perhaps the most fundamental puzzle is not why the settlement amount was so large, but why the companies paid off the states at all. Evidence to be examined in subsequent chapters indicates that cigarettes are self-financing at both the national level and the state level. If cigarettes in effect pay their own way and there are no net costs to society, why is it that the states reaped what would appear to be a windfall gain? Which costs count and how cigarette costs are tallied will, however, affect the assessment of the costs of cigarettes to the states. Cigarettes do in fact increase expected health-care costs. Whether the courts would conclude that cigarettes were on balance self-financing consequently depended on which other cost effects the courts would recognize in determining the economic loss to the states. The potential for punitive damages and runaway juries also presented the industry with a potentially unfavorable lottery outcome.

The settlement led to an enormous payoff to the states. The unprecedented size and scope of the settlement alone make it of considerable interest. The settlement also raises other intriguing issues regarding the structure of the payments and their disposition. To what extent is the settlement tantamount to an excise tax, as was the formula in the Proposed Resolution? Which states have gained the most from the settlement, based on estimates of the underlying medical costs that gave rise to the claims? How have the lawyers representing the states fared as a result of the settlement provision for attorneys' fees? Addressing these issues is pertinent not only to the cigarette litigation but also to all future litigation of this type.

Litigation versus Taxes

For market outcomes to be efficient, all costs associated with the use of a product must be borne by the consumer. If, for example, consumers impose costs on others that are not reflected in the price of a particular consumer good, they will consume "too much" of that good. Economists call such costs inflicted on others outside of the market transaction "externalities." A conventional solution to such externalities is to impose an appropriate tax. If, for example, consumption of a product imposes 25 cents per unit cost on others, then a tax of 25 cents per unit will create efficient incentives for the "correct" amount of product use. The tax may lead the consumers to generate an efficient amount of harm, but there is also the task of getting the 25 cent penalty to the party who is harmed. Such compensation for any loss in welfare is needed to ensure that the outcome is equitable. Even without such targeting of the payments, the penalty level itself will be sufficient to promote efficient levels of risk. For example, a properly set penalty on heavily polluting vehicles will lead consumers to recognize the costs of their pollution, which must be offset by some other valuable car attribute if the product is to remain attractive for purchase.

The lawsuits filed by the state attorneys general have similar economic underpinnings. The fundamental concern is with the financial cost smoking imposes on the states. The chief economic cost is that cigarettes have an adverse effect on individual health, boosting health-care costs and the associated financial burden on the states.

A key question raised by the litigation is why the states pursued a litigation strategy at all rather than following the economic textbook prescription of levying excise taxes. Unlike externality taxes in general, this tax would present no problem in directing the payment to the injured party because it is the state government itself that has suffered the financial harm. Thus, the state could tax the product at the time of sale rather than suing the cigarette industry after the fact for these costs. Were the states truly ignorant of the smoking–health cost linkage? Moreover, even if the states just learned of cigarette risks, they could impose a tax in the future, which is what the settlement primarily did.

Taxes have advantages over legal action. They create incentives at the time of sale for efficient use of the product. In contrast, unanticipated liability costs will not affect product prices. If, for example, the purpose of these suits is to recoup net costs incurred over the previous decades of cigarette consumption, then the prices consumers paid in the past for cigarettes did not reflect these costs, and people smoked too much given the costs of smoking. Appropriate taxes reflecting the social harm of current consumption will lead to correct consumption choices now. They cannot correct for past errors. However, is it really credible that the states were unaware of the adverse health effects of smoking until now and consequently did not foresee a potential role for taxes?

It is noteworthy that both the Proposed Resolution and the Master Settlement Agreement of the state attorneys general case each ultimately had a tax-like structure for collecting the settlement amount, insofar as payment is linked to the number of cigarette packs sold. If state legislatures impose excise taxes directly, they avoid the considerable litigation costs and attorneys' fees associated with the state suits. These costs are in the billions and represent a loss from what could have been paid to the states. Providing attorneys with billion-dollar legal bounties also creates incentives for more speculative litigation efforts.

Potentially superior policy routes could have been taken, but were not. What is the government failure that did not produce efficient taxation before the litigation? Why did not state legislatures levy the appropriate tax in the past to cover the costs of smoking? Or perhaps previous tax levels were already appropriate. Prospectively, why didn't the state legislatures simply tax cigarettes now in recognition of whatever the perceived costs of cigarettes are? The cigarette settlement will prove to be largely tantamount to an excise tax on future packs of cigarettes. State tax levies could have accomplished the same objective without incurring the enormous litigation costs and attorneys' fees. What was the market failure in the political arena?

Moreover, whatever tax was levied would have been the result of open legislative bargaining rather than a backroom deal involving state attorneys general eager for self-promotion. Mississippi attorney general Michael Moore intended to use the success of the settlement as a springboard to the governorship. Other attorneys general, such as Scott Harshbarger from Massachusetts and Skip Humphrey from Minnesota, featured their antismoking efforts in their unsuccessful 1998 gubernatorial campaigns. Senator McCain used the visibility from the tobacco in his unsuccessful bid for the Republican nomination for the presidency. It is not coincidental that the broad settlement agreement was reached shortly after the 1998 elections. Governors in liberal strongholds such as Massachusetts waited until after the election before signing on because they did not wish to risk the ire of the extreme anti-smoking forces who opposed any settlement.

Cigarette executives likewise may have been subject to a variety of incentives other than the national interest. Because tobacco company stock prices jumped whenever the prospects of a settlement appeared likely, there was a strong financial rationale for ending the litigation. Indeed, Philip Morris stock continues to perform quite strongly in the postsettlement period. If, however, the companies had beaten market expectations and won these suits, then that would have been an even better financial outcome that would also have affected the firms' fortunes favorably. Cigarette executives did not take any of these cases to a verdict, as they were perhaps fearful of the legal uncertainties.

A settlement agreement whereby in effect the industry agrees to a higher excise tax to end the litigation has an additional advantage as well. If the industry was likely to face political pressures to incur a higher excise tax, then a settlement that imposes a virtual tax may dampen the political impetus for even higher actual taxes.

Another reason for imposing a cigarette tax through the guise of a complex legal settlement is that legislators would not have to suffer the political fallout from having imposed a tax. Rather, the attorneys general seem to be punishing the cigarette companies, whereas it is the smokers who will bear the preponderance of the tax.[1] Although cigarette companies nominally pay the penalty, its linkage to sales ensures a tax-like structure.

The question nevertheless remains as to why the damages payment was in the form of a tax. This is not the norm for damages. The more typical form would be in the form of a lump sum payment equal to the value of the damages award. In some instances, parties may agree to a structured settlement, such as an annuity for an accident victim. Phasing payments over time also does reduce the size of the immediate financial effect.

However, the Master Settlement Agreement does not simply spread the payments out over time. It also links these payments directly to cigarette sales. Doing so is of tremendous economic importance. Tax-like structures alter future incentives to buy the product and will be largely borne by consumers. Such a structure is only appropriate if one believes that cigarette prices continue to be too low given their true social costs. Estimates in the next two chapters do not indicate that this was the case. Moreover, from the standpoint of the litigation, only the portion of costs due to wrongful conduct should be counted in setting the tax. However, the estimates by the states did not single out only a part of the costs due to wrongful conduct as being bad. Smoking more generally was viewed as being costly and harmful.

Would it have been preferable to simply levy a lump sum penalty on cigarette companies? Taxes that are invariant with respect to cigarette sales would fall on the company and its shareholders, not the consumers. Some antismoking forces favored this structure as a means of punishing the companies. However, this penalty approach does not raise the cost of cigarettes to smokers and does not discourage smoking. If we act under the assumption that the penalty is related to prospective harm cigarettes inflict on the states, then the tax-equivalent form of penalties is preferable because it provides appropriate economic incentives to smokers to discourage their smoking behavior. It also will be more lucrative for the states than having the industry make a fixed damages payment now.

The Resolution of the State Attorneys General Suits

Because of the substantial litigation costs and legal uncertainties associated with litigating these suits in a variety of state jurisdictions, the cigarette industry sought a negotiated settlement of this litigation in 1997. As the previous chapter indicated, the Proposed Resolution of the tobacco litigation would have provided for $368.5 billion in payments over twenty-five years, substantial regulatory changes, and shielding of the companies from litigation by the states, class actions, and punitive damages claims. After this agreement failed to receive approval from Congress, the industry negotiated an agreement directly with the states. How did the industry fare and in what way did this outcome differ from the Proposed Resolution?

At the end of 1998 the industry did reach a separate settlement agreement with the group of forty-six attorneys general who had not yet settled. It had already settled with four states in separate agreements in 1997 and earlier in 1998. Mississippi received $3.6 billion, Florida $11.3 billion, Texas $15.3 billion, and Minnesota $6.6 billion.[2] Most of these settlements occurred after the prospects of the June 1997 Proposed Resolution effort began to dim, as the tobacco industry sought to resolve the litigation with each individual state. The industry's settlement efforts were baffling to those involved in the tobacco litigation. The first such settlement was for the Mississippi case where, as in all other state cases, I was serving as an expert witness for the industry on whether smokers were aware of the risks of cigarettes. This case was just going to trial, and the lawyers litigating the case were optimistic. However, the negotiation decisions were being made at the corporate level, not by the litigators. Not only was the decision to settle surprising, but the amount of the settlement exceeded the damages that Mississippi sought in the case. All that seemed to matter was that Wall Street continued to regard such settlements favorably—irrespective of the wisdom of such deals. Indeed, no state suit ever made it to a court verdict as a result of this rush to settle the litigation.

The $36.8 billion in settlements for the four separate state settlements are not included in the overall announced price tag of $206 billion, which was the most highly publicized figure from the Master Settlement Agreement. Thus, the total settlement value with all fifty states is $243 billion.

The Master Settlement Agreement included substantial regulatory reforms. Whereas ideally one might want these reforms to emerge from a national policy discussion and federal legislation, these reforms are the result of the decentralized bargains by the state attorneys general. Unlike the Proposed Resolution, the settlement did not include a new set of rotating cigarette warnings or broad FDA authority to regulate cigarettes. The regulations in the settlement included prohibition of targeting youths in cigarette marketing, a ban on the use of cartoons (e.g., Joe Camel, who had already been retired voluntarily by R. J. Reynolds in 1997), limitations on corporate sponsorships of events, elimination of outdoor advertising and advertisements, no payments for product placements, ban on tobacco brand name merchandise, ban on youth access to free samples, and lobbying limits. Cigarette companies are, for example, not permitted to lobby against measures to reduce youth smoking. It is difficult to envision situations in which this restriction would be necessary, because of the broadly based public consensus against underage smoking. The industry also had to dissolve the Tobacco Institute and the Council for Tobacco Research—U.S.A. as well as the Center for Indoor Air Research, but it had the freedom to form new trade associations so that this lobbying limit may be largely symbolic.[3]

Limiting advertising may not be in society's interest. If the primary effect of advertising is to influence brand choice rather than consumption of a broad class of products, as a considerable economic literature suggests, then banning advertising or restricting it in important domains has the effect of locking in the current market shares to the extent that firms cannot advertise new brands. Firms with a high market share at the present time, notably Philip Morris, will presumably tend to benefit more from advertising restrictions than firms with a more modest market share. New market introductions by these firms will be more difficult, so that it will be harder to get smokers to switch brands or to switch to different types of cigarettes by making consumers aware of the properties of these new products.

This disadvantage is troublesome for two reasons. Restricting advertising decreases market competition, leading to increased concentra-

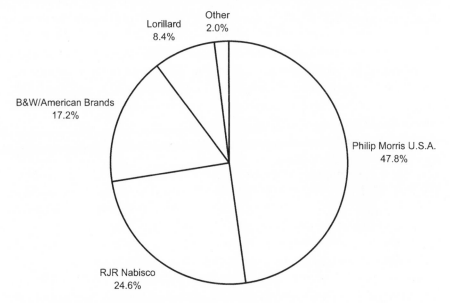

Figure 1 Tobacco industry market share: top 7 multinational tobacco companies. Source: Philip Morris Companies Inc. 1996 Year End Financial Fact Sheet.

tion and higher prices. It is anticompetitive. Second, advertising is a mechanism for providing information to consumers about safer cigarettes that may be developed in the future. In an environment with stringent restrictions on advertising, an alternative mechanism must be found if consumers are to be alerted to the changing safety characteristics of cigarettes.

Even before the settlement agreement and its likely anticompetitive effects, the U.S. tobacco industry was becoming increasingly concentrated. Figure 1 summarizes the market shares. By 1996 Philip Morris U.S.A. controlled 47.8 percent of the domestic tobacco market.[4] R. J. Reynolds was next, with 24.6 percent market share. The two largest firms consequently controlled almost three-fourths of this major industry, which reflects a high degree of concentration. Brown and Williamson/ American Brands controlled much of the remainder with 17.2 percent market share, and Lorillard (8.4 percent) and other brands (2.0 percent) made up the rest.

The antismoking objective is consequently at odds with the usual antitrust norms to foster market competition. If the companies had colluded on their own to eliminate wasteful advertising expenditures so as to lock in current market shares and save billions in marketing costs, there would have been immediate legal actions by the government to prevent it. Once these restraints were specified as part of the Proposed Resolution and the Master Settlement Agreement, government officials lauded them as an effort that will stop smoking, ignoring their consequences for market competition. Anticompetitive efforts are not the exclusive concern, just as decreasing smoking is not the only avowed policy objective. However, if advertising primarily affects brand choice rather than cigarette consumption, the anticompetitive consequences will loom larger in terms of the social costs.

The imposition of a cigarette tax through the settlement leaves existing companies vulnerable to new entrants. If the tax is intended to discourage smoking and prospective harms, it should be borne by new entrants as well. If the tax is truly only for past harms, as was claimed in the lawsuits against the cigarette companies, then more conventional damages payment rather than a tax would have been warranted.

To prevent existing companies from being undercut by new entrants, the Master Settlement Agreement also included provisions that would reduce the payments by the company if existing sales went down. The states that did not adopt so-called Qualifying Statutes would incur the reduced value of these payments. Such Qualifying Statutes would require new entrants to post pro rata damages based on cigarette sales. New entrants for whom there are no allegations of past wrongful conduct consequently would have to make payments into a damages fund. Whether one views this approach as anticompetitive in nature depends on how one views the appropriateness of the tax-like structure. If a cigarette tax mechanism is appropriate and actually pertains to future harms, all cigarettes of comparable riskiness should bear the tax. However, the cigarette tax is not linked in any way to cigarette safety. Should cigarettes free of nicotine and all cancer risks ever be marketed, they would be subject to the same tax as other cigarettes. Thus, even if the tax is viewed as a prospective penalty on a risky product, it is not structured appropriately.

Legal challenges to the agreement that were under way in 2001 sought to strike the portion of the agreement that imposed penalties on new entrants. These firms were not parties to the original settlement, which was purportedly for past harms. Ultimately, the failure of the financial structure of the settlement can be traced to the fact that it imposes an excise tax, and such taxes are the appropriate province of the legislature.

The original participating manufacturers in the settlement included the four major producers: Philip Morris Incorporated, R. J. Reynolds Tobacco Company, Brown and Williamson Tobacco Company, and Lorillard Tobacco Company. As a result of the settlement, these firms were released of all claims relating to the state suits. In particular, they were released of all claims for past conduct targeted in the state suits, where these claims were based on sale, research, and statements regarding tobacco products. Similarly, the firms were released of state suit claims for future conduct, and monetary claims relating to tobacco product exposure. Unlike the Proposed Settlement, this agreement included no restrictions on private tort actions or punitive damages. Suits by other entities, such as labor unions, insurance companies, and Native American tribes, were also unaffected. Each of these groups has since filed lawsuits based on the briefs prepared for the state cases.[5] Companies thus received less shielding from litigation than under the Proposed Resolution.

Because the Master Settlement Agreement and the settlement of the Minnesota case led to the release of voluminous tobacco industry documents, there also would be more information available for future plaintiffs' cases. Plaintiffs' attorneys armed with these internal company documents would claim that companies had withheld vital risk information. Whether such claims are true or not, the use of formerly secret internal documents gives such evidence a cloak-and-dagger mystique that enhances its impact on a jury. Moreover, the fact that the industry was vulnerable and had paid damages in the billions raised the expectations of potential plaintiffs and perhaps juror perceptions of liability as well. The multibillion-dollar payoff also may influence juror attitudes as well by establishing an anchor for future award levels.

The payments to be made under the agreement function very much like a tax per pack. Costs are to be based on the firm's market share, and in particular will be linked to the total number of individual packs sold. If, for example, the payment level were $8 billion annually, as it will be from 2004 to 2007, there would be a $0.33 per pack tax-equivalent charge associated with the agreement. Costs for the four states that reached separate agreements are in addition to that amount, bringing the total tax equivalent to about $0.40 per pack. The actual increase in the price per pack will be more due to the costs generated by attorneys' fees, wholesaler markup, and related expenses. This tax level bears no reasonable relationship to any of the estimated costs of cigarettes calculated in the next two chapters. Even if only medical costs incurred by the states enter the tally, and one excludes any cost savings due to cigarettes, the industry overpaid.

The focal point of the public discussion has been the publicized figure of $206 billion for the Master Settlement Agreement rather than on the per pack equivalent. In fact, the actual cost levels are much more complex than either a lump sum damages award or a simple payment per pack. The scope of the settlement with the states was quite broad and involved more than cash transfers. Many of the financial outlays also were targeted for specific purposes related to antismoking efforts. The lion's share of the money, however, goes to the states for unrestricted uses.

First, the cigarette industry will be funding a foundation to reduce youth smoking. The base payments were $25 million in 1999 and in the subsequent nine years for a ten-year total of $250 million.

Second, the cigarette industry will also fund a more broadly based national public education fund. The amount of funds going to this effort were set at $250 million in 1999, and $300 million beginning in the year 2000 and continuing for every year through 2003, for a total amount of $1.45 billion. Whereas there will be no inflation adjustments for the youth smoking payments, the national public education fund payments will be subject both to an inflation adjustment and to a volume adjustment based on the level of cigarette sales by the particular firm. Total allocations for the antismoking foundation and the national public education fund are under 1 percent of the total settlement price tag for the first twenty-five years. These measures are not the main point of the settlement, which is simply to transfer money to the states.

The third component of financial payments is for enforcement efforts related to the settlement agreement. In particular, the four major tobacco firms must contribute $150,000 annually to fund an executive committee to supervise the agreement, or $1.5 million over ten years. Moreover, the firms had to pay $50 million in 1999 for enforcement of the agreement. These payments are subject both to inflation adjustments and to volume adjustments.

Table 1 summarizes the payments the firms must make for the settlement agreement, not counting their payments for the various educational efforts mentioned earlier. The first column of payments lists the initial payment amounts for the years 1999–2003. These initial payments range from $2.4 billion to $2.7 billion. The next column of payments pertains to annual payments, and these begin at $4.5 billion in the year 2000 and rise to $9 billion in the years 2018 into perpetuity. Note that whereas the press has focused on payments over the initial twenty-five years, these annual payments do not stop in 2023 but continue forever. The final set of payments, which are designated additional payments, are for $0.861 billion from the years 2008 through 2017. These payments are distinguished in different categories in part because different kinds of volume and inflation adjustments pertain to them. The final column in table 1 lists the total payment amounts, which begin at $2.4 billion in 1999 and rise to a total of $9 billion by 2008 and remain at that level in perpetuity.

Table 1 also lists the twenty-five-year payment totals for each column of costs, where I take 1999 as the starting point. These amounts are

Table 1 Summary of Master Settlement Agreement Payments by Year
(in billions of dollars)

Year	Initial Payments	Annual Payments	Additional Payments	Total
1999	2.400	0	0	2.400
2000	2.472	4.500	0	6.972
2001	2.546	5.000	0	7.546
2002	2.623	6.500	0	9.123
2003	2.701	6.500	0	9.201
2004	0	8.000	0	8.000
2005	0	8.000	0	8.000
2006	0	8.000	0	8.000
2007	0	8.000	0	8.000
2008	0	8.139	0.861	9.000
2009	0	8.139	0.861	9.000
2010	0	8.139	0.861	9.000
2011	0	8.139	0.861	9.000
2012	0	8.139	0.861	9.000
2013	0	8.139	0.861	9.000
2014	0	8.139	0.861	9.000
2015	0	8.139	0.861	9.000
2016	0	8.139	0.861	9.000
2017	0	8.139	0.861	9.000
2018	0	9.000	0	9.000
2019	0	9.000	0	9.000
2020	0	9.000	0	9.000
2021	0	9.000	0	9.000
2022	0	9.000	0	9.000
2023	0	9.000	0	9.000
25-year total	12.742	189.890	8.610	211.242
2024	0	9.000	0	9.000
			0	
			0	
			0	
In perpetuity				

Table 2 Master Settlement Cost Summary over Twenty-five Years, 1999–2023

	Cost ($ Billions)	
	Undiscounted	**Present Value**[a]
Agreement payments		
Executive committee	0.002	0.001
Enforcement	0.050	0.050
Initial payments	12.742	12.000
Annual payments	189.890	130.671
Additional payments	8.610	5.798
Foundation and education		
Base payments	0.250	0.220
Additional payments	1.450	1.365
Total payments over 25 years	212.994	150.105

[a]Present value is based on use of 3% real rate of interest.

$12.7 billion for the initial payments, $190 billion for the annual payments, and $9 billion for the additional payments, for a total amount of $211 billion.

In terms of the total costs over the twenty-five-year period, one must also add in the base payments to the foundation of $0.25 billion and the additional payments of $1.45 billion. There are also the executive committee payments of $0.002 billion and enforcement payments of $0.05 billion. The net result is that the total payment over twenty-five years comes to $213 billion, as is summarized in table 2.

Payments made in the future have a smaller economic value than payments made today. Even though most cost components are indexed for inflation, current payments can be invested and are consequently more valuable than future payments. Using a 3 percent real (i.e., net of inflation) rate of interest, the present value of the losses over twenty-five years is $150 billion.

Viewed from any perspective, the average annual settlement amount is at an unprecedented level. Indeed, total general liability premiums paid by all U.S. firms for insurance of all liability risks were only $20 billion in 1997, or roughly double the annual settlement costs for any year listed in table 1.[6] Similarly, the annual payments in the settlement are about one-third the total value of U.S. workers' compensation insurance premiums, and the total settlement package is roughly an order of magnitude greater than all workers' compensation insurance premiums throughout the country. The staggering amount of the settlement, which is in addition to annual cigarette excise taxes of $13 billion,[7] dwarfs any damages award ever paid in litigation.

While these payments may appear to be an abstraction beyond our normal experience, they may have inadvertently sent a signal to potential jurors to view the cigarette industry as guilty of wrongdoing and to think in terms of higher stakes for cigarette case damages. The first evidence of such an anchoring effect occurred in a 1999 individual plaintiff's case in San Francisco that led to a $1.5 million compensatory award and a $50 million punitive award.[8] This amount was more than triple the value of the $15 million punitive award requested by the plaintiff's attorneys. This punitive award was subsequently reduced to $26.5 million by the California Superior Court.[9] Another San Francisco case led to a $1.7 million compensatory award and a $20 million punitive award.[10] A subsequent case in Oregon led to a $1.6 million in compensatory damages and $79.5 million in punitive damages—an amount that was subsequently reduced to $32 million.[11] These amounts were topped by the $3 billion punitive award for the 2001 Los Angeles case against Philip Morris by Richard Boeken, which thus far has been reduced to $100 million by the appeals process. Should other smokers whose illnesses are attributable to smoking receive similar awards, the costs quickly exceed the industry's resources. With class actions, the awards could escalate to enormous levels in only a single case. The Florida class-action case alone led to an award of $145 billion that is now under appeal.

Divvying Up the Settlement

The national settlement was a political deal in which the attorneys general bargained for their piece of the largesse. It specified the share of the settlement fund that would be received by each state. In particular, the settlement indicated a percentage share of the total annual payments that each state would receive. The second column of statistics in table 3 lists the state allocation percentages for the states participating in the agreement. The four states that negotiated separate agreements do not appear in the table. It is noteworthy that the highest shares are for the two largest states, California and New York, where each received an identical amount—13 percent. This symmetry was a political outcome of the bargaining process and was not driven by the states' respective medical costs. Relatively speaking, California profited and New York was shortchanged. The smallest share was for Wyoming, which received 0.25 percent.

Table 3 Ratio of the State Settlement Payment Share to the State Medical Care Cost Share for States Participating in the Settlement

State	Percentage Share of Medical Cost	Percentage Share of Settlement	Payment Share Divided by Medical Cost Share
Alabama	1.520	1.650	1.080
Alaska	0.280	0.350	1.263
Arizona	0.530	1.500	2.850
Arkansas	1.020	0.840	0.828
California	8.551	12.997	1.520
Colorado	1.229	1.396	1.136
Connecticut	1.948	1.890	0.970
Delaware	0.513	0.403	0.784
Georgia	3.154	2.499	0.792
Hawaii	0.212	0.613	2.886
Idaho	0.229	0.370	1.615
Illinois	5.609	4.739	0.845
Indiana	3.587	2.077	0.579
Iowa	0.983	0.886	0.901
Kansas	0.830	0.849	1.023
Kentucky	2.806	1.793	0.639
Louisiana	2.424	2.296	0.947
Maine	0.724	0.783	1.082
Maryland	2.048	2.302	1.124
Massachusetts	3.170	4.113	1.297
Michigan	3.326	4.431	1.332
Missouri	2.722	2.316	0.851
Montana	0.244	0.432	1.774
Nebraska	0.569	0.606	1.065
Nevada	0.521	0.621	1.191
New Hampshire	0.894	0.678	0.759
New Jersey	4.262	3.937	0.924
New Mexico	0.351	0.607	1.729
New York	15.170	12.995	0.857
North Carolina	3.491	2.375	0.680
North Dakota	0.211	0.373	1.764
Ohio	6.148	5.129	0.834
Oklahoma	1.199	1.055	0.880
Oregon	1.003	1.169	1.165
Pennsylvania	5.298	5.853	1.105

Table 3 *continued*

State	Percentage Share of Medical Cost	Percentage Share of Settlement	Payment Share Divided by Medical Cost Share
Rhode Island	0.736	0.732	0.995
South Carolina	1.422	1.198	0.842
South Dakota	0.256	0.355	1.389
Tennessee	2.874	2.485	0.865
Utah	0.220	0.453	2.058
Vermont	0.321	0.419	1.306
Virginia	2.766	2.082	0.753
Washington	1.498	2.091	1.396
West Virginia	0.978	0.903	0.923
Wisconsin	1.983	2.110	1.064
Wyoming	0.178	0.253	1.420

Note: Medical cost externality figures assume a 3% discount rate and cost levels for 1995.

All states made money relate to the medical costs of smoking, but did they get their fair share? The first step in assessing whether a state got its fair share is to determine the level of medical costs in each state. This can be done by multiplying the medical cost estimate per pack for the state, which will be presented in chapter 5, by the total number of packs of cigarettes sold in the state. After determining this amount for each state, one can ascertain the total medical costs to the states throughout the country by summing these medical costs per state figures. Using this value for total medical costs and the counterpart values for each state's specific medical costs, one can then calculate each state's proportionate share of the medical costs. These amounts appear in the first column of data in table 3. The medical cost share ranges from 0.18 percent in Wyoming to 15.17 percent for New York. It is noteworthy that California's share of medical costs is 8.55 percent, whereas both California and New York received an identical share of the agreement. This equality was a consequence of the political nature of the settlement shares, not the cost levels, which are in fact quite different. Bargains among the attorneys general produced the allocation, not simply recognition of the underlying economic costs.

An instructive measure of just how well different attorneys did in bargaining on behalf of their state's interests is the payment received relative to their share of medical costs, which is the ratio of the percentage share of the settlement agreement received by the state in column 2 of table 3 to the medical cost percentage share in column 1. This ratio indicates whether a state beat the average or performed worse than the average. Thus, if the ratio of the percentage share of the agreement to the percentage share of the medical costs is 1.0, then the state exactly breaks even in terms of its share of the settlement outcome, based on its medical costs. These ratios range from 0.58 for Indiana to 2.89 for Hawaii.

The performance of some key states is of particular interest. How well did the state of Alabama fare, given that its attorney general (and former deputy attorney general) William Pryor was a prominent holdout in terms of taking initiative against the cigarette industry? The state of Alabama recognized that cigarette smoking was dangerous, but did not believe that litigation by the states had merit. As the report of the task force headed by then Alabama deputy attorney general William Pryor observed:

> We recommend to the Governor and the Attorney General that the State of Alabama not file a Medicaid reimbursement suit. We do not believe that filing such a suit would serve the interests of the citizens of Alabama. First, such a suit would advance weak legal or equitable theories which, even if the State won the suit, would threaten to undermine Alabama law generally. Second, the State's burden of proving net harm is problematic, because widely respected economic studies conclude that there is no net harm to the State's treasury as a result of cigarette consumption. Third, this litigation would effectively raise taxes on tobacco companies without going through the ordinary legislative process. As a matter of judicial and political economy, if the State of Alabama wants to raise taxes on tobacco, the Legislature, not the judiciary, should do so.[12]

For the state of Alabama, the allocation percentage was 1.6 percent and the medical cost share was 1.5 percent. By dividing the allocation amount by the medical cost share, one finds that Alabama was paid $1.08 by this agreement for every dollar that it incurred in terms of its share of the medical costs. Attorney General Pryor was thus able to capture a disproportionate share of the settlement amount as part of the agreement among the attorneys general without having to incur the litigation costs associated with filing a claim against the tobacco industry.

A bigger winner was the state of Washington. Washington attorney general Christine Gregoire was the principal architect of the settlement proposal and was instrumental in gaining widespread support for the deal. This involvement yielded substantial dividends, as she apparently looked out for her state's financial interests when cutting the national deal that purportedly was in the interest of all states. The state of Washington received $1.40 in payments for every $1 of its medical cost share.

Brokering the agreement proved to be quite lucrative. Some might suggest that the state of Washington should have received some compensation for coordinating the deal. But was increasing Washington's fair share from $3.1 billion to $4.3 billion necessary? Did the other state attorneys general realize that Christine Gregoire was getting her state an extra $1.2 billion for making a few long distance phone calls? This extra effort bonus exceeded the total payments received by nine states.

The national deal proved to be a true windfall for the state of Iowa. That state's tobacco suit had been tossed out by the Iowa supreme court. However, the master settlement nevertheless included Iowa in the payoff, and Iowa got payments of $0.90 for each medical share dollar, or $1.8 billion of the settlement.

The plight of the three leading tobacco-producing states was not as favorable. In terms of the payment share per percentage share of medical cost, North Carolina received 0.68, Kentucky received 0.64, and Virginia received 0.75. Not only would these states have leading industries within the state penalized by the settlement, but they would be shortchanged by the drafters of the state settlement deal, as well.

These figures, as with those for all states, represent the percentage share of the deal relative to the percentage share of total medical costs. They do not imply that states are undercompensated in absolute terms. States are being compensated for more than their total medical costs because of the upward biases in the state medical cost estimates, which will be documented in chapter 5. Being compensated at less than the state's proportional share of medical costs consequently only implies that the state didn't receive its fair economic share of the payoff.

The settlement outcome was highly political in nature. No jury ever established an award level. Instead, the bargains were made in secret negotiations involving the attorneys general and cigarette industry officials. The way in which the state shares differed from the economic assessment of the proportional share is a reflection of the broad political character of the settlement outcome.

Paying Off the States' Attorneys

In personal injury cases, plaintiffs generally pay their attorneys on a contingency fee basis. If the case is unsuccessful, the lawyer gets nothing, but if the case is successful, the lawyer gets a share of the damages amount—often one-third. The expected payoff for the attorney is the probability of success multiplied by the contingency fee share and the damages amount. For a case with a given amount of legal effort, one can maintain the same expected level of compensation by altering the probability of success, the share, and the size of the award in various ways. Thus, the actual share of damages needed to recruit legal counsel will decrease as the size of the stakes and the probability of success rises, because the expected payoff to attorneys rises as the stakes and odds of success increase. Injured plaintiffs often find these arrangements attractive because their income is often reduced by the injury, and their medical expenses exert additional financial pressures. Paying lawyers on a contingency basis also reduces the need to monitor lawyers' efforts.

Somewhat surprisingly, the states did not use in-house legal counsel but instead farmed the tobacco litigation out to private law firms—some of whom had personal connections to the attorneys general. There was no advance public scrutiny of these sweetheart deals between the states and their lawyers. The terms were not even disclosed in advance. The fault, if any, lies with the attorneys general for negotiating overly generous terms, not with the attorneys who wanted the terms of the contract upheld once they had won. Unlike injured plaintiffs, the states are not strapped for funds. They don't need to rely on contingency fee arrangements because of inadequate resources. If they need additional resources, they can always seek additional funding from the legislature. These firms contracted for a substantial share of the payout—amounts so large that publicity regarding the fees led to considerable public outrage. The plaintiffs' lawyers were billing at levels estimated at over $100,000 or $200,000 per hour worked on the states' cases and typically never even presented tallies of hours worked to justify their bill. The Master Settlement Agreement provides for the tobacco companies to pay the fees of attorneys and paralegals and to compensate them "for time reasonably expended" for the government entities. Similarly, they must pay private outside counsel "reasonable attorney's fees." These amounts have a quarterly payment cap of $125 million, or $500 million annually, but these amounts will continue into perpetuity.[13] The lawyers' heirs, too, will be billionaires, leading some attorneys to try to cash in now by selling off the payment rights that continue forever.

The settlement with the states stipulated that attorneys' fees would be paid by the tobacco companies, not the states. However, this designation is largely a formality that disguises the true economic reality of who is actually paying the costs. Because the attorneys' fees will be borne by the tobacco companies rather than by the states, the settlement amount reflects the net take by the states including the expected legal costs. From a bargaining standpoint one would of course expect that the amount of the settlement given to the states would have been more if the cigarette industry did not also have to be paying the attorneys' fees of the states.

Thus, putting the attorneys' fees under a separate heading simply establishes a separate category of costs which the firms must ultimately bear. The costs may, however, have turned out to be more than anticipated. Making attorneys' fees not a part of the settlement also makes the payoff to the attorneys more politically acceptable to the constituents in these states.

The process of determining these fees after the settlement has been relatively hidden as well. The general public might be upset to see lawyers receiving billions of dollars in compensation; therefore the political salability of the agreement can be enhanced by making attorneys' fees a distinct and less visible component.

As attorneys' fee levels were resolved by the arbitration panels, lawyers representing the plaintiffs developed sometimes opposing interests. Beneficiaries of the billions in fees already awarded will not get these payoffs soon because of the annual cap of $500 million in attorneys' fee payouts by the industry. Once lawyers have had their fee levels set by a state, it is consequently in their economic self-interest to deny payments to lawyers in other states, because such payments will only delay their own reward, given the annual payout cap.

The arbitrators assigned lower levels of payment, in terms of the percentage of the state settlement, to lawyers of states that joined the litigation at a later date.[14] The lawyers of the lead state of Mississippi received $1.43 billion in legal fees, or 35 percent of the state award. The Florida lawyers received $3.43 billion, or 26 percent of the state settlement. The lawyers for the state of Texas, another early litigant, received $3.3 billion, or 19 percent of the state settlement. Lawyers in the larger states of Texas and Florida received more compensation than the lawyers in Mississippi even though it was the Mississippi case that broke the most legal ground that benefited all other states. Moreover, there is no reason to believe that lawyers' efforts were proportional to the size of the state. For example, my calculations of the cost estimates in chapter 5 for each state involved no significantly greater effort on my part for any of the states.

However, the justification for the fees is quite different for lawyers in different states. Lawyers in the lead litigation venues, such as Mississippi, took genuine risks. Once the tobacco companies settled out of court with these states, the prospects for success elsewhere soared. And when the Proposed Resolution was made public on June 20, 1997, it was all but guaranteed that there would be some broadly based deal.

The prospect of a big payoff and the need to create the illusion of substantial risky legal effort was not lost on the plaintiffs' lawyers. As these prospects for payoffs to the states' lawyers increased, my depositions in these cases that previously took less than a day expanded even though the ground had been covered in previous depositions already in the record. To pad the depositions and create the illusion of effort, the attorneys representing the states asked expert witnesses such as myself to spend hours reading voluminous documents into the record. Lawyers often went through the motions of the deposition, having already covered the same ground previously in other cases. For example, the law firm of Ness, Motley, Loadholt, Richardson, and Poole represented twenty-six states,[15] which often led to repeat appearances by the lawyers retreading the same ground with witnesses. To ease the burdens on its lawyers, some firms had their own private jets to ferry their lawyers to these depositions. Some now have the resources to purchase their own fleet of jets.[16]

In contingency fee contexts, not all legal effort should be treated equally. When it was performed is most critical. If there is a high likelihood of a payout, attorneys need not be compensated for long-shot risks. If, for example, the firms are risk neutral—as the states should certainly have been—the payoff should be inversely related to the probability of success. Suppose a firm's average hourly rate for legal services is $400 per hour. With a 50-50 chance of success, $800 per hour if there is a success and 0 if the suit fails gives the correct payoff to induce the firm to expend the hour of work on the case. If the chance of success is 1/10, $4,000 per hour is adequate; if 1/100, then $40,000 per hour is appropriate. Getting to even higher payoffs per hour requires an even lower chance of success, or odds that bear no relationship whatsoever to the excellent prospects of success after the Proposed Resolution and the initial state settlements were announced. Moreover, once the prospects of success were apparent, the need for a risk premium to induce lawyer effort disappears.

In Florida, the contractual formula for reimbursing the lawyers provided 25 percent of the settlement or verdict if they won.[17] The state of Florida's cigarette settlement was $11.3 billion over twenty-five years. The eleven lawyers involved in the trial eventually received their payoff of $3.4 billion, which at that time was the largest legal fee in U.S. history.[18] This legal fee award was in excess of $300 million per attorney involved in the trial.

Attorneys from the six firms representing the state in Texas were awarded legal fees of $3.3 billion, which was a substantial share of the state's $17.3 billion settlement.[19] While several billion dollars may seem like a generous reward, the lawyers had sought a fee of $25 billion—or roughly one and a half times the settlement amount.[20] In this never-never land of dreamlike awards, why not dream big? Had they been successful, those lawyers would have received an extraordinary contingency fee that exceeded the damages award. Estimates of the hourly rate implied by the legal fee they actually did receive put it at $150,000 per hour; the *Houston Chronicle* observed that this fee was the result of "enough backroom dealing to make Tammany Hall look like a Boy Scout meeting."[21] This hourly rate exceeds the annual salary of $136,000 for members of the U.S. Senate and House of Representatives and is three-fourths of the president's salary of $250,000[22] for which he must work the entire year. Surprisingly, the Texas lawyers got 19 percent of the settlement even though their contract called for 15 percent.[23]

Many of these issues have surfaced in the debate over setting the level of legal fees. Plaintiffs' attorneys in Massachusetts sought about $2 billion in fees over twenty-five years, and received just under half that. Their fee level of 9.3 percent of the total recovery is a substantial reward for lawyers that were not even in a lead state in the litigation.

Massachusetts had a $5 billion settlement with the tobacco industry and a 25 percent fee arrangement with the attorneys. Attorneys in Massachusetts were still taking expert depositions at the time of settlement and had not prepared their case. Because the firm of Ness, Motley was involved in this state and more than two dozen more, many of these depositions were repeat run-throughs of well-worn material. Indeed, for most experts, such as myself, the Commonwealth of Massachusetts relied on the depositions already taken in Minnesota and did not even take expert depositions. Moreover, most of the state's experts had been prepared for trials taking place in other states. Not only was the public not apprised of the deals, even the governor was left in the dark. Governor Paul Cellucci called this payoff to the attorneys "a closed-door arrangement that has been shielded from public scrutiny."[24] Calling the prospect of a billion-dollar-plus fee "obscene" and the ultimate $775 million payment "excessive," the governor proposed a bill to cap fees at $50 million.[25] The highly Democratic legislature did not pass this bill.

Officials believed that this fee award, which was well below that in other states, was the largest legal fee in civil litigation history for the Commonwealth of Massachusetts. As in the other states, these fees had no hourly justification, and in fact the lawyers did not present any hourly logs to justify their fee demands.[26]

The exorbitant fee scales and massive payouts has led to speculation about backroom dealings. Such ties were in evidence for Mississippi, which was the lead state in the litigation and was represented by a consortium of thirteen firms that were awarded $1.4 billion by the arbitration panel.[27] A prime beneficiary was the law firm of Richard Scruggs, who is a "close friend and ally" of Mike Moore, the Mississippi attorney general who launched the case and whose office drafted the terms of the lawyers' reimbursement.[28] Scruggs is also the brother-in-law of Senate majority leader Trent Lott. His personal take has been estimated to be as high as $900 million.

Epitomizing the mismatch between effort and reward was the situation of a lawyer whom neither side knew and who claimed he was involved in the Texas case. Marc Murr was a "good friend" of former Texas attorney general Dan Morales. He "came out of nowhere and demanded $519 million." After the lawyers in the Texas litigation indicated that they did not even know he was involved in the case, Murr was awarded $260 million by a state panel but only $1 million by the national arbitration panel, with the state of Texas being responsible for the remaining $259 million.[29] Even so, this was not a bad payoff for a case in which he played no role.

The state of Minnesota had a $6.1 billion settlement over twenty-five years, for which it too had a 25 percent legal fee arrangement with the lawyers. The attorneys accepted a $445 million settlement for their efforts.[30]

While these paydays for the plaintiffs' attorneys were the largest and most highly publicized, the legal teams have fared quite well as they have gone from state to state collecting their payoff. Recall that some lawyers were involved in more than a dozen suits, making it possible to collect multiple times for essentially identical legal efforts that became transportable from state to state. In Louisiana, the Tobacco Fee Arbitration Panel awarded $575 million to tobacco counsel. Once again the firms of Scruggs and Ness, Motley were among those awarded payoffs.[31] These same two law firms also shared in the arbitration panel award in Kansas made on the same day as the Louisiana award. The Kansas payoff was $54 million—low by tobacco lawyer standards, but an incredible windfall in any other context. Illinois added $121 million to the payouts, Hawaii added $90.2 million, and Iowa added $85 million. To paraphrase the late Senator Everett Dirksen: A hundred million here, a hundred million there, and pretty soon you're talking about real money.

Even though the legal fees are being paid as the result of suits brought by the states, there has been no general policy of disclosing the fee amounts. The U.S. Chamber of Commerce was forced to file Freedom of Information Act requests to obtain these figures. Reports from twenty-one states indicate legal fees of $11 billion.[32] Because the fees will be paid out in perpetuity, some attorneys have attempted to cash out their winnings by selling litigation bonds. One sale of $1 billion in future legal fees was for $308 million, reflecting both the risk and role of discounting in reducing the actual present value of the payments.[33]

The trial lawyers' winnings have also led to efforts on their part to protect their windfall gains and to promote their interests in future cases. Headlines in traditionally liberal papers proclaimed such messages as "Trial Lawyers Pour Money into Democrats' Chests."[34] The cigarette payoffs have potentially profound implications for future litigation as well.

Where Will the Money Go?

A useful check on the validity of the states' damages claims is to see how the damages payments were allocated. Are these funds truly needed to offset the higher Medicaid costs incurred by the state? The results in chapter 5 will show that the states' estimates included payment for federal costs as well as overpayment of costs to the states. According to my calculations the states would not need to devote the entire damages payoff to defray smoking-related medical expenses. It seems the agreement is almost all profit.

Indeed, public discussions of the states' allocation plans thus far have gone in a quite different direction than the health-care costs of smokers. Some states have suggested setting aside a token percentage amount for antismoking efforts generally and policies to cut youth smoking. These are smoking-related efforts, though they do not involve defraying medical costs directly.

Other states have attempted to emphasize expenditures that appear to be social services or education-oriented even though they have little to do with smoking. Still others have turned to public works efforts that have nothing whatsoever to do with cigarettes or health. A review of the states' allocations provides telling evidence of the lack of any need to siphon funds into bankrupt Medicaid programs.

The "feeding frenzy" over the Florida settlement prompted efforts to allocate the funds to reduce crowding in public schools.[35] Proposals in Oklahoma targeted schools as well, and Oregon sought to balance the state budget without raising taxes.[36] In Michigan, most of the funds were targeted to college scholarships and public education programs, not antismoking efforts.[37] Colorado favored spending on a third-grade reading program.[38] Illinois identified public works initiatives such as roads and bridges as being the most worthy targets for the tobacco suit winnings.[39] In other states, improved jails and other public works efforts headed the list.[40] Los Angeles earmarked most of its tobacco settlement money to improve wheelchair access for sidewalks, with the remainder used to build parks in poor neighborhoods.[41] Los Angeles subsequently advocated shifting some of the tobacco settlement money for an even more bizarre purpose. The mayor, Richard Riordan, proposed using much of its $300 million settlement for legal defenses of abuses by its police department. These cases involved officers who had been arrested for allegedly planting drugs and weapons on suspects, and in some cases beating or shooting unarmed suspects.[42] Support of such policies is a far cry from covering smoking-related Medicaid costs.

Even states in which there was some health-related emphasis strayed far from the purported need to siphon funds to pay smokers' Medicaid bills. Connecticut passed a public health measure that would fund AIDS testing for newborns, establish a Child Advocate Office, and make possible civil commitments of sex offenders.[43] Only $5 million was earmarked for antitobacco advertising and public education. West Virginia also launched a modest $4.5 million effort, but this included alcohol and drug prevention as well.[44] In Missouri the state legislators were torn between spending the money on health care or repairing the state's roads.[45] Alabama focused its energies on youth programs, including "boot-camp style detention centers,"[46] and North Dakota earmarked funds for flood-control projects.[47]

What is missing from these allocations is a concerted effort to fund smoking-related medical costs and antismoking efforts. Indeed, to the extent that smoking is a concern it is through token efforts that are largely symbolic. The states cashed in on a tobacco windfall and often launched spending sprees unrelated to tobacco. A spokesperson for the American Lung Association correctly observed the mismatch between the initial need for the state settlement money and how the tobacco windfall was being allocated: "It's been difficult for the tobacco prevention community to let people know that the reason we got the money was for reducing Medicaid costs. Unfortunately that message has been drowned out by a lot of special interests taking the money away from tobacco control."[48] The U.S. surgeon general also joined in the criticism of how the states have spent the money.[49]

Overall assessments of the allocations of the settlement money are in line with these case studies. Reports in 2001 by the National Conference of State Legislatures and the General Accounting Office estimated that only 5 percent to 7 percent of the money was being targeted to tobacco programs, such as those for smoking prevention and cessation. Mississippi attorney general Michael A. Moore, who launched this litigation, denounced this outcome as "moral treason."[50]

The financial interests of the states are at odds with those of the federal government. If the federal suit is successful or leads to a settlement that pushes up the price of cigarettes further, cigarette purchases will decline. The practical consequence of the state settlement being disguised as an excise tax is that the payments received by the states will decline as well. This economic linkage has not been lost on state governors. A group of five governors sent a letter dated July 15, 1999, to their fellow governors urging opposition to the federal suit and expressing the following fear: "The creative projects that you and others have developed for your state to use these funds will be cut back, perhaps sharply."[51] What this letter did not say is that these "creative projects" involved efforts such as sidewalk repair, delinquent youth programs, and highway construction rather than smoking-related health policies.

State legislators also realize the importance of protecting the compensation to be provided to the states. The state of Florida class action generated the greatest concern. After the punitive damages awards which turned out to be $145 billion, tobacco companies would have been required by Florida law to post a bond equal to 115 percent of the award. Doing so would bankrupt the industry, ending the infinite stream of revenues negotiated as part of the settlement with the states. The legislatures in North Carolina, Virginia, Kentucky, and Georgia all passed laws capping the amount that needed to be posted at levels such as $25 million.[52] The state of Florida also enacted a bill capping the bond the industry would have to post at $100 million.[53] Doing so protected not only the interests of the tobacco companies, but the states as well.

The bottom line of this budgetary inquiry is that smoking-related costs have come up almost as an afterthought. States have not rushed to allocate these funds solely to meet medical cost shortfalls due to smoking-related illness. Nor have they even restricted the funds to medical care generally. The settlement amounts dwarf the smoking-related health costs so the funds are not really needed to defray Medicaid costs. The norm has been to treat the tobacco winnings as the budgetary windfall that it is.

Is this spending on matters unrelated to smoking and health bad? Money is money, irrespective of its source. Shouldn't states be free to allocate it as they wish just as they would any other funds? While this freedom to spend is certainly true, the observed spending pattern is not consistent with the rhetoric that gave rise to the suits. Just as the Proposed Resolution was being marketed as a crusade against youth smoking, the state suits were touted as a mechanism to defray health costs and generate funds to discourage smoking. The principal antismoking component is the higher cigarette taxes resulting from the deal, not the substantive policies funded by the tax revenues.

Lessons from the State Settlement

The settlement of the state suits for more than $200 billion established a new reference point and potential anchor for runaway juries. As part of the settlement there was a broad release of the documents used in the litigation, which were placed on the Web and received substantial publicity. The flurry of antismoking efforts funded in part by the settlement and the expectation of multibillion-dollar awards have not only spurred the federal government into action but have also led to suits being filed by union pension funds as well as more private lawsuits.

Both the Proposed Resolution and the state settlement were comprehensive packages including substantial payments and legal protections. In making this gamble for a settlement, the industry may have thought that it was putting the litigation behind it. Instead, the payoff has simply fueled more litigation with me-too suits by Blue Cross Blue Shield, the federal government, the asbestos trust fund, and a series of class actions. Individual lawsuits have also been energized, and juries now think in billions rather than millions. Rather than putting the litigation behind it, the industry's settlement gamble has unleashed a torrent of litigation that threatens the industry's continuing viability. Major open questions remain about this entire type of litigation effort. A basic legal issue is why the federal government can file a claim based on its failure to appropriately recognize the health costs before, given that the surgeon general has issued annual reports on smoking hazards for over three decades.[54]

In terms of the prognosis for the tobacco industry, it is clear that the industry did not buy peace with this settlement but in fact stimulated further litigation. Moreover, no legal issues were ultimately involved, so the precedent for other industries is unclear. Which suits have standing? Is the tobacco industry experience in any way unique, or can it be readily transferred to other industries? Alcoholic beverages, cars, and other products similarly could emerge as targets for litigation. Lead paint, HMOs, and guns have already been targets.[55]

Because these issues were not resolved through the judicial process, there is also no resolution on how costs should be counted for such lawsuits. For example, is it appropriate to net out the nursing home cost savings and pension cost savings attributable to cigarettes or should one simply look at the increase in medical costs? Given that the Master Settlement Agreement is tantamount to imposing a higher tax rate on cigarettes, the question arises as to whether other excise taxes paid by smokers as a result of state tax levies also should be counted.

Most fundamentally, why is it that these matters are the province of the courts rather than the legislative process? The hazards of cigarettes are known. The state suits have generated no new knowledge on this front. It is possible to tax and regulate cigarettes now rather that relying on retrospective lawsuits to address the issue. Moreover, this regulation can emerge from a consensus process in which legislators formulate regulatory objectives and policies that represent the national interest. In contrast, the state lawsuits led to a resolution that reflected the interests of the state attorneys general. While they are public officials, they are not health officials. Their major concern was with the dollar amount reaped by the states as part of the settlement, which is their principal area of competence and responsibility, rather than formulating broadly based regulatory initiatives.

The competency of the judicial process to deal with such litigation also may be called into question. What is at issue in these suits is a very complex judgment regarding the economic ramifications of a product for an entire market. The question is not whether a manufacturer produced a defective product that harmed a particular individual. Rather, the state suits are being used to make an overall judgment regarding market outcomes and, ultimately, to formulate a market-wide regulatory policy. The technical nature of these judgments alone suggests that they might be better addressed by regulatory staffs with expertise in these matters. Moreover, there also appears to be a mismatch between the locus of expertise of a jury and the scope of the problems being addressed in these cases.

By settling this litigation out of court rather than by awaiting the ultimate judicial disposition of these cases, the cigarette industry sacrificed the opportunity to provide a knowledgeable baseline for estimating how future efforts such as this may fare. The likely result is that there will be a flurry of similar suits until there are definitive judgments regarding the underlying basis for this litigation.

IV

THE FINANCIAL COSTS OF SMOKING TO SOCIETY

Do cigarettes impose financial costs on society? The answer to this question is not simple. It depends on what gets counted as a cost, in what way the costs are counted, whom the cost affects, and whether taxes already paid should be recognized as part of the cost calculation.

My interest in the social costs of smoking began in 1994. Hillary Rodham Clinton and public health officials bandied about estimates of the medical costs of smoking—a dollar a pack, two dollars a pack, perhaps more. These estimates were often out of nowhere—claims with no support. When there was backup, it was usually from health-care analysts—people well versed in analyzing diseases but often with little economic training. In an effort to make sense of these numbers, I embarked on a study funded solely by the National Bureau of Economic Research, the independent research group based in Cambridge.

This study proved to be of more than academic interest, as it intersected with ongoing tax policy debates. As the antismoking fervor grew, legislators turned to cigarette taxes both as a mechanism for reflecting the social costs of cigarettes and as a means of raising revenues to finance other policy efforts. Although the federal cigarette tax has long been $0.24 per pack (and was recently raised to $0.39 beginning in 2002), legislation proposed in the 1990s would have increased these taxes even further. As it became obvious that tobacco was going to become a target for increased taxation, various legislators proposed multiple tax variations and profiles. The mid-1994 version of a plan proposed by President Clinton would have imposed a tax of $0.99 per pack, the bill proposed by then Senate majority leader George Mitchell would have imposed a tax of $0.69 per pack, and one draft health-care bill from the House Education and Labor Committee would have imposed a tax of $2 per pack. In 1997, Senator Ted Kennedy proposed a $1.50 per pack tax. The states impose their own substantial taxes as well. In December 1999, the New

York legislature passed a sweeping health-care reform bill which they funded with an additional $0.55 tax on cigarettes, increasing it to a total of $1.11, the highest in the nation, generating an additional $500 million a year.[1] The Proposed Resolution and the Master Settlement Agreement also have a tax-like structure.

There are many political reasons for imposing taxes. One is political expediency. Cigarette smokers now constitute a minority of the population. This minority group is not very well educated, is predominantly blue-collar, and is not as politically powerful as more affluent nonsmokers. Moreover, given the social controversy pertaining to smoking, they are a vulnerable minority and thus there will be lower political costs associated with cigarette taxation than, for example, with a more broadly based tax.

There may be other reasons for taxing cigarettes, wholly apart from the desire to raise revenues. Cigarette taxes and alcohol taxes are among the most common forms of "sin taxes." The economic rationale for such taxes is that imposing taxes discourages behavior that may be associated with inefficient decisions harmful to health. The potential inadequacies in behavior may pertain to the effects of smokers' decisions with respect to their own well-being or that of their families. Taxes could be imposed to align these decisions with rational self-interest.

A second impetus for taxation would be net external costs imposed on the rest of society by cigarette smoking. The financial costs of cigarettes could harm others in much the same way as pollution inflicts harm that the polluter may not recognize. In that case, cigarette taxes would reflect the incremental costs generated by a pack of cigarettes, leading smokers to internalize the external costs of their actions.

Although the possible rationales for cigarette taxation are clear, whether or not taxation of any kind is desirable from the standpoint of promoting efficient decisions is not theoretically obvious. Consider first inefficiencies regarding losses to smokers themselves. One might hypothesize that smokers ignore the externality to their future selves (and their family members) and make inadequate self-protective decisions. However, there may also be distortions of the opposite type, in which smokers overestimate the risk and place too great a weight on the losses involved. Appropriate tax levels can discourage smoking to the same degree as would accurate recognition of these harmful effects to the smoker. The efficient risk level is not necessarily zero for cigarettes or any other commodity. Rather, one should balance the competing benefits and costs associated with smoking activity, that is, the pleasure derived from smoking versus the financial and health costs.

A second type of inefficiency has to do with harm to society at large.

These external aspects of smoking likewise involve competing effects. Cigarette smokers have no private incentive to internalize all the effects that their own smoking may have on others, with the possible exception of family members, but these effects are not necessarily adverse on balance. What matters is the entire trajectory of all cost consequences, not just costs of a particular type at a particular time. To the extent that cigarette smoking is harmful to one's health, there will be higher health insurance costs associated with smoking-related illnesses, as well as other social externalities, such as life insurance costs.

However, adverse health effects have other cost implications as well. There may be offsetting cost savings from earlier mortality through reduced costs of pensions, Social Security, Medicare, and health expenditures later in life. It is not clear a priori whether the cost savings to society are exceeded by the costs imposed on society. Resolving these issues requires a detailed empirical assessment of the competing influences.

This chapter provides a careful examination of the social costs of smoking. Are there net social costs, and how do they compare with the taxes already paid? This comparison is fundamental because taxes should be levied to reflect any net social costs so as to create proper economic incentives. Exploring the functioning of the cigarette tax mechanism and its incidence is also essential to understanding the damages claims in the state lawsuits against the cigarette industry. The linchpin of the analysis is that cigarettes are expected to harm one's health. These adverse health effects often have surprising financial consequences. While my estimates will illuminate the value of the financial efforts at issue in the state and federal suits, my estimates were not prepared for that litigation and were not the subject of my involvement in those cases. My initial estimates were prepared before the first state suit was filed and long before the industry realized that these financial effects were matters of legal concern.

This focus on financial effects may seem too narrow. What about the harm to the smokers themselves and the adverse health effects of environmental tobacco smoke? Surely these consequences matter as well. These concerns do, in fact, matter for the social welfare calculation and will be addressed in subsequent chapters. However, they have nothing whatsoever to do with the damages claims by the states or the ongoing federal claim. These cases were about one thing only—money. How much do smokers cost these government entities financially? Health losses to smokers themselves were not the subject of the litigation in any of the governmental lawsuits. The litigation consisted of little more than a sophisticated accounting exercise to determine if smokers impose financial costs. Although my examination of the consequences of smoking will begin with this strictly financial perspective, subsequent chapters will broaden the assessment to include the health consequences of second-hand smoke and other policy-relevant concerns.

Profile of the Cigarette Tax

A useful starting point is to assess the financial contribution already made by cigarettes through excise taxes. Given the centrality of excise taxes in any financial assessment for cigarettes, determining whether cigarettes are a net financial drain ultimately may hinge on the amount of those taxes.

Beginning with excise taxes also pushes to the forefront the major issue raised by litigation. If cigarettes inflict financial harm on society, why were taxes not raised to reflect these costs? Because excise taxes are not the norm for consumer products, the proponents of "sin taxes" for cigarettes presumably must have had at least some vague idea that smoking was potentially harmful. Indeed, the existence of some smoking risk has been common knowledge for centuries, as cigarettes have long been referred to as "cancer sticks" and "coffin nails."[2] So why have we relied on the tax-like settlement generated by the litigation process rather than levying taxes directly?

One reason why legislators have repeatedly balked at raising cigarette taxes is that they are already high and also have very unattractive properties. Cigarettes are the most heavily taxed major category of consumer purchases. Relative to the purchase amount, tobacco products are subject to a higher tax rate than alcohol, three times the tax rate of gasoline, and over ten times the tax rate imposed on items such as utilities and automobiles.[3]

Since as of 1998, 24 percent of all American adults continued to smoke, the potential tax revenues associated with the cigarette tax are substantial.[4] The overall cigarette tax is shared roughly equally between the federal government and the states. For fiscal year 1998, the federal excise on cigarettes of $0.24 per pack of twenty cigarettes grossed a total tax revenue of $5,478,418,000.[5] For that fiscal year, federal, state, and municipal excise taxes on cigarettes amounted to $13,236,575,000—over $13 billion, or $50 per person in the country. The cost per smoker will, of course, be several times greater. Overall, the federal and state taxes totaled 28.2 percent of the retail price of cigarettes. Municipal taxes added an additional $196 million. Since almost all of the tobacco taxes are accounted for by cigarettes—97.7 percent in 1998—I will use the cigarette tax and tobacco tax label interchangeably.[6]

Although the absolute magnitude of cigarette taxes has never been higher than at present, these taxes have been higher as a percentage of the retail price. Cigarette taxes reached a peak of 51.4 percent of the total price of cigarettes in 1965, immediately after the initial government report on lung cancer and smoking. The percentage taxation varies over time because the tax is set in absolute amounts and is varied periodically. Over the past fifty years, federal cigarette taxes have held only five different levels, $0.07 per pack beginning in 1942, $0.08 per pack in 1951, $0.16 per pack in 1983, $0.20 per pack in 1991, and $0.24 per pack in 1998. The absolute level of the tax and the periodic nature of the tax revision have as a consequence resulted in swings in the cigarette tax as a percentage of retail price.

Who pays cigarette taxes? It is not legislators and the affluent who will foot the bill. The maintenance crew at the Capitol will bear more of the tax than will members of Congress who vote to boost it. The perverse distributional effect of cigarette taxes has been a principal source of caution in the political reluctance to boost the cigarette tax. While the poor may lack political power in their own right, there is often an altruistic concern with their welfare.

The usual economic measure of regressivity is whether the poor pay a higher proportion of their income for something than do the rich.[7] This standard test provides some hint of the overwhelming regressivity of cigarette taxes. Whereas, in 1990, people making $50,000 or more paid 0.08 percent of their income in cigarette taxes, those with incomes below $10,000 paid 1.62 percent of their income in cigarette taxes—or twenty times as high a percentage. The discrepancy is not solely a consequence of higher income, as smoking propensities also differ. Smoking was once the glamorous pursuit of the rich. Indeed, in some countries such as Spain that continues to be the case. However, only 19 percent of American adults with incomes of $50,000 or more smoke, as compared to 32 percent of those with incomes less than $10,000.

The regressivity of cigarette taxes is so great that the poor pay a higher absolute dollar tax amount than do the wealthy. Average taxes paid per person in 1990 in different income groups ranged from $81 for income levels under $10,000 to $49 for income levels $50,000 or above. These tax amounts are averaged across all members of each group, not all of whom smoke. Looking at only smokers would make the tax burden seem even more lopsided.

Tar Levels and the Changing Cigarette

Cigarettes are not all alike. Differences in tobacco blends, filters, and flavors are obvious differences at any given time. Cigarettes also change over time in their composition. The Marlboro and Camel of today are not the same as those of a half-century ago. And the market mix of cigarettes sold has changed, with venerable brands such as Lucky Strike, Pall Mall, and Chesterfield giving way to Lark, Merit, and generic cigarettes.

The increased public concern with the risks of smoking has led to two major changes in the characteristics of cigarette smoking. First, cigarette smoking is much less prevalent now than it was in the past. Second, the kinds of cigarettes people smoke are quite different from those smoked decades earlier. Filter cigarettes now dominate the cigarette market. Moreover, the "tar" level, which is the most frequently used composite measure of the chemical residues linked to cancer risks of smoking, has declined as smokers have switched to lighter cigarettes. Tar levels are defined by the United States Federal Trade Commission (FTC) as "total particulate matter in milligrams per cigarette less nicotine and water."[8] Tar and nicotine levels are measured using testing procedures and criteria established by the FTC. Moreover, since 1967 the FTC has published standardized tar and nicotine measurements for all cigarettes.[9] Many assessments of cigarette smoking have taken into account the changing frequency of smoking, but none of these studies has incorporated the shift in tar levels in these risk assessments.

The omission of changes in tar levels is quite fundamental, as it has broad ramifications for the assessed risks of smoking, the rationality of smoking decisions, and the magnitude of societal externalities. Lower tar levels imply that the risk levels associated with smoking will be less than has been estimated. This discrepancy is not a minor nuance. The pertinent smoking era currently used in reported scientific estimates of the hazards of smoking may be as much as a half a century out of date.

Two lags result. First, the studies used in formulating the risk assessments are often not based on current data, but instead on illnesses that occurred decades earlier. Second, the smoking exposures that gave rise to the risks identified in these studies preceded the publication dates for these studies because of the substantial latency period involved between exposure to carcinogens and incidence of the disease. If, for example, there is a three-decade latency period between cigarette smoking and the onset of lung cancer, and if the study estimating such a linkage is two decades old, then in effect there is a fifty-year lag in the pertinence of the evidence.

In this section I will review the changing history of the tar levels of cigarettes and the implications of this shift for the potential riskiness of cigarette smoking. The adjustments that I will make will be linear, since reductions in tar will be weighted proportionally.[10] These adjustments are likely to be overly conservative to the extent that there is a no-risk threshold for carcinogenic exposures, which is consistent with much of the evidence on the causation of cancer.[11]

The analysis below will consider two different assumptions—that health risks of smoking are proportional to tar levels and that the health risks are independent of the tar level. Those assumptions bracket the debate concerning the importance of tar levels as a risk indicator. Smokers of lower-tar cigarettes may inhale more deeply or take more puffs, thus diminishing some of the health benefits. Smokers of low-tar cigarettes may also smoke a greater quantity of cigarettes, which is an effect my calculations take into account because the costs are on a per cigarette basis.

The presence of a behavioral response that affects the net risk effects of safety innovations reflects the types of influences found in my own work on safety issues.[12] After the advent of safety caps, children continued to be poisoned, as parents were given a false sense of security by what I termed the "lulling effect." Because consumers equated having safety caps with being "childproof," they were less careful, to an extent that fully offset the beneficial effects of the caps. People who found the caps difficult to open also tended to leave the bottles open. My empirical analysis of a similar relationship for safety mechanisms for cigarette lighters showed diminished care, but not to such an extent that there would be a full offset of the safety benefit. Studies of driver responses to seat belts also suggest that there is some behavioral offset influence, but the extent of the effect and whether it is fully offsetting remains controversial. From an economic standpoint, very strong conditions must be met for the diminished care to be so great that it fully offsets the safety benefits.

In the case of low-tar and -nicotine cigarettes, suppose that smokers do in fact mute some of the benefits because of the way they hold the cigarette with their fingers covering the side air vents, how deeply they inhale, and how much of the cigarette they smoke. Even with all these behavioral responses, the risks of low-tar cigarettes may be lower, though not as much lower as they would be otherwise. Can any health expert seriously suggest that smoking a Gauloise cigarette is really no riskier than smoking a Vantage or other low-tar and -nicotine cigarette? Observing that there is an offsetting behavioral response does not imply that there is a full offset of the benefits of low-tar cigarettes.

The final behavioral response is in terms of numbers of cigarettes smoked. Smoking more cigarettes that are low in tar and nicotine than one would if one smoked regular cigarettes in no way implies that the tar and nicotine ratings are erroneous. The risks per cigarette are still down. However, the total risk reduction the smoker will achieve because of switching to low-tar and -nicotine cigarettes will be less. I will explicitly account for these quantity effects and fully incorporate them in my analysis below.

When all these effects are considered, how much safer are low-tar and -nicotine cigarettes? Available scientific evidence indicates that they are about 20 percent safer in terms of the lung cancer risk, but there is no comparable evidence indicating an effect for heart disease. On balance, these cigarettes appear to be safer, but perhaps not to the extent that one might hope.

Presumably because lower-tar cigarettes are safer, they should impose lower financial costs on society. It turns out that making the tar adjustment to assess the health costs of cigarettes will have some surprising implications that are the opposite of what one might expect.

Estimating the Societal Financial Costs

Calculating the social costs of smoking should be a relatively straightforward accounting exercise. However, if one's accounting principles are incorrect, then the cost estimates will be invalid as well. Public discussions of smoking costs have often been dominated by estimates of the social cost per pack of cigarettes, some of which are based on flawed analyses and others are based on no analysis whatsoever. Press accounts seldom scrutinize the documentation of these cost per pack estimates, which often seem to assume a validity simply because they are precise dollar figures.

The basic principles for calculating the social costs of smoking are simple and have not been the object of any controversy within the professional economics literature. First, the question to be addressed is what would the costs attributable to smokers have been but for their smoking behavior. This type of analysis is also the basic principle underlying economic damages calculations in the courtroom more generally. It is only the smoking-related increase in costs that is relevant, not smokers' gross medical costs. Moreover, for legal damages it is only the portion of those costs attributable to wrongful conduct that is consequential. If smokers have annual medical costs of $10,000 and they would have had annual medical costs of $6,000 had they not smoked, it is the incremental $4,000 in costs that is the smoking-attributable portion.

A second related principle is that the costs of smoking must be assessed on a lifetime basis. Suppose people start smoking at age twenty-one and never stop. If they had not smoked they would have had a lifetime trajectory of costs, such as medical expenses in each year. Because they do smoke, their trajectory of costs may be different and possibly higher, particularly for medical expenses. It is this difference that reflects the health consequences of smoking.

Acknowledging the adverse health effects of smoking has other ramifications as well. Cigarettes shorten one's expected lifetime. If smoking reduces one's life expectancy by six years, then the trajectory of smoking-related costs will be shorter as well. Consistent recognition of the health cost effects requires that one compare the cost trajectory without smoking to the shorter expected cost trajectory with smoking. These are the cost trajectories that have actually occurred and the costs that would have occurred had the person not smoked. Smoking may raise costs while alive, but it shortens the period in which these costs occur.

Is the shortened life expectancy good? Of course not. Losing part of one's life is obviously a real "welfare loss" to smokers themselves. However, if the only focus of the cost estimation exercise is on the financial costs to society, which has in fact been the exclusive emphasis of the lawsuits by governmental entities, then the shortened life expectancy is not a financial harm that society at large experiences. To the extent that the premature mortality enters the financial picture, it is by decreasing certain tax payments that would have been made, which will be accounted for in the tally below. Private welfare losses are of course relevant to overall policy judgments regarding the total welfare implication of smoking and will be the subject of chapters 7 and 9.

Critics of the procedure of taking life expectancy effects into account often suggest purported conundrums such as the following. If in fact society saves money by the early death of smokers, could one then not claim a credit for causing a fatal accident in which, for example, a busload of elderly citizens goes off a cliff? Aren't we saving society Social Security and Medicare costs? Such examples reflect a basic misunderstanding of the analysis of assessing the actual life expectancy consequences, which they often term a "death credit." In the case of the elderly citizens, one would still be liable for conventional economic damages to the families of the deceased as well as possible criminal sanctions for driving their bus off a cliff. The cost implications for Social Security would not enter at all as a potential offset in any damages estimate. Why then are they part of the analysis for cigarettes smokers? The difference is that the cigarette cases initiated by the government have nothing whatsoever to do with addressing wrongs done to the smokers. Their intent also has nothing whatsoever to do with compensating the survivors of the smokers. Rather, the focus of the litigation is solely on whether the government incurred financial costs as a result of cigarettes. Within the context of this narrow accounting exercise that has been framed in the government lawsuits, taking life expectancy effects into account is essential because otherwise the procedure will not capture the costs that actually were incurred, but rather the costs that might have happened had cigarettes not affected life expectancy. And if there were no effect of cigarettes on health and life expectancy, there would be no basis for this litigation. The fundamental principle guiding these lawsuits and my calculations is that cigarettes are very dangerous and cause significant harms to individual health. However, this principle must guide all calculations. One cannot recognize the hazardousness of cigarettes selectively for different aspects of the estimates out of fear that doing a proper analysis will lead to lower cost estimates.

It is also noteworthy that the lawsuits address the company's treatment of tar in contradictory ways. Many state lawsuits have used the alleged failure to market low-tar cigarettes aggressively as a basis for cigarette industry liability. Individual lawsuits in which the person smoked higher-tar cigarettes will invariably make this claim. Whether, in fact, it is the government or the industry that discouraged dissemination of information about low-tar cigarettes is a matter that will be addressed in chapter 9. Similarly, the lawsuits pending in England are known as "excess tar" cases, as the plaintiffs allege that the industry should have only marketed low-tar cigarettes. At the same time the industry faced these lawsuits in some jurisdictions, in other litigation, the plaintiffs have alleged that low-tar cigarettes in fact do not confer any additional safety benefits. According to these claims, by marketing low-tar cigarettes, the industry has deceived consumers regarding the cigarettes' safety. The alleged deception in this instance arises from suggesting that low-tar cigarettes confer a relative safety benefit. This low-tar deception argument was, for example, the approach used by the state of Minnesota in its suit against the industry and the federal government in its current claim. In 2001 the European Union banned marketing low-tar cigarettes using terms such as "light."[13]

The cigarette industry is consequently in the rather unusual position of having plaintiffs seeking to find the industry liable with respect to its marketing of low-tar cigarettes, with some plaintiffs claiming that the marketing efforts were too strong and others claiming that the marketing efforts were too weak. In the individual plaintiff cases, these differing points of view typically stem from the kind of cigarettes smoked by the plaintiff. If the plaintiff smoked low-tar cigarettes, the industry's error was in marketing such cigarettes, whereas if the plaintiff smoked conventional cigarettes, the injuries are blamed on a failure to market low-tar cigarettes sufficiently aggressively.

A third principle in counting costs is that the lifetime costs must be discounted back to their present value to put them in comparable terms in today's dollars. The health consequences of smoking are typically not immediate. Many of the most severe potential consequences, such as respiratory disease and cancer, may not be apparent until many years or even decades after the risk exposure. Each pack of cigarettes thus gives rise to the possibility of a series of long-term consequences at different points in time. These cost effects need to be converted into comparable terms.

The standard approach in all economic damages calculations for personal injury cases is to compute the present value of the losses so as to make them equivalent to losses in today's dollars. Thus, one discounts all future cost effects using a rate of interest that recognizes that money today is more valuable than receiving a deferred payment because these funds could be invested. The social costs of smoking will vary considerably depending on the rate of interest. As a result, I will show results for three different real (i.e., net of inflation) riskless rates of interest: 0 percent, 3 percent, and 5 percent. Riskless rates are those paid on U.S. Treasury bills, not stock market portfolios or mutual funds. The Treasury bill rates are nominal rates that must be adjusted for inflation for purposes of these calculations. A zero rate of interest in effect results in no discounting whatsoever, as cost effects today receive the same weight as deferred consequences. Decreasing the rate of interest toward zero boosts the weight on immediate cost effects and reduces the weight on long-term consequences. Of the three interest rates, 3 percent is most in line with the long-term riskless return. It is, for example, the rate that government agencies such as the U.S. Environmental Protection Agency prefer to use.

The fourth principle is that insofar as possible the calculations should reflect cost characteristics associated with cigarettes, not overall costs that smokers generate, which may or may not be due to smoking. Thus, the calculations will use as a reference point the costs generated by a "nonsmoking smoker."[14] Smokers differ from nonsmokers in a variety of ways—their education, employment, and health habits. To the extent possible one would want to purge the cost estimates of these confounding influences that are correlated with smoking status. The "nonsmoking smoker" has the same demographic and risk characteristics of smokers other than their smoking status.

All such efforts to control for risk characteristics tend to be incomplete; thus the resulting estimates may overstate the social costs. Research by Joni Hersch and myself found that smokers are more likely to select risky jobs and are much more risk prone than are nonsmokers, wholly apart from their smoking status.[15] Smokers are more likely to be injured for any given type of job, and require less pay to compensate them for the hazards of working on risky jobs. Smokers are also more likely to be injured at home, are less likely to floss their teeth, and check their blood pressure less often. Smokers are systematically different from nonsmokers. Purging the cost estimates of the influence of broad demographic differences correlated with smoking status based on information available in the usual survey data sets only partially eliminates these confounding influences.

A fifth principle is that the costs should reflect the riskiness of the cigarettes being valued. As the discussion of the tar estimates above indicated, cigarettes have changed dramatically over time. Risk estimates based on cigarettes smoked just after World War II may not accurately reflect the hazards posed by today's cigarettes. By presenting unadjusted cost estimates and estimates that adjust for the tar content in a proportional manner, the analysis below will bound the likely effects of any such tar adjustment. Those willing to credit changes in tar levels with some benefit but not a fully proportional effect can use estimates in the intermediate range.

Once we are armed with these basic principles, what then should be valued as part of this assessment? The tally should encompass all external costs to the federal government, state government, and private insurers. Medical expenditures and sick leave costs will reflect the health costs of smoking, as will the costs of nursing home care. Insurance costs related to fires started by cigarettes also may enter. The effects of smoking on life expectancy have ramifications for the costs of group life insurance and pensions. If the effects on the duration of receiving these retirement pensions is recognized, one must also recognize the loss of tax revenues as deceased smokers do not contribute to Social Security and Medicare.

This comprehensive review reflects all cost components that have been recognized in the professional economics literature. Moreover, while participants in the tobacco litigation have sometimes attempted to narrow the list of concerns, there has been no attempt in this litigation to expand the list.

Nevertheless, there are other items that one might think are relevant. If one counts the excise taxes paid by smokers, should one not also count the sales taxes paid on cigarettes and the income taxes derived from tobacco sales and production? These, however, are not net economic costs, as consumers would spend their resources on other goods in the absence of cigarettes. What about the decreased productivity and health losses of smokers? These are private costs of smoking, and to the extent that these are ramifications that affect others (e.g., the grief experienced by one's family), these are not the type of insurance and financial costs being considered in the lawsuits. Secondhand smoke costs are not private costs, but for the most part they are health losses, not financial costs. These costs are the subject of chapter 6. Finally, should lost income taxes be counted if one counts payroll taxes? Since smokers are not receiving government services after their death, it seems inappropriate to bill them for taxes after their death.[16] Taxes are paid on what people actually make, not what they could have made. Following much the same logic, one would bill people for taxes if they failed to fulfill their maximum earning potential because they chose early retirement or became a public interest lawyer or judge rather than a more handsomely rewarded Wall Street lawyer. Society does not intrude in these income-generating decisions generally, because they are reflections of personal trade-offs people choose to make.

Based on the approach outlined above, the costs of smoking exhibit a surprising pattern. In particular, even excluding the role of excise taxes, cigarettes are self-financing. This result is not an anomaly, but is a consequence of smokers' premature mortality. Shoven, Sundberg, and Bunker (1989) found that smokers generated substantial Social Security savings, which on balance provided a net gain to society. In a government-funded RAND Corporation study, Manning et al. (1989, 1991) found that social costs were lower overall for smokers. This study is a basic building block and reference point for my analysis. Finally, the Congressional Research Service study by Gravelle and Zimmerman (1994) likewise found that cigarettes are self-financing. As did these studies, I will omit influences such as costs associated with low-birthweight babies.[17]

Table 4 provides my estimates for these cost effects based on the levels of prices and other economic factors in 1995. Among the influences that change over time are health cost factors such as nursing home utilization rates.[18] The first panel pertains to costs without adjusting for tar content, while the second panel adjusts these costs proportionally to tar content. If there is a partial behavioral offset, the costs will lie between the estimates in these two panels. The bottom panel is a simple update of the Manning et al. estimates based on price changes alone.[19] Influences such as changes in community hospital expenditures and increases in federal pension levels are not, however, included, as these more fundamental shifts are captured in my first set of estimates.

Because the health-care costs associated with cigarettes tend to be more immediate than the insurance-related financial savings, the choice of the discount rate affects the present value of the cost per pack of cigarettes. Indeed, whether cigarettes save society money or impose losses depends on the discount rate. The cost estimates in table 4 do not represent the contemporaneous costs but rather the present value of the ultimate time stream of costs associated with a pack of cigarettes. In each

Table 4 Social Costs of Smoking per Pack of Cigarettes (dollar costs per pack)

Cost Category	Real Rate of Interest		
	0%	3%	5%
Estimates with No Tar Adjustment for Cigarette Risks			
Total medical care	0.754	0.580	0.533
Sick leave	0.000	0.013	0.021
Group life insurance	0.254	0.144	0.097
Nursing home care	−0.633	−0.239	−0.080
Retirement and pension	−3.046	−1.259	−0.386
Fires	0.015	0.017	0.019
Taxes on earnings	0.932	0.425	0.129
Total net costs	−1.724	−0.319	0.333
Estimates with Tar-Adjusted Risks			
Total medical care	0.634	0.481	0.437
Sick leave	0.003	0.012	0.018
Group life insurance	0.213	0.121	0.081
Nursing home care	−0.549	−0.207	−0.070
Retirement and pension	−2.553	−1.055	−0.323
Fires	0.015	0.017	0.019
Taxes on earnings	0.755	0.344	0.104
Total net costs	−1.482	−0.287	0.266
Estimates Based on Manning et al. Assumptions			
Total medical care	0.511	0.383	0.345
Sick leave	0.003	0.014	0.022
Group life insurance	0.170	0.097	0.065
Nursing home care	−0.341	−0.129	−0.043
Retirement and pension	−2.556	−1.057	−0.324
Fires	0.017	0.019	0.022
Taxes on earnings	0.937	0.427	0.130
Total net costs	−1.259	−0.246	0.217

Note: All estimates update the 1993 cost estimates in Viscusi (1995a) to 1995 data whenever possible.

case, estimates appear for three different real discount rates: 0 percent, 3 percent, and 5 percent. The long-run real riskless rate of return in the United States has been in the vicinity of 1 percent to 3 percent, so the intermediate case shown in table 4 is probably the most realistic. For simplicity, all discussions below will focus on results using the 3 percent assumption.

Consider the components of the cost estimates for the set of results without a tar adjustment. The total medical care cost externality averages $0.58 per pack, where about two-thirds of these costs are incurred before smokers reach age sixty-five. Sick leave and fires are relatively minor cost items, averaging only $0.01–$0.02 per pack. Group life insurance costs average $0.14 per pack, as smokers' earlier expected mortality increases the present value of life insurance costs.

The remaining cost components represent cost savings associated with cigarettes. Although the higher expected morbidity of smokers increases a variety of costs, because of smokers' earlier mortality smokers on average save society $0.24 per pack in nursing home care and $1.26 per pack in retirement and pension benefits. Social Security benefit savings constitute the lion's share of this enormous retirement and pension cost component.

The final cost component in the various calculations in table 4 is taxes on earnings, which involve a cost of $0.43 per pack. This tax figure reflects only the payroll taxes for programs such as Social Security, not income taxes. The rationale for excluding income taxes is that since deceased smokers do not reap the benefits of public spending once they are dead, it would be inappropriate to hold them responsible for income taxes they did not pay.[20] Payroll taxes that finance retirement and medical care programs for the aged merit inclusion in the analysis because the cost savings for premature mortality are recognized.

To calculate the net financial costs associated with smoking, one must recognize both the forgone benefits not received and the forgone tax revenues. A straightforward updating of the assumptions made in a past analysis by Manning et al.[21] indicates that the net social cost of cigarettes is −$0.25 per pack, which is a cost savings. If this analysis is updated to reflect changes in program structure, benefit utilization rates, and similar factors, then the net social costs associated with smoking average −$0.32 per pack without any tar adjustment. With a tar adjustment, the net costs are −$0.29 per pack. Because of the lower risk potency of cigarettes after the tar adjustment and the smaller mortality cost savings, the cost estimates are scaled down with the tar adjustment. The tar adjustment has the surprising effect of making smoking more costly from a societal standpoint.

That is to say, the cost savings are greater in my analysis without the tar adjustment, which is perhaps surprising because in that analysis the total medical care costs are also the highest. By contrast, the analysis with the lowest total net cost savings is the update of the previous Manning et al. study, for which the total medical care cost impositions are the lowest of the three sets of estimates. Although the shifts in the analysis are not exactly proportional, the updating procedures that increase estimates of the total medical care costs also tend to increase the estimates of the cost offsets of smoking, with the net result being that there is a greater cost savings when cigarettes are potentially more costly. It should be emphasized that these cost savings reflect only the financial externalities associated with smoking. They do not also capture the $0.56 per pack excise tax value paid on each pack of cigarettes during this time period.

A potentially significant economic externality that has been omitted from the cost calculations is the cost associated with environmental tobacco smoke. These costs are much debated, highly uncertain, but of great consequence based on the expected risk levels assessed by government agencies. Chapter 6 estimates these costs, almost all of which are direct health costs rather than the financial externalities that are the focus of the calculations here.

If one were to organize the cost effects (without tar adjustment) into the most important cost impositions and cost reductions, the cost imposition side of the ledger would include medical care ($0.58), forgone taxes on earnings ($0.43), group life insurance ($0.14), and sick leave and fires ($0.01). Total costs are consequently $1.18 per pack. The cost reduction side of the ledger includes retirement pension ($1.26) and nursing home care ($0.24) as insurance cost savings, as well as $0.56 revenue in excise taxes. Thus, the total cost reductions and excise taxes equal $2.06. The total net cost effect is an overall savings of $0.88 per pack.

By these calculations one might view cigarettes as a financial profit center, not a costly imposition on society. The dollar stakes involved are enormous. In 1995 the public purchased 23.2 billion packs of cigarettes.[22] A total cost savings of $0.88 per pack including excise taxes implies a total societal cost savings of $20.4 billion. If one focuses only on the financial effects exclusive of excise taxes, the cost per pack savings of $0.32 implies an aggregate cost savings for society of $7.4 billion.

In view of the considerable financial gains, what could be the basis for the litigation by the state governments and the federal government? Several influences are at work—the governmental scope of the calculations, the cost components included, and the method of calculating costs.

The estimates in table 4 are for the overall costs of smoking to all of society, not just the government. The costs to each government entity will hinge on their different programmatic structures. If there is a large nursing home and retirement pension/Social Security cost component, there is likely to be net savings. However, if the only program of consequence is medical insurance, then there is a cost increase. Other differences arising with respect to the cost calculations will be the subject of chapter 5.

The temporal character of the cost effects is interesting as well. Medical costs tend to be relatively near term, as compared to the pension and nursing home cost effects, which are longer term. Thus, raising the discount rate increases the emphasis on the loss components. For the no-tar-adjustment case in table 4, even excluding excise taxes cigarettes generate a net savings of $1.72 per pack if there is no discounting, but at a high real discount rate such as 5 percent, there is a net cost increase of $0.33 per pack excluding excise taxes. At a real discount rate of 4 percent cigarettes become a break-even proposition. Recognition of excise taxes of $0.56 per pack, however, would make cigarettes still self-financing even at a rate of 5 percent, where the total savings including taxes would be $0.23 per pack. Public health officials generally present medical cost estimates without discounting, making the medical costs appear to be large. However, if one adopts the zero discounting approach for all cost components, doing so makes cigarettes more attractive from a cost standpoint.

These results concerning cigarettes' self-financing are even stronger in other countries with a different medical cost structure. In the Netherlands, for example, within the health care cost domain alone cigarettes are self-financing because the mix of illnesses affected and the associated health care costs differ from those in the United States.[23] Thus, calculations of retirement savings and excise taxes are not even needed in that country to produce the self-financing result. In the United States there is no complete cost offset unless one includes other cost components such as retirement pension savings. Other medical cost estimates that have appeared in the press have generated numbers as high as $2.06 per pack, of which $0.89 is a publicly funded cost. These estimates not only do not discount the costs to their present value, they also do not adjust for the different health risk profile of smokers and their shorter life expectancy.

A similar study by Philip Morris prepared for the Czechoslovakian government created substantial controversy when it was released in July 2001.[24] As in the United States and the Netherlands, cigarettes did not impose net financial costs on the Czech government because of the role of taxes and premature smoker mortality. Indeed, smoking leads to annual cost savings of 5,815 mil. CZK. Industry critics suggested that the company was touting the deadliness of its product as a benefit. However, these calculations in no way imply that the riskiness of cigarettes promotes social welfare. Rather, they simply address the financial consequences to society, which is an issue that was first raised by the Czech government and U.S. government officials, not the industry.

Cost Estimate Implications

What are the implications of these estimates for social policy? Should we begin to subsidize cigarette consumption to foster additional savings arising from smokers' premature mortality? Such unfounded policy inferences stem from a misinterpretation of what these estimates capture. The financial cost estimates do not represent a social welfare calculation. They are not meant to provide a comprehensive assessment of what one might term the economic costs and benefits of smoking to society, which would also include private benefits and costs to smokers as well as consequences such as health effects of environmental tobacco smoke. Rather, their focus is solely on the financial costs to society, chiefly on the insurance ramifications. Framing the question in this manner may seem overly narrow, which it is. But it should be emphasized that it is the antismoking forces and the governmental lawsuits that initiated this framing. To be able to address the financial cost issues that have been raised, it is necessary to confront those cost issues even though doing so does not capture all pertinent concerns. Subsequent chapters will broaden the inquiry substantially.

These societal financial cost estimates also serve as a building block for estimating the effects on the states and the federal government. Whether cigarettes are self-financing for these entities, which have been prominent in the cigarette litigation, depends on the particular set of programs in place in each locale as well as the role of excise taxes. The basic conclusion regarding self-financing will continue to hold, but not always with the same strength as in the overall cost estimates.

My estimates of the national costs of smoking were funded by the National Bureau of Economic Research, without the knowledge or support of the cigarette industry. When my initial estimates of the social costs of smoking appeared in the *New York Times*, they were not embraced by the tobacco industry. Indeed, the leading attorney representing Philip Morris explicitly disavowed my study and its methodology.[25] The plaintiffs in the cigarette litigation were even more reluctant to embrace the analysis.

Outside of the litigation arena, the study was well received. The Associated Press made one excerpt its quote of the day, and my appearances on the news shows such as *20/20* and the *CBS Evening News* with Dan Rather treated the calculations in a positive manner. Most of the uneasiness with my calculations stems from a misunderstanding of what they capture. Focusing solely on the financial costs of smoking, smokers pay their own way and, in fact, generate net cost savings. The premature death of smokers is not a desirable social outcome. However, the focus of the public debate on cigarette financial costs and the exclusive emphasis of the litigation on financial costs have brought to the forefront a dimension on which cigarettes perform quite well.

V

THE FINANCIAL COSTS TO THE STATES
AND THE FEDERAL GOVERNMENT

The most costly litigation in U.S. history was the series of tobacco-related lawsuits filed by more than forty states and by the federal government.[1] However, did these government entities in fact suffer increased costs because of smoking?

To the extent that cigarette smoking adversely affects health, there will be higher health insurance costs, including higher costs borne by the states, which share in the costs of Medicaid and other health programs. But the estimates in chapter 4 showed that, on the whole, cigarettes are not a net financial drain to the country. The fact that cigarettes are self-financing when viewed on an overall national basis does not, necessarily, imply that the federal government or any given state also did not suffer financial harm. Their program structures and tax mechanisms differ substantially and are affected in different ways. Even if there had been no net costs, the courts might have found the companies liable for increases in medical costs.

Many of the cost savings, such as reduced Social Security costs, benefit the federal government and not the states. The states, therefore, could potentially be net losers. Furthermore, the distribution of the costs and the excise taxes on cigarettes are not uniform, so that some states may lose financially while others gain. Consequently, one cannot necessarily conclude from the evidence in the previous chapter that the individual states are not adversely affected financially by cigarettes.

Whether the legal focus should be on the consequences for specific governmental entities or on the national consequences is a different matter. From the standpoint of efficient social policy, the net national consequences are paramount. The extent to which one could conclude that the states and the federal government have incurred costs associated with cigarette smoking may depend in part upon which cost components are recognized in calculating the damages amount. Here I will explore these various cost components for the states as well as for the federal government to assess the governmental distribution of the insurance consequences of cigarettes.

How States Count Costs

At the outset of the litigation, the principal issue was not what the damages were, but whether such suits had standing at all. Suing the industry to recover costs of adverse health effects was an untested legal approach, which could potentially affect a wide range of products. Indeed, many observers regarded such suits as highly speculative and lacking a sound legal basis. To help bolster the states' cases, the state legislatures in Florida[2] and Maryland[3] passed laws that would establish a legal basis for standing of the suits so as to assist the states in their litigation efforts. We thus have the curious situation of states passing laws now to provide a legal basis for a current claim to obtain damages for acts that were immune to such claims at the time they were taken decades ago. In effect, states created retroactive liability from which they would directly profit. Eminent legal scholars such as Judge Stephen Williams of the D.C. Circuit have observed that there are considerable dangers presented if states are able to restructure legal rules to promote litigation that is in their financial interest.[4] From an economic standpoint, such retrospective shifts in the legal regime will not serve any deterrence role. The cigarette industry behavior in question took place before the shift in the legal rules so that there could be no anticipation of such sanctions and consequently no effect on safety-related behavior. The past behavior that was the subject of the litigation cannot be altered retrospectively.

Even if there were no external costs attributable to smoking, the legal rationale for the suits is unclear. Suppose that smokers voluntarily assume the risk and consequently have no individual claim against the cigarette industry. If the assumption of risk defense is valid against claims by the smokers, this defense would also travel with such claims recast as independent claims by the state for medical assistance to smokers. A principal basis for the state suits was consequently a claim by the states that alleged deceptive practices by the industry prevented consumers from knowing that smoking is dangerous. Risk awareness issues were consequently central to the states' suits in determining liability and setting damages. Only the portion of the economic costs of cigarettes attributable to wrongful behavior can be recovered. Chapter 7 will examine the evidence on smoking risk awareness. However, an upper-bound estimate of cigarette industry liability is to assess all cigarette costs, not simply those due to wrongful behavior. If these costs are zero, then one need not distinguish the portion of the costs due to wrongful behavior.

The courts' assessment of the costs of smoking depends critically on what they choose to recognize as cost components. Though the analysis in chapter 4 focused on total net costs, in their litigation the states focused on a narrower question of whether the state health-care costs alone are positive. The prospective federal suit will probably also focus on health costs alone, excluding excise taxes and components such as nursing home care, but the nature of the federal damages claim is not yet clear. Both taxes and nursing home care are components for which the states are net gainers, not losers. Thus, the states sought to exclude from consideration cost components that on balance may be negative. The states also excluded excise taxes from their tally. The emphasis here is on a more complete social accounting because there is no economic justification for selective inclusion of the different cost components when determining net financial consequences. What costs matter from a legal standpoint is a different issue that has yet to be resolved. By looking at information on all cost effects, one can see how the size of the damages would vary depending on which costs are included.

A simple summary of the states' position is that they wanted to count only the increased costs for Medicaid. Even if one accepts this framing of the damages claim, these are serious and fundamental flaws with how the states estimated costs. First, in calculating the increased medical costs, states counted not only the costs incurred by the states but also the federal government's share of Medicaid expenditures. As a matter of program structure, Medicaid costs are shared between the state and the federal government, where the state's share depends on the income level in the state. All states sought reimbursement for both the state and the federal cost components, although it is only the state portion of the claim that represents a true cost increase for the state budget. In justification for including the federal share, the states maintained that the tobacco companies cannot include federal payments as an offset. In the states' view, the federal contributions are payments by a source independent of the tobacco companies, that is, they are a collateral source.[5] However, the federal payments are not a collateral source in the usual sense, as Medicaid costs are simply shared by the state and federal governments as a matter of policy. The federal contribution is not akin to the usual type of collateral source for an accident victim, such as the person receiving health insurance coverage as well as a tort award for accident-related medical expenses. If the states were compensated for the federal share, the states would collect these funds twice—once from the tobacco companies and once from the federal government. Including the federal share has additional complications as well. Now that the federal government has also filed a claim, if the companies lose they will end up paying twice for the federal cost share—once to the states and a second time to the federal government.

The double payment of the federal share is also noteworthy in that the states vigorously objected when President Clinton and federal budget officials suggested that the federal government should share in the value of the 1997 Proposed Resolution of the cigarette litigation, if in fact it had been passed by Congress. Such sharing was not an unprincipled money grab by the Clinton administration, as the state governors characterized it. Rather, such sharing would have been entirely consistent with the nature of the damages claim filed by the states. The 1999 federal budget assumed that the federal government would ultimately share in these funds, but the compromise outcome Clinton proposed to the governors was that they make expenditures in certain designated areas, which has turned out to be a largely symbolic gesture.[6]

The second shortcoming in the analysis of medical costs by the states is that these claims are not restricted to costs actually incurred by smokers, but instead charge smokers for costs as if they had nonsmokers' life expectancy. Proper recognition of the life expectancy of smokers is not a "death credit," as the states have labeled it. Rather, it simply represents appropriate recognition of costs that the state actually incurred. There are no additional damages to the state in terms of higher Medicaid costs once smokers are dead. These factors will account for most of the difference between my estimates and higher publicized figures.

The fallacy of the states' logic in ignoring life expectancy effects can be shown with a simple hypothetical example, illustrated in figure 2.[7] Suppose that nonsmokers live for two periods, and incur medical costs of $2,000 in each period. Suppose that smokers live only for one period because of the effect of smoking on their health and their mortality, but because they are sicker they have medical costs of $5,000 in period 1. Ignoring the role of discounting, the incremental medical costs of smoking are $1,000. However, the states' method of calculating medical costs is to carry smokers forward into period 2 after they are dead, assuming that they will incur the same level of costs in period 2. Thus, the states charge them for $5,000 in costs that they never even generated. Based on the states' calculations, the increased medical costs are $6,000, not $1,000. However, $5,000 of these costs never even occurred because smokers were dead so that the states did not suffer this financial loss.

Accounting for the shorter life expectancy of smokers is not a con-

Nonsmokers:

Total calculated costs: $2000 + $2000 = $4000

Smokers:

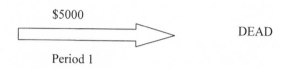

DEAD

Total actual costs: $5000

Total costs as calculated by the state: $5000 + $5000 = $10,000

Incremental medical costs of smokers: $1000 Actual
                                              $6000 Calculated

Figure 2 Structure of how states calculate medical costs

troversial "death credit." Rather, it is the only legitimate way to account for possible damages attributable to smoking. The appropriate legal test is what were the damages to the state but for the wrongful conduct of the cigarette industry. There are no damages to the state in terms of higher Medicaid costs once smokers are dead.

By making smokers in effect die twice, the states exaggerated medical costs in another way as well. Most medical expenses are incurred in the last years of life. To count these expenses again by making smokers die a second time after having normal life expectancy creates a bizarre distortion in the cost estimates, leading to substantial overestimation of the expected medical costs attributable to cigarettes.

The impetus for the state suits was a series of allegations of wrongful behavior on the part of the cigarette industry. Consider, for example, some of the allegations by the state of Minnesota. The state claimed that there has been a decades-long combination and conspiracy of willful and intentional wrongdoing by the leading cigarette manufacturers and their trade associations. . . . These same defendants have known for decades from their own internal studies that their products are deadly and addictive. Instead of disclosing this knowledge, these defendants intentionally chose to engage in a unified campaign of deceit and misrepresentation. This course of conduct was intended by the defendants to control and maintain their market, to maximize their profits, and to minimize their legal exposure—all for the "self-preservation" of the industry. . . . The defendants' collective conduct has resulted in an unprecedented impact on the public health, in both human and economic terms. . . . Despite the duration and the severity of the misconduct, the industry has enjoyed virtual immunity because of its economic and political power, its scorched-earth litigation tactics, and its fraudulent concealment of unlawful conduct.[8]

From a legal standpoint, the costs for which the cigarette companies should be liable are those attributable to their wrongful behavior, such as that alleged in the Minnesota brief. Thus, to the extent that deceptive advertising, antitrust violations (for example, the alleged conspiracy to suppress development of safer cigarettes), or other illegal practices led to additional smoking-related costs, the state can seek to obtain damages for the portion of such costs attributable to the wrongful behavior. However, the states' suits did not distinguish the influence of such wrongful behavior, but instead included all smoking-attributable costs, which implicitly assumes that smoking rates would be zero had it not been for the alleged wrongful conduct of the cigarette industry.

The nature of the federal claim for damages is in many respects similar to that for the states.[9] The federal government is pursuing various allegations of unlawful conduct such as those alleged in the state suits, where these actions are taken pursuant to the Medical Care Recovery Act, the Medicare Secondary Payer Provisions of Subchapter 18 of the Social Security Act, and the Racketeer Influenced and Corrupt Organizations provisions.[10] The federal government claim is that the "tortuous and unlawful conduct" of the tobacco industry has caused the federal government to spend "more than $20 billion annually for the treatment of injuries and diseases caused by defendants' products."[11] Whether this cost estimate, in fact, distinguishes the incremental influence of the wrongful behavior, as opposed to being a gross estimate is unclear. No details regarding this damages figure have been released. We consequently do not know what the estimate includes or where it came from.

The most striking aspect of the federal Complaint is the treatment of the company's marketing of low-tar and low-nicotine cigarettes. Ide-

CHAPTER FIVE

ally, one would want to encourage the companies to market cigarettes that posed lower health risk, as do lower-tar cigarettes. Indeed, many individual suits against the cigarette industry, the state suits, and the British suits are based on the claim that the cigarette industry did not market such lower-risk products aggressively enough. In the federal suit, on the other hand, there is a denial that there is any evidence that low-tar and low-nicotine cigarettes are safer, notwithstanding scientific evidence to the contrary. Moreover, tar and nicotine levels are measured and sanctioned by the Federal Trade Commission, and federal law requires that companies disclose these levels. The position taken instead is that the very act of marketing low-tar and -nicotine cigarettes constituted racketeering violations.

Indeed, fairly innocuous claims on behalf of low-tar cigarettes become racketeering violations according to the federal suit. For example, one of the purported racketeering acts cited in the federal Complaint is that in marketing its Vantage cigarettes, R. J. Reynolds sent out an advertisement that included the following language: "If you're like a lot of smokers these days, it probably isn't smoking that you want to give up. It's some of that 'tar and nicotine you've been hearing about.'"[12] Similarly, another racketeering violation in the view of the federal government is the Vantage ad that states "Vantage cuts down substantially on the 'tar and nicotine' you may have become concerned about."[13] Other products also came under criticism for similar claims. The alleged racketeering violation in the marketing of True cigarettes was an advertisement stating "I thought about all I'd read and said to myself, either quit or smoke True. I smoke True."[14] Similarly, Merit cigarettes, marketed by Philip Morris, also are associated with alleged racketeering acts. One of these acts, according to the federal brief, was the advertisement stating that Merit's "ability to satisfy over long periods of time could be the most important evidence to date that MERIT science has produced what it claims: The first real alternative for high tar smokers."[15] Another racketeering violation in the view of the federal government is the Merit ad: "Merit taste eases low tar decision."[16]

These racketeering acts alleged in the federal Complaint are but a sample of the overriding concern in the complaint over the marketing of low-tar and low-nicotine cigarettes. Legitimate and quite restrained marketing statements become racketeering violations. While the scientific evidence suggests that there may be some offsetting behavior on the part of smokers, on balance low-tar and low-nicotine cigarettes do pose reduced risk. The fact that the government is not applauding these attempts to market low-tar cigarettes but instead views them as racketeering violations shows how far government policy has drifted from its more responsible role of fostering market innovations that promote safety. Mischaracterizing legitimate marketing efforts as a racketeering conspiracy seems so far removed from what racketeering laws were meant to address that it appears to be a desperate effort to establish a legal basis for a speculative legal claim.

Whether the federal suits have standing and what portion of the tobacco-related costs are in fact attributable to wrongful behavior by the cigarette industry are unclear. Moreover, unlike the state suits, there has yet to be any calculation of the estimated damages released as part of the litigation.

One can, however, establish an upper bound on the cost. In thinking about the annual cost, how far should one go back in time in examining these cost levels? Is it all the cigarette consumption that has occurred historically and all the associated state and federal costs? That approach would be correct if smoking would have dropped to zero had this wrongful behavior not occurred. However, that clearly is not that case. Indeed, the first wrongful acts that are even alleged in the federal suit and in most of the state suits did not begin until 1954 with the release of the advertisement entitled "A Frank Statement to Smokers," which appeared in various newspapers.[17] Thus, the extent of the damages is limited in time and does not predate the wrongful behavior. A second pertinent concern is that within the period after wrongful conduct began, only smoking behavior attributable to this conduct is relevant in calculating damages. Over the past half century, there has been considerable new research on smoking and the release of an enormous amount of information concerning cigarettes, including all the confidential documents from the cigarette industry that were made public after the Minnesota cigarette litigation. Notwithstanding this public release of the confidential files and the extensive publicity given to the cigarette industry in general, smoking rates have not plummeted. Assuming there would be no smoking whatsoever in the absence of wrongful industry conduct will overstate the actual costs due to such behavior. My calculations below that estimate the total cost attributable to cigarette consumption will consequently provide an upper bound on the amount of damages that would be appropriate if only the smoking due to wrongful conduct were eliminated.

Smoking affects the states in ways other than medical costs. Pension costs, nursing home expenditures, and other nonmedical components of state allocations are among these other cost effect categories. On balance, such cost effects are beneficial to the state because the premature deaths of smokers will reduce the total costs of many of these programs. The states have resisted such considerations, claiming that they are a "death credit." In its litigation *Memorandum*, the state of Mississippi launched the state litigation effort with the following critique targeted at my 1995 cigarette article in its working paper form:

> A credit to the cigarette industry for any monetary savings in elderly health care, as well as other savings resulting in the premature deaths of smokers, is utterly repugnant to a civilized society and must be rejected on grounds of public policy. . . . The contention of entitlement to an 'early death' credit is, on its face, void as against public policy. That policy and basic human decency preclude the defendants from putting forth the perverse and depraved argument that by killing Mississippians prematurely, they provide an economic benefit to the State. No court of equity should countenance, condone, or sanction such base, evil, and corrupt arguments. . . . The defendants' argument is indeed ghoulish. They are merchants of death. Seeking a credit for a purported economic benefit for early death is akin to robbing the graves of the Mississippi smokers who died from tobacco-related illnesses. No court of law or equity should entertain such a defense or counterclaim. It is offensive to human decency, an affront to justice, uncharacteristic of civilized society, and unquestionably contrary to public policy.[18]

What was striking about the Mississippi attack on my work was that they equated my analysis with the defendants' position. The Mississippi memorandum was in fact the opening salvo in the litigation effort by the states. At that point in the litigation, the defendants had no stated position and had not even discussed my cost estimates with me. Moreover, when my study was covered in the press, the tobacco industry did not endorse it.

Shortly after the Mississippi memorandum outlined the basis for their case, I was contacted by lawyers representing Philip Morris and R. J. Reynolds, who asked me to explain what I had done. They were curious as to what my methodology was and whether in fact it would be pertinent to the litigation. Perhaps my cost accounting merited a more careful examination than took place with the initial industry reaction to press coverage of my study.

Other portions of the Mississippi memorandum question aspects of the methodology or attempt to discredit it. If the states truly believe that the cigarette companies are "merchants of death," one wonders why they have not banned cigarettes rather than sought profits through excise taxes and the recent litigation. The controversial exercise of tallying the financial consequences of smoking was initiated by the states, not the defendants. The objective of such an effort should be to calculate the true financial costs to the state, not to focus selectively on the positive components and to ignore the negative, cost-reducing effects. Suppose, for example, that Medicaid consisted of Medicaid Part 1, for which cigarettes raised the costs by $1,000, and Medicaid Part 2, for which they reduce the costs by $1,500. Is the net effect of smoking that the states are entitled to collect the $1,000 cost increase, or should one include the reduced cost as well? From the standpoint of efficient deterrence and optimal insurance, it is always the net economic damage that is the appropriate matter of concern. However, the logic of the damage claims would be to count only the cost increase.

The final major component of concern consists of the cigarette-related taxes. The states all maintained that income taxes paid and general sales taxes paid because of cigarette consumption should not be credited to cigarettes. This argument has a sound economic basis. Presumably, if consumers were not purchasing these products they would be buying other goods that would also be generating similar sales or income taxes.

But the states' effort to exclude all taxes falls short by not distinguishing the incremental additional taxes paid by cigarettes—the excise taxes. One can view the excise tax mechanism as an ex ante substitute for the ex post damages payments in the courts. Suppose, for example, that cigarettes imposed some positive costs per pack. If this relationship were known on a prospective basis, the state could charge smokers at the time of purchase for these costs through an excise tax mechanism. Recouping these costs through litigation is simply the analog of excise taxes, except that it is done after the fact and involves much higher levels of transaction costs. Indeed, the structure of the actual settlement functions as an excise tax, not a lump sum settlement. The mechanism of collecting for the costs imposed on the state is not a matter of economic consequence other than with respect to accounting for transactions costs, which are higher in litigation contexts. Would, however, states have levied higher excise taxes had the health effects of cigarettes been known to the state, assuming they were not? Also, from a legal standpoint, is this distinction consequential? Such key issues were never resolved because of the out-of-court settlement.

Perhaps at the most fundamental level, do such suits have legal standing at all? Is it appropriate for the states to collect payments for the costs associated with legal risky products? If that is acceptable, are other products such as automobiles, barbecue grills, and alcoholic beverages subject to the same legal sanctions? Recent litigation has added guns,[19] lead paint, and HMOs to the cigarette model of litigation.[20]

The guiding principle for my calculations is to assess the net differential costs specifically linked to cigarettes. The approach here will be to undertake a comprehensive cost-accounting framework that recognizes excise taxes as well as all insurance-related consequences of cigarette smoking for states.[21] To the extent that excise taxes are based on the state of information at the time of the smoking decision and litigation is based on retrospective assessments, excise taxes will be better suited to providing appropriate levels of deterrence based on the expected social costs of smoking at the time those decisions are made.

The arguments against counting excise taxes largely reflect a misunderstanding of fundamental economic principles. The first argument made by the state of Mississippi is that "tax revenue is the sole domain of the legislature, not the defendants." The fact that legislatures set taxes and not the cigarette companies is irrelevant for determining the net economic cost to the state. For taxes used to correct external damages, it will be the legislature rather than the companies themselves that set the tax level since that is the policy mechanism by which taxes are levied.

The states' second argument against excise taxes is that they were "not paid by the *defendants*. They were paid by the consumers of cigarettes and those who treated them."[22] All taxes are shared by the consumers and producers, depending upon the relative elasticities of supply and demand. However, whether it is the producer or the consumer that bears the brunt of the tax is irrelevant from the standpoint of social efficiency. From that standpoint, the object is not to punish particular groups, but rather to have the price of a product reflect its full social cost. Questions of tax incidence are irrelevant to determining the optimal tax level to reflect any external costs imposed by a product. What matters is that the tax reflects the external economic damage. We want consumers to have to pay more for harmful products so as to discourage their purchase.

The argument against excise taxes that should have been made, but was not, was that perhaps the states were not aware of the costs until recently. Had they been aware of the cost effects, excise taxes would have been higher. As it turned out, however, the companies never paid a damages payment for past actions but agreed to a future excise tax to settle the litigation. Why such an excise tax should not have been the province of the state legislatures was never addressed in any of the states' cases.

Externality Estimates for the State of Mississippi

The basic building blocks of the following analysis will be the estimates of the national externalities associated with cigarette smoking presented in chapter 4. The essence of my methodological approach will be to adjust the national estimates in various ways to reflect the different cost level for the states and the federal government. Thus, for each category of expenditures this approach distinguishes to the extent feasible the state and federal share of these expenditures as well as factors that influence the state share differently across states, such as differences in per capita income levels or nursing home care utilization rates.

The costs for the state of Mississippi, which was the first state to file a suit against the industry, provide a useful starting point. Table 5 presents the state of Mississippi counterparts to the national estimates presented in chapter 4; the data are for 1995. The estimates address three different scenarios—the health effects invariant to tar level assumption, estimates with the tar changes recognized, and a simple update of an earlier analysis but on a state-specific basis.[23]

The tax per pack of cigarettes in Mississippi in 1995 was $0.18. The question is whether the net social externalities exceed that amount. As can be seen by the summary of these costs, the total net cost of smoking in Mississippi is the cost savings of $0.03 per pack with tar adjustments and $0.04 per pack without tar adjustments, excluding the excise tax payment amount. The update of the Manning et al. (1989, 1991) study on a state-specific basis leads to a cost savings of $0.02 per pack for Mississippi.

These cost estimates reflect a variety of adjustments from the national estimates presented in the preceding chapter. The procedure used for transforming the national estimates into state estimates represented straightforward application of a series of adjustment factors to reflect state cost shares and state differences, and the factors affecting those adjustments are quite diverse.[24]

To see the general approach for developing these cost estimates, let us begin with the focal point of the state litigation efforts—medical care costs. Medical care costs for the states include two main components: Medicaid and other medical expenditures, which consist of uncompensated care in community hospitals and any other state medical expenditures. Medicaid costs are shared by both the federal government and the states, where the average federal share for all states was 60 percent in 1995. The rate of federal matching differs by state and is a critical component in determining the state cost share. This rate is higher for Mississippi than for the United States as a whole due to the Medicaid formula that increases the federal matching rate as the per capita income of the state declines. Thus, in Mississippi the federal matching rate is 79 percent.

Since Mississippi is poorer than the national average, the need-based Medicaid program serves a larger fraction of its citizenry—roughly one and a half times the national average. However, the state of Mississippi

Table 5 State Burden of Insurance Externalities of Cigarettes for the State of Mississippi (dollar costs per pack)

Cost Category	Rate of Interest		
	0%	3%	5%
Estimates with No Tar Adjustment for Cigarette Risks			
Total medical care	0.026	0.020	0.019
Sick leave	0.000	0.001	0.001
Group life insurance	0.010	0.005	0.004
Nursing home care	−0.076	−0.029	−0.010
Retirement pension	−0.124	−0.051	−0.016
Fires	0.000	0.000	0.000
Taxes on earnings	0.039	0.018	0.005
Total net costs	−0.125	−0.036	0.003
Estimates with Tar-Adjusted Risks			
Total medical care	0.022	0.017	0.015
Sick leave	0.000	0.001	0.001
Group life insurance	0.008	0.005	0.003
Nursing home care	−0.066	−0.025	−0.008
Retirement pension	−0.104	−0.043	−0.013
Fires	0.000	0.000	0.000
Taxes on earnings	0.031	0.014	0.004
Total net costs	−0.109	−0.031	0.002
Estimates Based on Manning et al. Assumptions			
Total medical care	0.018	0.013	0.012
Sick leave	0.000	0.001	0.002
Group life insurance	0.006	0.004	0.002
Nursing home care	−0.041	−0.015	−0.005
Retirement pension	−0.104	−0.043	−0.013
Fires	0.000	0.000	0.000
Taxes on earnings	0.039	0.018	0.005
Total net costs	−0.082	−0.022	0.003

Note: All estimates are for 1995.

also has lower operating costs (wages, rent, contracted services), and it uses less technologically advanced medical procedures, which account for a lower cost per Medicaid recipient.

The estimates adjust for state differences in non-Medicaid expenditures similarly. I divided these expenditures into uncompensated care in community hospitals and other state medical expenditures. For each of these categories, I calculated the relative value of expenditures in Mississippi as compared to the rest of the country. The final step is to take the average state share of hospital, physician, and drug payments and apply this measure to the medical costs assessments presented in table 4 to determine the Mississippi state share of that cost, which is shown in table 5.

Next, we consider that workers in ill health may suffer higher sick leave costs. These costs were relatively minor for the nation as a whole—about $0.01 per pack for the estimates using a 3 percent rate of interest—and are considerably less for the state of Mississippi. To make these estimates specific to the state of Mississippi, the calculations reflected the relative earnings of Mississippi workers relative to the U.S. average, the percentage of the labor force employed by the state, and the average state share of sick leave costs per employee.

In the case of group life insurance, there is no information available to make separate estimates for the state of Mississippi as opposed to the average state. This calculation consequently simply divides the life insurance costs proportionally among federal employees, state employees, and other employee groups based on their employment share.

Nursing home costs are one of the most important external costs associated with cigarettes. However, this category represents a cost savings, not a cost imposition. The starting point for this calculation is to reflect the average state burden of nursing home care costs, which is 33 percent, as the federal government pays the remainder. One can then adjust this amount to reflect factors specific to the state of Mississippi. In particular, the estimates adjust for the relative percentage of the Mississippi population in nursing homes, which is only 86 percent of the national average. The cost of nursing home care is also less than the national average as measured by covered charges per day. Finally, the calculations reflect the Medicaid share paid for by the state of Mississippi in proportion to that paid by the average state.

The largest component in the total societal externality costs is pension costs, chiefly Social Security. To calculate the Mississippi pension cost savings because of smokers' premature mortality, one first assesses the proportion of pension payments paid by each level of government and by the private sector. The adjustment relative to the average state consists of two parts. First, many states augment federal Supplemental

Security Income (SSI) payments. Mississippi does not. As a result, one must assess the gross state pension expenditures to reflect the omission of SSI payments from total costs. The second adjustment is to correct for differences in the average state pension payment per recipient. The net result is pension cost savings of $0.04 to $0.05 per pack for the state of Mississippi depending on the particular assumptions used. This amount is a small fraction of the total societal pension cost savings.

The taxes on earnings reflect direct state employee payments into the system to cover costs of health care, sick leave, group life insurance, and pensions. The starting point for the calculations consists of the state employee's hourly benefit cost. One then can adjust these amounts by the relative benefits for the state of Mississippi, taking into account all different components of workers' pretax contributions.

Certain combinations of the insurance externalities are of interest as well. For the set of estimates without tar adjustments, total medical care costs are $0.02 per pack, whereas nursing home cost savings are $0.03 per pack. Thus, even within the medical component alone there is no net cost imposition if one includes both medical care and nursing home care in the calculations. In addition, the retirement pension cost offset exceeds the cost associated with medical care.

On balance, table 5 indicates that cigarettes are self-financing for Mississippi. Whereas the cost savings generated by cigarettes were substantial for society as a whole, for the state of Mississippi these savings only averaged $0.03 per pack. The results for the state of Mississippi and other states are, however, sensitive to the rate of discount. Cost savings from smoking increase if there is no discounting, and cigarettes are a break-even proposition at a 5 percent rate. These results paralleled those for other states. Note that these estimates do not reflect the role of the $0.18 per pack excise taxes in the state of Mississippi.

Effects by State and Overall Federal Costs

The state of Mississippi is unrepresentative in a variety of ways, chiefly because of the lower per capita income and the consequences this has for the structure of state programs and the demands on them. As a result, it is useful to assess the costs for an average state and to distinguish the costs for the federal government as well.[25] Table 6 presents the three sets of such calculations for both the state's costs and the costs to the federal government. As before, one assumes that health effects are invariant to the tar level, a second set recognizes changes in tar content, and a third set updates an earlier analysis.[26] For both the federal and state govern-

Table 6 Average State Governmental and Federal Governmental Burden
of Insurance Externalities of Cigarettes (dollar costs per pack)

Cost Category	State Cost Estimate Rate of Interest			Federal Cost Estimate Rate of Interest		
	0%	3%	5%	0%	3%	5%
Estimates with No Tar Adjustment for Cigarette Risks						
Total medical care	0.043	0.033	0.030	0.306	0.236	0.217
Sick leave	0.000	0.001	0.002	0.000	0.001	0.002
Group life insurance	0.010	0.005	0.004	0.008	0.004	0.003
Nursing home care	−0.206	−0.078	−0.026	−0.383	−0.145	−0.049
Retirement pension	−0.189	−0.078	−0.024	−2.048	−0.847	−0.259
Fires	0.000	0.000	0.000	0.000	0.000	0.000
Taxes on earnings	0.058	0.027	0.008	0.486	0.221	0.067
Total net costs	−0.284	−0.090	−0.006	−1.631	−0.530	−0.019
Estimates with Tar-Adjusted Risks						
Total medical care	0.036	0.027	0.025	0.258	0.195	0.178
Sick leave	0.000	0.001	0.002	0.000	0.001	0.001
Group life insurance	0.008	0.005	0.003	0.006	0.004	0.002
Nursing home care	−0.179	−0.068	−0.023	−0.333	−0.126	−0.042
Retirement pension	−0.158	−0.065	−0.020	−1.717	−0.710	−0.217
Fires	0.000	0.000	0.000	0.000	0.000	0.000
Taxes on earnings	0.047	0.022	0.007	0.393	0.179	0.054
Total net costs	−0.246	−0.078	−0.006	−1.393	−0.457	−0.024
Estimates Based on Manning et al. Assumptions						
Total medical care	0.029	0.022	0.020	0.208	0.155	0.140
Sick leave	0.000	0.001	0.002	0.000	0.001	0.002
Group life insurance	0.006	0.004	0.002	0.005	0.003	0.002
Nursing home care	−0.111	−0.042	−0.014	−0.207	−0.078	−0.026
Retirement pension	−0.158	−0.065	−0.020	−1.719	−0.711	−0.218
Fires	0.000	0.000	0.000	0.000	0.000	0.000
Taxes on earnings	0.059	0.027	0.008	0.488	0.223	0.068
Total net costs	−0.175	−0.053	−0.002	−1.225	−0.407	−0.032

Note: All estimates are for 1995.

ment, the costs due to fires are assumed to be zero since these are largely private costs.

The cost effects are similar for both the unadjusted estimates and those that reflect tar adjustments. Because of the similarity, I will focus on the tar-adjusted estimates, which reflect somewhat smaller cost savings. As before, I will focus on the 3 percent rate of interest. The total federal cost savings are $0.46 per pack, whereas the total state cost savings are $0.08 per pack. This average state cost savings amount is more than double the cost savings for Mississippi because the greater affluence of these other states largely has the effect of scaling up the benefits and the cost savings involved.

Cigarettes impose $0.20 per pack of medical care costs on the federal government, as compared to $0.03 per pack for the average state. Sick leave costs and group life insurance are relatively small effects. The nursing home care cost savings are $0.13 per pack for the federal government and $0.07 per pack for state governments. As expected, federal retirement pension savings from smokers' early mortality equal to $0.71 exceed the $0.07 per pack value for the states. Taxes on earnings are similarly scaled higher for the federal government than for the states, as one would expect.

There are some differences in the composition of the cost with respect to the cost offsets. Whereas the nursing home care cost savings to the states exceeds the total medical care cost increase, this is not the case for the federal government. In each instance, however, the retirement pension cost savings exceed the medical care cost increase. Moreover, the $0.32 average excise tax for the states and the $0.24 excise tax for the federal government each exceeded the higher value of medical costs.[27]

These estimates of the cost savings are, however, sensitive to the discount rate. Cigarettes are self-financing at the federal level for all rates shown in table 6, with cost savings ranging from $0.02 per pack at 5 percent interest to $1.39 at 0 percent. For all states the cost savings range is much narrower—from $0.01 at 5 percent interest to $0.25 at 0 percent. Nevertheless, the self-financing status holds true even without the inclusion of excise taxes.

One can undertake a similar set of calculations as was undertaken for Mississippi for each state. These values appear in table 7. For simplicity, I have summarized only the most salient cost components and the total effects for the no-tar-adjustment case. Column 1 summarizes the state excise tax rate for each of the states as well as for all states as a group. The next series of four columns presents the principal cost components for the externality costs per pack for the scenario in which costs are

Table 7 State Cigarette Smoking Externalities (dollar costs per pack)

State	State Excise Tax Rate per Pack	External Costs per Pack by Category				
		Medical Care	Nursing Homes	Pensions	Taxes on Earnings	Total Externalities
Alabama	0.165	0.025	−0.044	−0.075	0.019	−0.075
Alaska	0.290	0.035	−0.038	−0.136	0.021	−0.118
Arizona	0.580	0.012	−0.047	−0.094	0.015	−0.114
Arkansas	0.315	0.026	−0.069	−0.057	0.019	−0.081
California	0.370	0.033	−0.112	−0.132	0.021	−0.190
Colorado	0.200	0.028	−0.097	−0.104	0.019	−0.154
Connecticut	0.500	0.052	−0.103	−0.129	0.026	−0.154
Delaware	0.240	0.040	−0.081	−0.065	0.022	−0.084
Florida	0.339	0.031	−0.086	−0.063	0.020	−0.098
Georgia	0.120	0.031	−0.050	−0.089	0.020	−0.088
Hawaii	0.600	0.027	−0.047	−0.097	0.019	−0.098
Idaho	0.280	0.018	−0.047	−0.046	0.017	−0.058
Illinois	0.440	0.039	−0.120	−0.070	0.022	−0.129
Indiana	0.155	0.032	−0.095	−0.048	0.021	−0.090
Iowa	0.360	0.026	−0.162	−0.031	0.019	−0.148
Kansas	0.240	0.025	−0.143	−0.034	0.019	−0.133
Kentucky	0.030	0.029	−0.051	−0.071	0.020	−0.073
Louisiana	0.200	0.037	−0.119	−0.039	0.022	−0.099
Maine	0.370	0.040	−0.068	−0.071	0.022	−0.077
Maryland	0.360	0.037	−0.060	−0.095	0.022	−0.096
Massachusetts	0.510	0.047	−0.113	−0.093	0.024	−0.135
Michigan	0.750	0.029	−0.047	−0.082	0.020	−0.080
Minnesota	0.480	0.037	−0.089	−0.075	0.022	−0.105
Mississippi	0.180	0.020	−0.029	−0.051	0.018	−0.042
Missouri	0.170	0.029	−0.143	−0.068	0.020	−0.162
Montana	0.180	0.022	−0.052	−0.059	0.018	−0.071
Nebraska	0.340	0.028	−0.113	−0.036	0.019	−0.102
Nevada	0.350	0.025	−0.052	−0.084	0.019	−0.092
New Hampshire	0.250	0.035	−0.120	−0.055	0.021	−0.119
New Jersey	0.400	0.046	−0.067	−0.098	0.024	−0.095
New Mexico	0.210	0.022	−0.034	−0.079	0.018	−0.073
New York	0.560	0.082	−0.066	−0.091	0.033	−0.042
North Carolina	0.050	0.028	−0.045	−0.073	0.019	−0.071
North Dakota	0.440	0.029	−0.058	−0.047	0.020	−0.056
Ohio	0.240	0.034	−0.086	−0.080	0.021	−0.111
Oklahoma	0.230	0.023	−0.118	−0.090	0.018	−0.167
Oregon	0.380	0.024	−0.070	−0.059	0.019	−0.086
Pennsylvania	0.310	0.032	−0.102	−0.065	0.020	−0.115

Table 7 *continued*

State	State Excise Tax Rate per Pack	External Costs per Pack by Category				
		Medical Care	Nursing Homes	Pensions	Taxes on Earnings	Total Externalities
Rhode Island	0.560	0.056	−0.082	−0.130	0.026	−0.130
South Carolina	0.070	0.025	−0.035	−0.075	0.019	−0.066
South Dakota	0.230	0.025	−0.084	−0.043	0.019	−0.083
Tennessee	0.130	0.031	−0.058	−0.047	0.020	−0.054
Texas	0.410	0.029	−0.080	−0.038	0.020	−0.069
Utah	0.265	0.016	−0.032	−0.067	0.016	−0.067
Vermont	0.200	0.031	−0.064	−0.064	0.020	−0.077
Virginia	0.025	0.028	−0.070	−0.073	0.019	−0.096
Washington	0.565	0.029	−0.095	−0.037	0.020	−0.083
West Virginia	0.170	0.032	−0.049	−0.052	0.021	−0.048
Wisconsin	0.380	0.029	−0.089	−0.102	0.020	−0.142
Wyoming	0.120	0.023	−0.065	−0.053	0.018	−0.077
Averages	0.315	0.031	−0.077	−0.072	0.020	−0.098

Note: All figures assume a 3% discount rate and are for 1995. These statistics are averages weighted by the packs of cigarettes sold per state rather than simple averages, which are used in table 4. All estimates are for the costs invariant to the tar level. Figures in the first column are based on p. 9 of the Tobacco Institute, *The Tax Burden on Tobacco*, Vol. 30, 1995.

invariant to the tar level. The final column presents the total net externalities per state.

The implications of table 7 are quite dramatic. In every instance the excise tax level roughly equals or exceeds the medical care cost per pack. Moreover, even excluding excise taxes, the total net external cost per pack is always negative. Indeed, even if one only looks at the medical care and nursing home components, from the standpoint of these two medical-related effects, cigarettes are self-financing in almost every instance.

As is evident from table 7, the medical care costs per pack are somewhat less for Mississippi than for other states, but the pension cost savings and the nursing home cost savings are lower as well. On balance, the net costs per pack of cigarettes in the state of Mississippi represent a $0.04 per pack cost savings. This amount ties for being the lowest net cost savings per pack for any state in the table. It is consequently not surprising that the Mississippi lawsuit to recoup the externality costs was the initial state litigation effort.

Because of the substantial heterogeneity across states, the net consequences of cigarettes for the states differ substantially. The average net cost savings is $0.10 per pack, but this value ranges from a low of $0.04 per pack in the state of Mississippi to a high value of $0.18 per pack in the state of California.

It is useful to consider some extreme states in this table. Virginia, a leading tobacco producer, has the lowest excise tax rate, which is $0.025 per pack. However, even this low level of excise tax roughly equals the state's smoking-related medical care costs. Moreover, the nursing home cost savings associated with smoking are over double the value of the medical care cost increases. On balance, cigarettes save the state of Virginia a $0.09 per pack as well as the value of the excise taxes.

Another extreme case is that of New York. That state has the highest value of medical care costs associated with smoking, which are $0.08 per pack. Nevertheless, the nursing home cost savings offset is almost as great as this amount. Moreover, even for the state of New York there is a net insurance cost savings of cigarettes of $0.04 per pack. The medical cost amounts are also dwarfed by the value of the state excise taxes imposed on cigarettes in New York, which were $0.56 per pack. The doubling of the New York state excise tax in 1999 to $1.11 a pack raises the excise tax amount to a level that is an order of magnitude greater than the medical care costs.

Conclusion

The state and federal breakdown of the financial consequences of cigarette smoking does not simply involve scaling down the national estimates. The distribution of the effects across different cost categories is not symmetric. States, for example, receive over half of the total excise taxes levied on cigarettes. However, states receive only a small fraction of the total decrease in pension costs associated with smokers' premature mortality.

The striking economic result is that cigarettes are self-financing for every state and for the federal government when viewed from a variety of insurance cost perspectives. Nursing home cost savings resulting from smokers' early mortality typically exceed the increase in medical costs. Similarly, pension cost savings associated with smokers' premature mortality exceed the increase in medical costs. Finally, excise taxes on cigarettes equal or exceed the medical care costs associated with smoking. At the time smokers purchase cigarettes, they are paying an excise tax fee that fully covers the adverse state medical insurance consequences of their smoking behavior.

My analysis also indicated that the net gains to the federal government from cigarette smoking are greater than those to the states. This result illuminates one potential reason why the federal government was not a party to the initial lawsuits against the cigarette industry. In addition to the excise taxes received by the federal government, the nursing home and pension cost savings fully offset the increase in medical costs. However, the driving force of the state suits and the out-of-court settlement was gross medical costs, not net financial externalities. From that standpoint, the stakes of the prospective federal lawsuit are considerably greater. Although my analysis did provide a general economic framework similar to some industry arguments, I never presented these results as part of any litigation.[28] Rather, my cost estimates by state and for the federal government were of independent research interest.

When the initial state suits were filed, I asked a prominent legal appointee of the Clinton administration why there was no similar federal suit. His response was that with the large Social Security cost effect there was a fear that the huge net cost savings aspect of the federal effects would undermine the state cases. However, the cigarette industry settled the state claims without ever obtaining a legal resolution of whether such effects could be recognized. With the state suits resolved, there was no longer any risk of muddying the waters with the federal claim. Moreover, the willingness of the industry to pay off the states without insisting that the negative cost effects be included suggested that the Social Security effects would not loom large in any litigation or settlement of the federal claim.

One puzzle raised by these results is why the cigarette companies would settle such suits rather than litigate them. Whether the industry would have won such suits would have depended on whether the suits had legal standing and on which costs counted and which did not. In many but not all jurisdictions, preliminary rulings excluded recognition of excise taxes. In some instances, the cost implications of smokers' premature mortality were excluded. Making the cost savings argument based on the early death of the product's consumers also is an uncomfortable argument for any industry to make, even if the courts permit this approach. The approaches taken in different states varied considerably in terms of what could be counted and how costs would be counted, but these issues were never resolved. Instead, the industry gambled on an out-of-court settlement as the cure for its litigation ills, and it lost.

In 2001 the Bush administration indicated that it wanted to settle the federal claim against the industry, as it viewed the case as weak. If there is in fact no legitimate basis for a claim, it should be dropped altogether rather than being used to extract concessions from the industry. However, if the U.S. Department of Justice believes the claim is valid, it should pursue the case to its legal resolution. Doing so will have tremendous benefit beyond the tobacco litigation, as it will begin the process of establishing meaningful legal precedents to guide litigation that will continue to emerge against a whole range of other hazardous products.

VI

ENVIRONMENTAL TOBACCO SMOKE

The hazy, smoke-filled airport lounges in the eighties are a thing of the past, and there are now few public places in the United States inundated with environmental tobacco smoke (ETS). Almost all types of public and private enterprises have initiated some kind of smoking restriction. Outside the United States it is still possible to find areas with substantial exposures to ETS—far more than the whiff of tobacco smoke that often provokes strong reactions by nonsmokers in the United States.

The regulation of public smoking has become an increasingly prominent policy issue. Many public and private institutions have instituted no-smoking policies or have restricted smoking to particular areas. Hospitals, as one might expect, were among the leaders in banning smoking, which they did in 1993.

We now witness smokers huddled outside no-smoking buildings attempting to smoke during brief work breaks. Even hospital patients have been observed smoking outside in the snow and rain.[1] At the federal level, in 1994 the Occupational Safety and Health Administration (OSHA) proposed but never enacted a ban on all public smoking in the workplace, except for smoking in lounges that meet highly restrictive requirements. Subsequently, the U.S. Environmental Protection Agency (EPA) also issued a report in support of legislation banning all public smoking. Some states, notably California, have instituted very strong antismoking bans in places such as bars and restaurants. Friendship Heights, Maryland, even banned all public smoking, and, after being given a warning, smokers will be slapped with a $100 fine for smoking in public.[2] Whether or not such policies make sense depends on the level of the hazards posed by environmental tobacco smoke.

Smoking restrictions are a sensible and targeted policy tool for limiting exposure to cigarette smoke. However, that does not necessarily mean that all public smoking should be banned. The key policy issues are how broad such public smoking restrictions should be and who should have the responsibility for setting the restrictions. As with all regulatory policies, to be desirable they should be in society's best interests. In particular, the overall benefits to society from such efforts should exceed the costs they generate for the policy.

Popular support for smoking restrictions has increased even though exposures to ETS have declined. As the percentage of nonsmokers in society has risen, the expectations of nonsmokers with respect to antismoking policies have steadily risen, as well. Consider the following Gallup Poll results.[3] In 1978 only 43 percent of all respondents believed that smoking on commercial airplanes should be banned completely. Similarly, in 1977 only 16 percent of respondents believed that smoking in public places should be banned. By 1987 the fraction of respondents supporting a complete ban on smoking in all public places had risen to 55 percent, and in 1988 it reached 60 percent. Within the course of only a decade there was dramatic surge in the strength of public support for smoking restrictions.

The presence of environmental tobacco smoke is a classic externality problem. Smokers derive pleasure from smoking, but it gives rise to a side effect that is undesirable for those exposed to the smoke. Clearly, we can restrict smoking activity to benefit nonsmokers, but doing so will decrease the welfare of smokers. How should we think about regulating smoking, and what is the appropriate extent of the regulation?

To design or evaluate public policies toward ETS we must understand the nature of the risks and trade-offs. How substantial are the hazards? Are the main concerns the financial costs associated with ETS or the health impacts? What are the losses incurred by smokers from smoking restrictions? Do people understand the degree of the hazard involved or do they overestimate or underestimate the risk?

Many of the key questions pertaining to ETS involve issues of risk analysis and economics. My involvement in public smoking regulations has included serving as a consultant to EPA on secondhand smoke and testifying on behalf of the tobacco industry at the OSHA hearings on smoking restrictions. In each case, the task was to provide a comprehensive perspective on the consequences of ETS regulations, including the health effects on nonsmokers, the welfare loss to smokers, and the costs of the regulation. My OSHA testimony addressed the loss to smokers; it was prepared in response to a request by the chief economist for the U.S. Department of Labor, who did not believe that these effects had been given sufficient attention by the agency. This chapter examines some of the most salient components of the ETS debate.

The Risks of Environmental Tobacco Smoke

For many years nonsmokers viewed ETS as a smelly annoyance. The odor is unpleasant to many. In some cases there are mild allergic reactions, and there is also the problem of tobacco smoke odor on clothing exposed to ETS or in rooms where smoking is permitted. Such consequences are real economic losses. Indeed, the economic value of these nuisance effects may be the most significant cost of ETS. However, the dollar equivalent of these costs has not been estimated, though possibly it could be, using the same kinds of survey techniques used to value environmental amenities.

More recently, the focus has shifted from nuisance effects to health. The stakes have been raised as opponents of smoking have characterized ETS as a significant threat to individual health. The health dimension has changed the terms of the debate, greatly increasing the moral authority that nonsmokers are bringing to bear, even though the nuisance effects may be of greater economic consequence. It is therefore useful to inquire whether ETS is in fact a major threat to the health of nonsmokers.

Cancer researchers observe that the human body is tough. It is resilient in the presence of some carcinogens. One whiff of ETS is proportionately less likely to be risky than massive and sustained exposures. There may be no risk at all below some threshold amount. Government agencies such as the Environmental Protection Agency and OSHA have not made such a distinction, assuming instead a linear dose-response relationship with no safe exposure level. This way of characterizing the risk relationship is often an analytic convenience arising from our lack of detailed knowledge that would enable us to pin the relationship down more precisely. Despite the rudimentary nature of our knowledge, it is nevertheless instructive to assess the extent of the risks that the agencies have estimated. It should be noted at the outset that most economics researchers in the cigarette area, including the Congressional Research Service, believe that the state of science with respect to ETS is too uncertain to warrant reliable estimation of the health consequences.

Because cigarette smoking is quite risky, it stands to reason that ETS may pose some health risks as well. However, this conclusion is not as straightforward as it may seem.[4] Sidestream smoke (smoke that goes directly into the air from a cigarette; for instance, from a cigarette burning in an ashtray) and smoke that a smoker exhales into the air (smoke that has been inhaled and then exhaled) both differ in a variety of ways from mainstream smoke (smoke as it is inhaled by the smoker directly from the cigarette). Their chemical constituents are not identical, and have different amounts of water vapor. Some of these compounds react chemically with the air and change over time. Moreover, the quantity of ETS exposure is starkly different from the amount of mainstream smoke inhaled by a cigarette smoker. If the body is more resistant to minor assaults, then there may be some level of ETS exposure that in fact poses zero risk of harm.

The underlying difficulty is that the level of the risk is hard to ascertain. Scientific studies attempting to track a comparatively small risk level need a very large sample of the population to make reliable estimates and must be able to distinguish the effect of ETS from other exposures and lifestyle factors. To complicate matters further, the health risks occur with a substantial latency period and are not signature diseases. Heart disease and lung cancer, for example, can result from many exposures and personal risk factors other than ETS. Failure to find a significant ETS risk consequently does not necessarily imply that ETS exposures are risk-free. Both OSHA and members of the U.S. Congress, with the support of a report by EPA, have proposed stringent regulation of environmental tobacco smoke. In each case, these agencies have asserted that there is a causal link between environmental tobacco smoke and adverse health outcomes, such as lung cancer and heart disease.

In contrast, previous economic assessments of the external costs of smoking have not included environmental tobacco smoke except through illustrative sensitivity analyses in which analysts make assumptions about the riskiness of ETS. Both OSHA and the EPA have issued reports analyzing environmental tobacco smoke risk estimates based on this literature. Notwithstanding these agencies' willingness to issue such judgments, there is little question that the linkages are not as strong or as well documented as the primary risks to smokers themselves.

Having stated these caveats, I will present estimates of the costs imposed by environmental tobacco smoke based on the EPA and OSHA studies. I will then adjust these estimates to account for factors such as the change in the tar level of cigarettes that were ignored in these governmental studies. Calculating these estimates in no way implies acceptance of their validity. As a consequence, I will review some of the most salient limitations of these studies in the course of presenting them. Readers who wish to make alternative judgments, such as setting these risks at a lower level or even equal to zero, can utilize the results presented here in doing so.

There are two major environmental tobacco smoke risks—lung cancer and heart disease. Most of the debate in the literature and the battles in the popular press have been over the validity of the lung cancer risk estimates. Of the two classes of risk effects, these are the more thoroughly researched. However, as will be indicated below, even the lung cancer estimates are the object of substantial, legitimate controversy. The heart disease estimates have been regarded as being highly speculative by the authors of the heart disease studies as well as by the agencies employing these results. Because all parties have given less credence to the heart disease estimates, these risk estimates have not been the object of as much public discussion. However, because the heart disease mortality rates are considerably larger than those for lung cancer, it is important both to recognize their potential implications as well as the limitations associated with their estimation.

Lung Cancer Risks

The first class of ETS risks to be considered is that associated with lung cancer.[5] The scientific evidence that led to the lung cancer risk assessments by EPA consisted of a selection of eleven studies of family members exposed to ETS. The entire literature on lung cancer is much larger, but these are the studies EPA chose to include in making its risk assessment. Eight of the eleven studies indicated that ETS led to a higher risk relative to the risk level of those not exposed to ETS, and three indicated that ETS led to a lower relative risk. Of these studies, only one showed statistically significant effects at the 90 percent confidence level, which is a less demanding statistical test than the 95 percent confidence interval that is usually applied in the scientific literature.[6] None were significant at the 95 percent level. "Significant" results such as this may occur on a random basis, particularly if one examines the results from a large number of studies. "Significance" also does not imply "large" effects. Rather, significance relates to testing statistical hypotheses. In particular, are the results large enough and estimated with sufficient precision that we can reject the hypothesis that the effect is zero?

Comparisons among the studies are difficult because the eleven studies were undertaken with data adjusted in different ways and collected from the 1960s through 1988. Moreover, the sample sizes were relatively small, and such small samples simply aren't well suited to analyzing such low risk events.

Without controlling for the differences among the studies, EPA pooled the estimates to make an overall ETS risk assessment. Doing so is problematic given the difference in samples and methodologies. Even after pooling studies in this manner, EPA concluded that the ETS risks are at least two orders of magnitude smaller than the risks to smokers themselves.

Table 8 Lung Cancer Relative Risks Associated with Passive Smoking

Study	Year	Risk: Original Data	Risk: Adjusted EPA Data	Original Confidence Interval (95%)	Recalculated EPA Confidence Interval (90%)
Brownson	1987	1.68	1.50	(0.39, 2.97)	(0.48, 4.72)
Brownson	1992	1.00	not analyzed[a]	(0.8, 1.2)	not analyzed[a]
Buffler	1984	0.80	0.68	(0.34, 1.81)	(0.32, 1.41)
Butler	1988	2.00	2.01	N/A	(0.61, 6.73)
Correa	1983	2.07	1.89	(0.81, 5.26)	(0.85, 4.14)
Fontham	1991	1.28	1.28	(0.93, 1.75)	(1.03, 1.60)
Garfinkel	1985	1.12	1.27	(0.94, 1.60)	(0.91, 1.79)
Garfinkel	1981	1.17	1.16	(0.85, 1.89)	(0.89, 1.52)
Humble	1987	1.78	2.00	(0.6, 5.4)[b]	(0.83, 4.97)
Janerich	1990	0.93	0.79	(0.55, 1.57)	(0.52, 1.17)
Kabat	1984	0.90	0.73	(0.46, 1.76)	(0.27, 1.89)
Stockwell	1992	1.60	not analyzed[a]	(0.8, 3.0)	not analyzed[a]
Wu	1985	1.20	1.32	(0.50, 3.30)	(0.59, 2.93)
11 EPA studies	—	—	1.19	—	(1.04, 1.35)

Source: Huber, Brockie, and Mahajan 1993, 51. This article provides a review of all studies listed above.
[a]Data from these studies were not included in the EPA risk assessment.
[b]Humble and coauthors were the only U.S. study to report data with confidence intervals of 90 percent; all other studies reported their results at the conventional level of 95 percent confidence intervals.

Consider the nature of the EPA exercise in detail.[7] Table 8 summarizes the results of the studies selected by the EPA in its analysis of ETS, along with two additional, more recent studies they omitted. The two studies in table 8 not listed in the EPA study were those by Brownson et al. (1992) and by Stockwell et al. (1992). This recent study by Stockwell et al. was undertaken at the National Cancer Institute and concluded that for lung cancer "We found no statistically significant increase in risk associated with exposure to environmental tobacco smoke at work or during social activities." Somewhat curiously, this study from the leading government cancer research agency did not make the list.

The first column of statistics in table 8 presents the relative risk to passive smokers based on the original study. A relative risk of 1.0 indicates that people exposed to passive smoking face the same risk as those without such exposures. A relative risk above 1.0 indicates some additional risk. In standard tort liability cases, the critical relative risk cutoff is usually at least 2.0, indicating that the disease was more likely than not caused by the particular exposure. Otherwise, the plaintiff would not have a valid claim. These values are close to 1.0, whereas primary smoke risks to smokers often yield relative risk values as high as 10 or 20. From the standpoint of regulatory policy, a risk that is significantly greater than 1.0 but falls short of 2.0 could nevertheless be a basis for some form of policy intervention to the extent that the risk can be distinguished statistically from a relative risk of 1.0. We should be cautious in taking these relative risk figures at face value, however, recognizing that in many instances there were not detailed statistical controls for other aspects of the personal risk exposure.

The next column of statistics in table 8 indicates how EPA chose to adjust the results based on a variety of subjective adjustment factors. In some cases, this adjustment increases the relative risk estimate and in other cases decreases it. However, there appears to be no evident bias in the EPA adjustments. These point estimates (i.e., the single best estimates of the risk) indicate a relative risk in excess of 1.0, but some of the point estimates are below 1.0, which would imply the presumably implausible result that exposure to ETS reduces the risk of lung cancer.

The second to last column of statistics gives the 95 percent confidence interval reported in the original study. What a 95 percent confidence interval indicates is that based on the sample of results, we have 95 percent confidence that the true value of the relative risk lies in the estimated range. The use of a 95 percent confidence interval is the standard scientific reference point in the medical and economics literature for making statistical judgments. Indeed, in only one of the studies did the authors of the original study fail to report data with respect to the conventional 95 percent confidence interval. In every instance shown in table 8, the 95 percent confidence interval includes 1.0 within the risk range. Thus, at conventional levels of statistical significance, it is always impossible to reject the hypothesis that there is no increase in the relative risk due to passive smoking. Put somewhat differently, there is no valid statistical evidence supporting a passive smoking—lung cancer linkage. The courts generally use a more demanding cutoff of whether a risk exposure is more likely than not to have contributed to the person's disease —or a relative risk value of 2.0. In only five of these studies is a relative risk value of 2.0 even within the fairly broad 95 percent confidence intervals.

Armed with such weak statistical results, one could certainly not proceed with an ambitious regulatory policy. As a result, the EPA chose to alter the usual standards for statistical tests and focus on a 90 percent confidence interval. Doing so shrinks the range of relative risk values, as we are only 90 percent confident that the true value of the relative risk lies in the estimated range calculated by EPA. Even with this approach, in only one of the eleven studies analyzed by EPA was the agency able to construct a 90 percent confidence interval in which a relative risk of 1.0 did not lie within the interval. Thus, it could not reject the hypothesis of no additional relative risk except for one study.

The final row of the table indicates that EPA combined the various studies' results, using a meta-analysis. This meta-analysis involved little more than pooling the results of the studies as if they came from one large study. The component studies all involved highly different methodologies and samples. EPA provided no details as to how it combined these studies or whether it ever took into account the study differences. EPA concluded that the 90 percent confidence interval for the pooled studies ranged from 1.04 to 1.35, thus putting it just above a relative risk value of 1.0.

EPA's set of studies is also not comprehensive, as the agency selected the studies most likely to demonstrate the existence of a risk. The selective nature of the EPA evidence subsequently contributed to the judicial rejection of the EPA study of ETS as a sound basis for policy. In a 1998 decision by Judge Osteen in the *Flue-Cured Tobacco* case, the United States District Court for the Middle District of North Carolina criticized the EPA approach on several scores:

> EPA's study selection is disturbing. First, there is evidence in the record supporting the accusation that EPA "cherry picked" its data. Without criteria for pooling studies into a meta-analysis, the court cannot determine whether the exclusion of studies likely to disprove EPA's a priori hypothesis was coincidence or intentional. Second, EPA's excluding nearly half of the available studies directly conflicts with EPA's purported purpose for analyzing the epidemiological studies and conflicts with EPA's Risk Assessment Guidelines. . . . Third, EPA's selective use of data conflicts with the Radon Research Act. The Act states EPA's program shall "gather data and information on all aspects of indoor air quality. . . ." In conducting a risk assessment under the Act, EPA deliberately refused to assess information on all aspects of indoor air quality.
>
> At the outset, the court concluded risk assessments were incidental to collecting information and making findings. EPA steps outside the court's analysis when information collection becomes incidental to conducting a risk assessment. In making a study choice, consultation with an advisory committee voicing these concerns would have resulted, at a minimum, in a record that explained EPA's selective use of available information. From such record, a reviewing court could then determine whether EPA "cherry picked" its data, and whether EPA exceeded its statutory authority.
>
> Plaintiffs raise a list of objections asserting that EPA deviated from accepted scientific procedure and its own Risk Assessment Guidelines in a manner designed to ensure a preordained outcome.

Given the ETS Risk Assessment shortcomings already discussed, it is neither necessary or desirable to delve further into EPA's epidemiological web. However, two of Plaintiffs' arguments require mention. The first contention is EPA switched, without explanation, from using standard 95 percent confidence intervals to 90 percent confidence intervals to enhance the likelihood that its meta-analysis would appear statistically significant. This shift assisted EPA in obtaining statistically significant results. Studies that are not statistically significant are "null studies"; they cannot support a Group A classification.[8]

The court expanded its critique, disputing the EPA analysis claiming a demonstrated link between lung cancer and ETS. The court concluded that "[u]sing its normal methodology and its selected studies, EPA did not demonstrate a statistically significant association between ETS and lung cancer," "EPA could not produce statistically significant results with its selected studies," and "[t]he studies EPA selected did not include a significant number of studies and data which demonstrated no association between ETS and cancer."[9]

The EPA estimates also neglected a variety of fundamental aspects of the risk. They did not, for example, account for the change in the tar content or per smoker consumption of cigarettes over time. These adjustments will be made below, using the same weighting system of the studies adopted by EPA. Another principal drawback of the ETS studies is that they pertain to risks to other household members. Those exposed to public ETS will typically be exposed to lower concentrations of ETS as well as shorter durations of exposures than the family members of a smoker. To the extent that there is a no-risk threshold, low levels of exposure to ETS may cause no risk whatsoever to the exposed population.

The character of the studies also is quite different from what economists might envision. There were, for example, no detailed multivariate controls to capture differences in demographic characteristics or location, though some studies did make a few primitive demographic adjustments.[10] If smokers choose to live in highly polluted areas, and if they and their families get lung cancer because of their broader environmental exposures, this type of relationship would be captured in these studies and incorrectly attributed to ETS. Similarly, smokers will more likely be married to other smokers. To the extent that studies do not control for such factors, higher mortality rates from ETS may reflect smoking behavior of other family members rather than ETS.

The results of the research are also difficult to interpret. In some instances, inconsistent research results have been treated in a way that reflects advocacy of an ETS-cancer link rather than a scientific assessment of causality. One 1992 study found that spouses of low and moderate smokers had a 30 percent lower probability of lung cancer, whereas spouses of heavier smokers had a 30 percent higher probability of lung cancer, than spouses of nonsmokers.[11] Thus, some smoking is health-enhancing, but more smoking harms one's health. Such results clearly don't make sense. Although the authors stress the health damage effect, taken at face value their results imply an implausibly shaped dose-response relationship between ETS and cancer that is initially negative and then positive.

In making its estimate of the number of people exposed to ETS, EPA also understates the extent to which workers have already been prevented from being exposed to ETS, thus overstating the potential risk. Many workplaces have installed special smoking lounges and banned work-place smoking. EPA figures underestimate the number of workers covered by bans since larger establishments are most likely to have bans or designated smoking areas (74 percent of firms with 750 or more employees versus 55 percent with 50–99 employees).[12] EPA, however, did not adjust for workplace size. The EPA estimates recognize only the efficacy of the 20 percent of the smoking lounges that meet the strict standards proposed in recent legislation (HR 3434). However, if the other lounges have some partial efficacy, then one would want to take this influence into account as well. As a result, in assessing the extent of the passive smoking risks, I will also explore the sensitivity of the results to the assumption one makes about the prevalence of bans and smoking lounges.

A final caveat that will be noted before exploring the number of fatalities implied by the risk estimates is that there is an inconsistency between the EPA and OSHA risk estimates.[13] EPA estimates that each year 1,694 people die from lung cancer due to ETS exposures outside the home. When analyzing deaths in the workplace, OSHA estimates that 140–722 deaths per year arise from workplace exposures. In this case, OSHA did not follow EPA's procedure of pooling the results of the risk studies irrespective of their statistical significance. These numbers can be linked, since EPA estimates that 82 percent of nonhome exposures occur at work. If one were to apply this workplace exposure estimate to the OSHA mortality estimate, one obtains an OSHA-based risk estimate of 171–880 lung cancer deaths from total nonhome exposures, far less than the EPA figure of 1,694. Thus, there is considerable inconsistency even within the federal government in terms of the assessment of the lung cancer risk levels, as EPA pegs the ETS risks at a much higher rate than does OSHA.

The calculations below will turn the estimated number of smoking-related deaths into financial costs. Here the financial costs will also include the financial equivalent of the individual health losses. Whereas health effects are private effects for smokers, they are appropriately regarded as externalities of ETS exposures. To obtain the estimate of the value of statistical lives, I utilize the $5 million value per statistical life from Viscusi (1992a, 1993). These values capture the value of risks to one's health, not just the financial and insurance consequences considered previously. This value is the midpoint estimate of the estimated value of life range based on wage-risk trade-offs. This value of life is pertinent for a worker with an average life expectancy of 36.5 years that will be lost because of an on-the-job injury. In contrast, an individual who contracts lung cancer because of ETS exposures will incur much less of a loss in life expectancy than would a worker suffering an acute injury. The average life expectancy loss conditional on being a victim of a smoking-related disease is 12.1 years (see Centers for Disease Control and Prevention 1993). For concreteness, I have used the discounted estimated life expectancy loss for smokers in making the calculation. Thus, the pertinent value of life is $5 million, multiplied by the ratio of the discounted expected life years lost from smoking divided by the discounted expected number of life years lost by a worker. One should also, however, adjust this lost value for the fact that it is deferred. People exposed to environmental tobacco smoke are not killed instantaneously, so that there must be appropriate recognition of the time lags involved in making these assessments.

Table 9 provides the lung cancer risk estimates for ETS if the OSHA and EPA estimates are taken at face value. Panel 1 in the table provides estimates based on EPA risk assessments, and the bottom panel provides estimates derived by extrapolating the OSHA ETS risk estimates for the workplace. Within panel 1, the bottom two sections adjust for the discrepancy between EPA's estimate of the number of people at risk and the estimated number of people at risk derived from the OSHA study. All risk assessments in panel 1 are based on EPA estimates. In contrast, panel 2 in table 9 utilizes both the OSHA risk estimates and the estimates of the population at risk based on OSHA's assessment. For each of these assessments, the columns indicate the differing assumptions that have been made with respect to the latency period. The first column assumes that the ETS risks are immediate. The second column reflects the estimates for which the risk was calculated on the basis of a 20-year latency period before the risks are manifested.

The first two rows in table 9 indicate the total number of lung cancer deaths and the associated costs attributable to ETS using the EPA assumptions in which there is no tar adjustment. The mortality estimate is a constant value of 1,694 with either latency assumption, but the mone-

Table 9 Lung Cancer Deaths Caused by Environmental Tobacco Smoke outside the Home (assuming 23 percent effectiveness of smoking restrictions)

	Risk Latency Assumption	
	No Lag	20-Year Latency
Panel 1: Estimates Using EPA Risk Assumptions		
EPA-based exposure estimates		
With no tar adjustment:		
Number of deaths	1,694	1,694
Cost (in billions)	$2.80	$0.83
With 100% tar adjustment:		
Number of deaths	1,171	696
Cost (in billions)	$1.19	$0.34
OSHA-based exposure estimate—lower bound		
With 100% tar adjustment:		
Number of deaths	374	223
Cost (in billions)	$0.62	$0.11
OSHA-based exposure estimate—upper bound		
With 100% tar adjustment:		
Number of deaths	970	577
Cost (in billions)	$1.60	$0.28
Panel 2: Estimates Using OSHA Risk Assumptions		
Lower bound		
Number of deaths	171	171
Cost (in billions)	$0.28	$0.18
Upper bound		
Number of deaths	880	880
Cost (in billions)	$1.46	$0.43

tized value of the lives lost differs because the time frame affects the discounted value of these losses. A discount rate of 3 percent is used throughout. The next two rows indicate the mortality costs if one makes an adjustment that is proportional to the tar level. If the reduction in tar leads to less than a proportional reduction in risk, such as half of the reduced tar amount, one can simply calculate the death and cost estimates that reflect the appropriate percent improvement by interpolating using the results in table 9.[14]

For purposes of illustration, consider the set of results for the twenty-year latency estimate. The original EPA estimate of 1,694 deaths is reduced to 696 if the entirety of the tar change is recognized. The value of the mortality costs changes similarly, because it decreases from $0.83 billion in the base EPA case to $0.34 billion if risks are proportional to tar levels.

If instead one utilizes the EPA risk estimates in conjunction with the OSHA estimate of the population at risk, one obtains considerably lower estimates of the mortality cost. For the tar adjustment case, estimates based on the low end of the OSHA risk assessment are 223 deaths and a monetary cost of $0.11 billion, with the high estimate being 577 deaths and a monetary cost of $0.28 billion.

Table 10 adjusts the outside-the-home ETS lung cancer estimates by assuming that current smoking restrictions are 50 percent effective rather than using EPA's assumption that restrictions are 23 percent effective (U.S. Environmental Protection Agency 1994, 28). Indeed, recent estimates suggest that smoking restrictions have had a much greater effect. Measured by levels of cotinine (a product of nicotine) in blood, secondhand smoke effects all but disappeared in the 1990s, as cotinine levels dropped from 0.20 nanograms per milliliter in 1988–91 to less than 0.05 in 1999.[15] If smoking restrictions are 50 percent effective, then one obtains estimates summarized in table 10 that are roughly two-thirds the size of those in the top panel 1 of table 9.[16] The OSHA-based estimates in table 10 reflect the population adjustment, not OSHA's risk value adjustment. If additional restrictions on smoking in the workplace are enacted, as would be the case if OSHA enacts its proposed regulation banning workplace smoking except in designated areas, then these cost estimates would be reduced even further.

Table 10 Lung Cancer Deaths Caused by Environmental Tobacco Smoke outside the Home (assuming 50 percent effectiveness of smoking restrictions, with 100 percent tar adjustment)

	Risk Latency Assumption	
	No Lag	20-Year Latency
EPA-based exposure estimates		
Number of deaths	760	452
Cost (in billions)	$1.25	$0.23
OSHA-based exposure estimates—lower bound		
Number of deaths	199	119
Cost (in billions)	$0.33	$0.06
OSHA-based exposure estimates—upper bound		
Number of deaths	516	307
Cost (in billions)	$0.86	$0.15

Table 11 Lung Cancer Deaths Caused by Environmental Tobacco Smoke inside the Home

	Risk Latency Assumption	
EPA Estimates	**No Lag**	**20-Year Latency**
With no tar adjustment:		
Number of deaths	800	800
Cost (in billions)	$1.32	$0.39
With 100% tar adjustment:		
Number of deaths	553	329
Cost (in billions)	$0.91	$0.16

In much the same manner, one can calculate the lung cancer deaths caused by ETS inside the home. Table 11 provides these estimates. There are no OSHA-based estimates for table 11, since OSHA did not address risks within the home. Making the tar adjustment reduces the estimates by an average of about one-half. It should be emphasized that including any lung cancer death risk estimate for ETS inside the home within an externality assessment may overstate the amount of the externality that is not recognized in smokers' decisions. These costs may be internalized by the smoker to the extent that there is recognition of the well-being of family members when making the smoking decision.

Virtually all the costs in tables 9–11 reflect direct health losses to the individual, not financial costs. Indeed, analysis of the total financial externality associated with ETS indicates that this value overall is negative—that is, there is a net cost savings just as there is with primary smoke. These results are consistent with the direct estimates by Moore and Zhu (2000), who found that there is no apparent effect on the health costs for those exposed to environmental tobacco smoke. To the extent that ETS merits a health-based concern it is through the effect on individual welfare, not finances. Perhaps it was because of this that none of the state lawsuits raised ETS as an issue.

Heart Disease

Despite the central role of lung cancer in the ETS debates, the heart disease linkage may be greater, and the risk levels much larger. The problem is that we know even less about the heart disease effects than about the lung cancer linkage. The overall mortality costs associated with the ETS–heart disease linkage are much greater than for lung cancer. EPA estimates that from 8,760 to 17,520 deaths per year from heart disease are due to ETS exposures outside the home.

Although these estimates are higher than those for lung cancer, they are based on much more preliminary scientific evidence. However, the study by Steenland (1992) that provides the scientific basis for EPA's estimates includes a myriad of caveats and cautionary notes that should make one reluctant to attach much precision to these estimates.[17] The most telling signal of a need for caution is that the ratio of heart disease risk to lung cancer risk for ETS is too great when compared to the comparable relative risk values for smokers. Whether the heart disease–ETS risk ratio is too high or the estimates of the lung cancer–ETS risk are too low is not clear. To deal with what the author termed "considerable uncertainty" regarding the results, EPA simply scaled down the mortality estimates. Although EPA adopted the Steenland (1992) findings, it should be noted that it did not adopt Steenland's conclusion that 55 percent of heart disease deaths from ETS are due to nonhouse exposures, but instead adopted a 73 percent assumption, which produced a higher estimated public cost from passive smoking.

Subsequent analysis by Steenland et al. (1996) likewise found a heart disease risk, but the results are not in a form that permits an update of the magnitude of the EPA estimates. Nevertheless, it did provide additional evidence of a significant heart disease–passive smoke linkage. Steenland's study had 353,180 females and 126,500 males, so small sample size is not a problem. As part of the American Cancer Society's cancer prevention study, this analysis is the largest study to date examining this association.

The EPA estimates of heart disease risk based on the scientific literature had the same classes of deficiencies as did the lung cancer risk estimates. In particular, they did not take into account the lag time between exposure and the onset of disease, and they ignored changes in the tar level and composition of cigarettes.

Table 12 summarizes the estimates of heart disease mortality as a result of ETS exposure outside the home. In each case, the table presents low and high estimates based on the EPA assumptions. If one uses the nonhome exposure amount advocated by Steenland (1992) of 55 percent rather than the 73 percent estimate used by the EPA, one reduces the mortality estimate and associated costs. Both cases appear in table 12. Table 12 also includes low and high estimates based on OSHA's estimates of the mortality costs of ETS. The annual total number of deaths in every instance is much higher than the lung cancer mortality rate.

The discounted cost associated with these deaths, based on EPA estimates and the 73 percent nonhome exposure, has a value ranging from

Table 12 Mortality Costs of Heart Disease Deaths Caused by Environmental Tobacco Smoke outside the Home (number of deaths and discounted cost of deaths in billions of dollars)

	Risk Latency Assumption	
	No Lag	20-Year Latency
Panel 1: Estimates Based on EPA (1994) Risk Assessments		
With 73% nonhome exposures:		
Low		
no tar adjustment	8,760	8,760
	$14.45	$4.28
100% tar adjustment	8,360	4,867
	$13.80	$2.38
High		
no tar adjustment	17,520	17,520
	$28.91	$8.58
100% tar adjustment	16,721	9,733
	$27.59	$4.77
With 55% nonhome exposures:		
Low		
no tar adjustment	6,600	6,600
	$10.90	$3.23
100% tar adjustment	6,299	3,667
	$10.40	$1.80
High		
no tar adjustment	13,200	13,200
	$21.78	$6.46
100% tar adjustment	12,598	7,333
	$20.78	$3.59
Panel 2: Estimates Based on OSHA (1994) Risk Assessments		
Low		
no tar adjustment	2,554	2,554
	$4.21	$1.25
100% tar adjustment	2,554	1,665
	$4.21	$0.81
High		
no tar adjustment	15,855	15,855
	$26.16	$7.76
100% tar adjustment	15,855	10,340
	$26.16	$5.06

$4.3 billion to $8.6 billion in the twenty-year latency period. These estimates are based on the assumption that the extent of life lost due to heart disease from ETS exposures is the same as the life expectancy loss of a smoker whose death is caused by smoking. If one adopts a 100 percent tar adjustment, these estimates decline to $2.4–$4.8 billion. The importance of the latency period is apparent, because the discounted value of the deaths is considerably greater based on the assumption that there is no lag.

Table 13 presents analogous findings for heart disease deaths caused by ETS inside the home. Results appear assuming 27 percent of exposures are inside the home (EPA's assumption) and 45 percent (Steenland's estimate). These mortality amounts are also substantial, since the death toll range even in the lowest scenario presented is 3,240 annual deaths. Even with a twenty-year latency period before these deaths occur, the mortality costs are $1.69 billion if one makes no tar adjustment. As with the public ETS risks, tar adjustments substantially decrease these values.

Table 14 summarizes the passive smoking costs evaluated at a 3 percent discount rate. These are the ETS values that I will use in calculating the total externality costs of cigarettes. Three categories of costs are considered: insurance externalities, ETS mortality costs, and fire-related mortality. The insurance externalities from ETS are the first estimates of this kind and are the analog of the insurance externalities from smokers themselves. The inside-the-home heart disease death estimates are excluded for two reasons. First, deaths inside the home may well be internalized by the smoker and consequently are not externalities. Second, as in the case of the other heart disease estimates, the range of estimates is broad, so the assumptions one adopts are consequential. For the median

Table 13 Mortality Costs of Heart Disease Deaths Caused by Environmental Tobacco Smoke inside the Home (no tar adjustment)

EPA-Based Risk Estimates	Annual Deaths	Discounted Cost of Deaths (in Billions)	
		No Lag	20-Year Latency
With 27% home exposures:			
Low	3,240	$3.11	$1.69
High	6,480	$6.22	$3.38
With 45% home exposures:			
Low	5,400	$5.19	$2.82
High	10,800	$10.37	$5.64

Table 14 Total Annual Social Costs of Environmental Tobacco Smoke (in billions of dollars)

	Risk Latency Assumption	
	No Lag	20-Year Latency
Net ETS insurance externalities		
No tar adjustment		
Low	−$0.25	−$0.25
Median	−$0.36	−$0.36
High	−$0.46	−$0.46
With 100% tar adjustment		
Low	−$0.26	−$0.21
Median	−$0.37	−$0.30
High	−$0.48	−$0.39
ETS mortality smoking costs		
Lung cancer (nonhome)		
Low	$0.28	$0.06
Median	$1.25	$0.27
High	$2.80	$0.83
Heart disease (nonhome)		
Low	$4.21	$0.81
Median	$12.10	$3.20
High	$27.59	$8.58
Fire deaths		
(nonresidential)	$0.03	$0.03

Note: These estimates assume a 3% discount rate.

estimates and a twenty-year latency assumption for the tar adjusted case, the net financial ETS cost is a $0.30 billion savings per pack. The mortality costs are $0.27 billion for lung cancer and $3.20 billion for heart disease.

Table 14 also adds the costs of nonresidential fire-related mortality, which are the first such estimates in the literature. These calculations assumed a value of life of $5 million, and yield a fire death cost of $0.03 billion. What is striking about the results in table 14 is that ETS saves society money based on the insurance implications alone. However, the welfare consequences of individual health losses are quite substantial. Thus, the policy concerns with ETS are somewhat different from what has driven the litigation of the state attorneys general. Individual health effects are the main externality, not financial losses.

Public Perceptions of Passive Smoking Risks

How strong is the public's belief in the hazards of secondhand smoke? Answering this question is of considerable interest because of people's general sensitivity to hazards imposed on them by others. More importantly, public risk beliefs have a critical influence on ETS policies and ETS exposures. If nonsmokers believe that ETS is dangerous, they will seek out nonsmoking areas in restaurants and bars, and more generally will attempt to limit their exposures. Smokers who consider ETS exposures dangerous to others will attempt to smoke in circumstances that do not pose a great threat to their family, friends, or the public. Substantial beliefs in the hazards of ETS will also determine the political pressures that are brought to bear on policies to restrict smoking. Are these perceptions accurate, or have we perhaps overreacted concerning these risks?

Ideally, it would be useful to have information pertaining to the public perceptions of passive smoking risks that would enable us to determine whether these risk perceptions were too high or too low. We know in general that people will respond in an exaggerated manner to risks that have been highly publicized. Small identified risks will also be prone to overestimation, as will involuntary risks imposed by others. Passive smoking risks possess each of these characteristics. To what extent do people properly assess these risks?

While there are no data available for the United States to enable us to make precise judgments, in conjunction with a group of professors in Spain I have developed estimates of ETS risk perceptions for a sample of 2,571 respondents in Spain.[18] Moreover, the survey of the Spanish population used questions pertaining to lung cancer risks and life expectancy loss to smokers that were modeled after those that I present in chapter 7 for the United States. Comparison of the different risk assessments that people have for the primary risk to smokers in these two countries yields some sense of the difference in the informational environments. There may, of course, be other differences as well because passive smoking has received considerable attention in the United States, much more than in Spain. Spain does, however, include passive smoking risks among the on-product cigarette warnings. The findings below are suggestive of the potential problems of overreaction to the risks of passive smoking.

Consider first the primary risks of lung cancer to the smoker due to smoking exposures. The Spanish population overall believes that 50 out of 100 smokers will get lung cancer because they smoke, and current smokers in the Spanish population believe that 46 out of 100 smokers will get lung cancer because they smoke. These estimates closely parallel my estimates in chapter 7 for U.S. risk beliefs. As a consequence, one might expect the risk beliefs in Spain regarding ETS to be at least somewhat similar to the view in the United States. Does the Spanish population regard ETS as a significant risk? Somewhat incredibly, the general Spanish public believes that 25 out of 100 members of the population will get lung cancer because of their exposures to passive smoke, and even current smokers rate the passive smoking risk as being 21 out of 100.[19] The perceived risks of passive smoking are about half as great as the perceived risk to smokers themselves.

These risk estimates are off the charts by any reasonable standard. If one took the upper bound lung cancer estimates from EPA and OSHA studies, one would only have a few thousand lung cancer deaths per year attributable to ETS—or one-hundredth of the death toll of primary smoking. Even these scientific risk estimates may greatly overstate the actual risks because the studies all fail to indicate any statistically significant risk based on the usual standards for statistical significance. In contrast, based on these same kinds of studies, public health officials suggest that over 400,000 smokers die annually from smoking. Not only is the total death toll to smokers about two orders of magnitude greater than that to the passive smoking population, but the size of the smoking population is smaller as well, making the risk probability to the general public from passive smoking even lower. Even an upper bound assessment of the lung cancer risks from passive smoking would put this risk at considerably under 1 case per 100 people exposed to passive smoking.

Much the same pattern is exhibited with respect to the Spanish public's belief of the risks of heart disease from ETS.[20] The general Spanish population estimates that 45 out of 100 smokers will get heart disease because of their smoking behavior, and smokers estimate this risk at being only slightly lower at 42 out of 100. These are the primary risks to smokers, which in fact are substantial. Once again, the passive smoking risk perceived by the general population is roughly half the perceived primary risk to smokers. The general public in Spain believes that the risk of heart disease from passive smoking is 25 out of 100, and current smokers believe it is 22 out of 100. While people's estimates of the primary risk to smokers of heart disease are consequently a bit lower than their estimates of the primary risk to smokers of lung cancer, the public's estimates of the risks due to passive smoking are roughly the same for lung cancer and heart disease.

Because these results are in terms of a risk out of a population of 100, it may be that a different risk scale would provide additional insight into the exact character of the public's risk beliefs regarding passive smoking. Thus, rather than focusing on the risk probability, the survey

CHAPTER SIX

then examined the public's perceived life expectancy loss due to smoking. In the case of the primary risks to smokers, the general public in Spain estimated the life expectancy loss to be 11 years, with smokers estimating the loss to be 8.5 years of life expectancy. What then is the life expectancy loss that the general public exposed to environmental tobacco smoke will experience because of these exposures? The general Spanish population estimates that a member of the general public will lose 6 years of life expectancy, and current smokers believe that the life expectancy loss will be over 4 years. In each case, there is an estimated life expectancy loss from passive smoking that is comparable to the actual estimated loss of life expectancy that smokers themselves will experience based on the evidence of the medical literature. These findings all indicate that in the Spanish population there is an alarmist response to the hazards of passive smoking. People believe ETS is comparable to the Black Plague.

The disparity between the public's perception of ETS risks and the actual level of those risks found in Spain is borne out in the analysis of U.S. data by Moore and Zhu (2000). They found that whereas active smoking affected both perceived health status and actual health expenditures, exposure to ETS affected perceived health status but did not significantly increase use of medical care or lead to loss of work. This belief in the risks of ETS is almost universal throughout different population groups. In California, 89 percent of adults and 97 percent of all tenth-grade students believe that breathing secondhand smoke is bad for your health.[21] These statistics indicate extremely high risk awareness.

Public perception of the risks of ETS are more in line with the hazards of primary smoking than of secondhand smoke. Given the considerable risks posed by cigarettes to smokers themselves, people may be equally wary of passive smoking. Nevertheless, it is clear, on the basis of the existing scientific evidence, that the perceived risks of passive smoking exposures grossly distort whatever actual risks there may be. This overreaction in turn may create substantial pressures for government policies that are, in fact, addressing a much more minor hazard than other potential targets of intervention that, if addressed, would do much more to advance the public health and safety.

How Should We Regulate ETS?

Public smoking has been restricted by private entities, such as corporations and universities, as well as by public regulations that either prohibit or restrict smoking in restaurants. Perhaps the most extensive national initiative of this type was the 1994 regulatory proposal by the Occupational Safety and Health Administration (OSHA) to ban smoking in the workplace except in designated areas that met stringent ventilation requirements. Examination of this major proposal, which the agency has let languish, highlights the competing interests at stake in regulations restricting public smoking.

In justifying its regulatory initiative with respect to public smoking in the workplace, OSHA maintained that it is obligated by its enabling legislation and related court decisions to regulate all "significant" risks. OSHA concluded that the lung cancer risks alone, which are the better established of the ETS risks, are significant, and consequently merit regulation. OSHA's interpretation of its regulatory mandate differs from the usual economic prescription that agencies should take a balanced view and pursue regulations that are in society's overall best interest, recognizing both benefits and costs. Consequently, it is instructive to examine this risk-based rationale more closely and explore how ETS risks relate to it.

In terms of the statistical significance of the effects, ten of the eleven studies cited by OSHA to justify the regulation fail to indicate a statistically significant linkage, as with the EPA analysis cited above. As in the case of the EPA lung cancer studies, the underlying lung cancer risk studies do not show statistically significant effects at the 95 percent confidence level. At conventional scientific standards, OSHA cannot reject the hypothesis that the risks are zero.

A quite different issue is the size of the point estimates or the risk. Is the magnitude of the effects substantial, although perhaps not precisely established? How big must the effect be to be a "significant risk"? Taking the point estimates of the ETS risk at face value, do they pass the test of being big enough to warrant regulation? Chlorine in drinking water poses a very low risk of death from cancer. In the 1980 OSHA Benzene case (*AFL-CIO v. American Petroleum Institute*), the Supreme Court indicated that a one-in-a-billion risk from drinking chlorinated water would not be considered significant, but a one-in-a-thousand risk from exposure to gasoline vapors would be significant.[22]

An interesting test of ETS risks is to use the Supreme Court's risk levels for significance as a reference point to see how ETS fares. While the Court may not have intended this example to provide precise numerical guidance, putting ETS risks in these terms will provide some sense of what magnitude of risk is involved. Viewed from a lifetime risk standpoint, how large is the lifetime equivalent of the Supreme Court's reference point that a one-in-a-billion risk of death from a single glass of chlorinated water would not be significant? The amount of water people drink per day from different sources ranges from 2.1 to 2.9 quarts. To be conservative, I will assume that people drink nine glasses of chlorinated water per day (that may come, for example, from sodas or other products). I will also assume that the risk is linear with the number of glasses and that there is no cumulative effect. The individual who drinks nine glasses per day each year for an assumed lifetime of seventy years will drink 229,950 glasses during his or her lifetime. If the risk per glass is one in a billion, as hypothesized by the Court, the lifetime risk of death from the water is two in ten thousand.

Now let us consider the level of risks that OSHA claims are posed by ETS. OSHA estimates that between 144 and 722 people will die from lung cancer each year because of ETS. If the 74 million nonsmoking American workers exposed to ETS are exposed over their entire forty-year employment expectancy, their lifetime risk ranges from one in ten thousand to four in ten thousand. Thus, the risk of drinking chlorinated water falls between the two bounds of the ETS risk range estimated by OSHA for ETS. These calculations translate into lifetime risks as opposed to risks from a particular exposure, so that both the ETS risks and the chlorinated water risks being discussed by the Court are in the same time dimension. The risks of ETS are quite comparable to the level of risks that the Supreme Court views as not significant enough to warrant regulation.

Even if the highly uncertain scientific evidence cited by OSHA is taken at face value, without regard to the lack of statistical significance, the case for banning smoking in the workplace on risk-based grounds is not compelling. Quite simply, there are more important and fundamental threats to workers' lives than ETS. That does not mean that ETS should not be a matter of policy concern, or that smoking restrictions are not warranted. Rather, the main costs to nonsmokers may be in terms of the nuisance cost of cigarette smoke that the agency should attempt to measure. Moreover, one should take a balanced view and assess the overall merits of such regulation and how one can advance the welfare of both nonsmokers and smokers rather than launching a regulation driven solely by a belief that the risks are so great that cost and smoker well-being should be ignored. Recognition of these competing concerns will increase the potential desirability of accommodating smokers through smoking lounges and smoking areas as compared to complete smoking bans.

Benefits and costs will be reflected at least partially in market processes. The market will in fact respond to ETS as it does to other environmental conditions. University of Chicago law professor Ronald Coase received the Nobel Prize for his work on the potential efficiency of voluntary market bargains for externalities. Although these mechanisms may not be perfect and may need to be augmented, one should not lose sight of the constructive role of voluntary actions. Consider the role of smoking in restaurants. ETS is not the only aspect of the restaurant business that partakes of a public goods character; others include the music that is played and the general ambiance of the restaurant. If the restaurant is unpleasant, whether it be because the music is too loud or the ETS is annoying to nonsmokers, the customers will go elsewhere. Restaurants in turn will establish nonsmoking areas, because they have a financial interest in keeping their nonsmoking customers.

Such market bargains have a constructive role to play but may not always be perfect. Once you are seated for dinner at a restaurant on a Saturday evening, you may be reluctant to go elsewhere even though smoke from the bar area is drifting near your table. If you are traveling in a small town and the only option to see a major sports event is at a sports bar, it may be hard to make other arrangements after learning that the evening will be spent inhaling environmental tobacco smoke. These problems come under the general heading of transactions costs and are a well-established reason why voluntary bargains may not be ideally efficient for dealing with externality problems. Additional regulation often can play a role.

For private-sector responses to be effective, there must be information to enable the parties to make sound decisions. Inasmuch as ETS has an unpleasant odor, its presence is readily monitorable. Although risk perceptions may not be perfect, the systematic bias, as discussed above, is that people tend to overestimate the risk level. Spain is not unique in its attention to ETS. Most workers are aware of the ETS debate. Indeed, in its regulatory proposal, OSHA cites evidence indicating that "88 percent of nonsmokers are aware of the negative health consequences of ETS."

Restrictions on workplace smoking are already quite widespread. A 1991 survey of company smoking policies found even before the increase in smoking restrictions in the 1990s that 85 percent of all firms had smoking policies. Of those policies, 34 percent were bans, and another 34 percent involved prohibition of smoking in all open work areas. Moreover, over 90 percent of nonmanufacturing establishments also had smoking policies. As one might expect, smoking policies are more common in larger establishments than in small enterprises. There should be economies of scale in providing smoking areas in larger work environments and also a greater need to standardize smoking policies as opposed to letting the voluntary discussions of small workers' groups address the appropriate smoking policy on a decentralized basis.

Losses to Smokers from Smoking Bans

Virtually all of the public debate over smoking restrictions has focused on the costs borne by nonsmokers. However, any restrictions will necessarily reduce the welfare of smokers, who will have to forgo a consumption activity they enjoy. If smoking is banned in the workplace or substantially limited, smokers will have fewer opportunities to smoke. If smokers are relegated to a specific smoking area, their welfare will also be decreased, and their productivity may be affected as well. These consequences are legitimate economic effects that warrant consideration.

Consider first the magnitude of the lost consumers' surplus (i.e., the difference between how much consumers pay for cigarettes and what they would be willing to pay) from the decrease in the demand for cigarettes that will result from limitations on workplace smoking. Estimates of the amount of the consumers' surplus for the market depend critically on the shape of the consumer demand curve. More specifically, what is the elasticity of demand, or the percentage change in the quantity of the good purchased that will result from a unit percentage change in its price?

Table 15 presents estimates of lost consumers' surplus for different elasticities of cigarette demand. Most of the demand elasticities in the literature cluster in the range of −0.4 to −1.0, where these values refer to the percentage change in quantity purchased in response to a 1 percent increase in price. For illustrative purposes, I will focus on the demand elasticity of −0.4, meaning a 10 percent increase in cigarette prices generates a 4 percent drop in the quantity of cigarettes purchased.

At that demand elasticity, before the enactment of the OSHA regulations, consumers would reap a surplus of $53 billion annually. In other words, smokers would be willing to pay $53 billion more for cigarettes than they are actually charged to have the ability to smoke cigarettes. The loss in consumers' surplus from ETS policies depends on the effect of the smoking restrictions on the level of smoking. The estimates in table 15 pertain to three different scenarios in which restrictions reduce the total consumption of cigarettes by 10 percent, 20 percent, and 30 percent, respectively. In the midpoint of this range, after the smoking reduction one has a consumers' surplus of $34 billion, leading to a total consumers' surplus loss of $19 billion annually.

The second party that loses because of the decrease in smoking is the tobacco industry or, more specifically, the shareholders of those firms. Panel 2 of table 15 reports a series of calculations that assume for simplicity's sake that total company profits are proportional to overall

Table 15 Annual Losses from Smoking Restrictions

Panel 1: Loss of Consumers' Surplus

Elasticity	Billions of Packs Sold	Average Price	Pre-Ban Consumers' Surplus (in Billions)	Post-Ban Consumers' Surplus (in Billions)			Loss of Consumers' Surplus from Ban (in Billions)		
				Assumed Smoking Reduction			Assumed Smoking Reduction		
				10%	20%	30%	10%	20%	30%
−0.4	25.1644	$1.693	$53.25	$43.14	$34.08	$26.09	$10.12	$19.17	$27.16
−1	25.1644	$1.693	$21.30	$17.25	$13.63	$10.44	$4.05	$7.67	$10.86

Panel 2: Loss of Producers' Surplus

	Tobacco Industry Profits[a] (in Billions)	Loss of Producers' Surplus		
		Assumed Smoking Reduction		
		10%	20%	30%
Fortune 500	$0.91	$0.09	$0.18	$0.27
Forbes 500	$1.17	$0.12	$0.23	$0.35

Panel 3: Loss of Tax Revenue

	Tax Revenue (in Billions)	Loss of Revenues (in Billions)		
		Assumed Smoking Reduction		
		10%	20%	30%
Federal	$5.53	$0.55	$1.11	$1.66
State	$6.18	$0.62	$1.24	$1.85
Local	$0.19	$0.02	$0.04	$0.06
Total	$11.89	$1.19	$2.38	$3.57

Note: Estimates use 1993 data, which was the most recent available at the time of the OSHA proposal.
[a]Profits are for U.S. sales only.

sales. A 20 percent reduction in cigarette consumption will lead to a loss in profits of approximately $0.2 billion per year. That calculation excludes the lost profits to tobacco farmers and other groups whose economic well-being is dependent on the tobacco industry.

The final component of the societal loss that I have calculated is the lost tax revenue from a reduction in smoking. If there is a 20 percent reduction in cigarette consumption, the total loss of tax revenues will be $2.4 billion, with the loss being roughly evenly split between federal and state governments.

My calculations suggest that the effect of OSHA's proposal to reduce smoking in the workplace will be nontrivial. Moreover, the group with the greatest amount to lose will not be the tobacco industry, but rather the individual smokers who will suffer an annual welfare loss on the order of $19 billion. The group that will suffer the second greatest loss will be the governmental entities that receive the cigarette taxes. The federal and state tax loss will exceed the loss in profits to companies by a factor of 10. None of those effects of the proposed OSHA regulation were addressed in the regulatory impact analysis prepared by OSHA.

The stakes of the smokers themselves ultimately led OSHA to scrap the regulatory proposal. Labor union opposition on behalf of smokers translated the then neglected cost components of harm to smokers into political reality. Industry groups likewise did not support the regulation. With opposition from both labor and industry groups as well as from the tobacco industry, OSHA tabled its proposal and has yet to resurrect it.

OSHA's failure to recognize the costs of the regulation goes beyond neglect of the losses to smokers. OSHA estimates the overall cost of eliminating ETS exposures ranges from zero to $68 million. How could the costs be zero? Could a regulation really be free? One might wonder how the agency could ban smoking in the workplace and mandate restricted smoking areas meeting stringent ventilation requirements without imposing any costs. OSHA's strikingly low cost figures should serve as a red flag for anyone considering the reasonableness of the cost estimates.

How did OSHA get such low numbers? It assumed that there were no capital costs for creating nonsmoking areas. Although OSHA did recognize that there may be costs involved in setting up appropriate ventilation systems, it assumed that every workplace in the country, ranging from barber shops and greeting-card stores to large factories, had available (at no cost) rooms that could be converted to smokers' lounges. In effect, OSHA treated office space as a free good in excess supply. The notion that every enterprise in the country has 150-square-foot rooms available at no cost to set aside for smokers is certainly implausible.

More generally, the indoor air quality regulation, which includes restrictions other than those pertaining to ETS, has associated direct costs estimated by the agency to be $8.1 billion annually. However, OSHA estimates that there will be cost savings of $15 billion to firms annually from improving workplace air quality. In effect, OSHA claims that the regulation is not only a no-lose proposition for business, but will in fact be a profit center.

One might wonder why American entrepreneurs are so ignorant that they fail recognize an opportunity to make almost two dollars for every dollar expended by implementing smoking restrictions. Such entrepreneurial shortcomings cannot be attributed to market imperfections such as an alleged lack of worker information about the risks of ETS, since the cost savings that OSHA projects yield productivity gains and other effects on firms' profitability. If a regulation has positive net financial effects, even if we do not take into account any of the health benefits, then surely profit-seekers would jump at the opportunity. However, even after reading OSHA's optimistic projections, industry groups lined up against the regulation. The fact that firms have to be coerced into taking such measures is a signal of the lack of internal consistency and plausibility of the cost estimates that have been put forth.

The California Policy Effort

The initiatives against passive smoking are not restricted to federal agencies. Several states have launched ambitious initiatives, perhaps chief among them the set of policies in California.

Whereas most states have instituted limited bans on smoking, the state of California has promulgated sweeping policies that both restrict smoking and provide information to the general public about the hazards of environmental tobacco smoke. California has undertaken informational policies as well as a complete ban on smoking in restaurants and bars, each of which was front-page news throughout California. Moreover, 79 percent of Californians were aware that there was less smoking after a 1995 law prohibited smoking in work areas other than bars and taverns, indicating that the publicity regarding smoking policies has also fostered awareness of passive smoking risks.[23]

Another informational mechanism at work is negative in character. As a result of the Master Settlement Agreement with the state attorneys general, there is now a prohibition on cigarette advertising in all states except in adult facilities and publications. The state of California has gone even farther than these national efforts. In the 1980s the voters passed a vaguely defined resolution known as California Proposition 65 in which firms were required to warn the public regarding exposures to carcinogens and reproductive toxicants. The state agency implementing this law established its list of potential carcinogens and included cigarette smoke. As a result, warning signs were posted throughout the state in locations where smoking was permitted. Establishments had to post these signs no later than April 1, 1989. These signs were in restaurants, bars, outside smoking lounges, and in other public areas. Indeed, in many instances one can still find today warnings that are permanently affixed to the sides of buildings alerting the public that entering the building places them at risk of exposure to environmental tobacco smoke because smoking is permitted within the building.

The text on the warning signs implemented in response to California Proposition 65 was "WARNING: This Facility Permits Smoking and Tobacco Smoke Is Known to the State of California to Cause Cancer." Warnings were also posted regarding the reproductive toxicity effects of cigarette smoke, which stated: "WARNING: This Area Contains Chemicals Known to the State of California to Cause Cancer, Birth Defects or Other Reproductive Harm." Thousands of these warning signs were posted throughout the state of California alerting the general public to the potential hazards of tobacco smoke.[24] These Proposition 65 warnings contain language that conveys a much higher risk than is warranted by the low levels of potential hazards associated with environmental tobacco smoke. Indeed, my field tests of this warnings language with a sample of Illinois consumers suggests that this language leads the general public to believe that the risks are comparable to one's smoking from a half a pack to a whole pack of cigarettes per day.[25] Thus, the warning disseminated under Proposition 65 was widely available and conveyed a very strong message to consumers.

Although the subsequent smoking ban in restaurants and bars led to the removal of the warnings in some locations, the fact that environmental tobacco smoke is viewed by the state of California as being hazardous enough to warrant such a ban in itself provides an informational signal to people. Awareness of the ban on smoking in bars is almost universal among bar patrons, as 98 percent have heard of the California law prohibiting smoking in bars. Moreover, 79 percent of nonsmokers approve strongly or approve somewhat of the ban. The ban was front-page news so that there was wider public awareness as well.[26]

The state of California has also undertaken vigorous antismoking campaigns in the media and in schools beginning in 1988 with the passage of Proposition 99, which is a referendum passed by the voters that taxes cigarettes and uses these funds for antismoking efforts. The Centers for Disease Control and Prevention ranked the program in California as being among the most effective of any state. These efforts have included community programs, school programs, state media campaigns, and grants for tobacco control projects. Many publications and videos are made available through schools, health agencies, community groups, and other organizations, such as the American Lung Association and the American Heart Association. These materials are often targeted at specific audiences, as in the case of videos in Spanish, Korean, and Cantonese.[27]

Education of youth with respect to the potential hazards of tobacco smoke has occurred through the general media coverage as well as textbook materials required for use in schools and teacher presentations. These textbooks discuss the role of cigarette smoke generally as well as risks of ETS. For example, the "Tobacco" chapter in a text used in California written by Ted Tsumara, *Health and Safety for You* (McGraw Hill, 1987), p. 263, states:

> Passive (involuntary) smoking occurs when a nonsmoker unwillingly inhales smoke from a burning cigarette, cigar, or pipe. In a smoky environment, the nonsmoker breathes many of the same particles in tobacco smoke that a smoker inhales. The chemical components in smoke-filled surroundings come from two sources— mainstream and sidestream smoke. Mainstream smoke is the smoke inhaled then exhaled by the smoker. Sidestream smoke is the smoke that goes directly into the air from the burning end of a cigarette, cigar, or pipe. Sidestream smoke can be seen, for example, when a cigarette is burning in an ashtray. The sidestream smoke is not filtered in any way. Many substances, including those known to cause cancer, are therefore found in much higher concentrations in sidestream smoke than in mainstream smoke.

Similarly, the "Tobacco" chapter in the textbook *Health* (Prentice-Hall, 1997) has an extensive discussion of passive smoking, including the following summary statistics (p. 480):

Sidestream Smoke: The Grim Statistics

- As many as 3,000 lung cancer deaths annually are caused by sidestream smoke.
- The concentration of carbon monoxide is 2.5 times higher in sidestream smoke than it is in mainstream smoke.
- Nonsmokers exposed to 20 or more cigarettes a day at home are twice as likely to develop lung cancer.
- Nonsmokers married to heavy smokers are two to three times more likely to develop lung cancer than those married to nonsmokers.

- Up to one million existing cases of childhood asthma get worse each year due to passive smoking.
- Passive smoking increases the risk of heart disorders, triggering 35,000 deaths a year.

In addition, the public health community, stimulated in part by Proposition 99 grants, has disseminated voluminous brochures and pamphlets throughout the state of California dealing with environmental tobacco smoke.[28]

Public awareness of ETS risks has been rising over time. A 1995 California Field Poll found that 86 percent of all respondents believed that work sites should be smoke-free and 85 percent preferred smoke-free restaurants. Also in 1995, 86.9 percent of nonsmokers believed that ETS caused lung cancer, and 95.4 percent believed that ETS harmed the health of babies and children.[29] Similarly, the Gallup-Stanford-USC report on smoking risk perceptions found that "in 1996, community awareness of the dangers of ETS remained extremely high with 89 percent of adults and 97 percent of 10th-grade youth believing that breathing secondhand smoke is bad for your health." Moreover, the report concludes, "The public is transferring lessons learned about exposure to secondhand smoke to smoking policies in their homes and cars."[30]

In short, there is almost universal awareness of the risks of environmental tobacco smoke in California. Given the extensive nature of the publicity, it would not be surprising if there was not also substantial overestimation of the risk, as there is in Spain. These risk perceptions in turn have been mirrored in the kind of antismoking policies adopted in the state of California.

In some areas, the extent of coverage of no-smoking policies has escalated to very high levels. By 1996, 87 percent of all California workers reported that their workplace had some official no-smoking policy, which represented a 10 percent increase since 1993.[31] Of those workers with a workplace no-smoking policy, 78 percent of workers in 1996 reported that there was a total ban on smoking in the workplace, as contrasted with 61 percent in 1993.[32] Although California is one of the more aggressive states in terms of its antismoking efforts, this kind of trend in business practices in other states as well will tend to reduce the OSHA risk estimates.

Similarly, even in homes there has been a dramatic increase in no-smoking policies, as the percentage of California homes that do not allow smoking rose from 5 percent in 1993 to 75 percent in 1996.[33] These trends will reduce the EPA risk estimates of risks in the home to the extent that private behavior has limited ETS exposures.

ETS Litigation

Secondhand smoke has also been the focus of a limited amount of litigation. By far the best-known case was the 1997 suit by flight attendants who claimed that they suffered from diseases attributable to the ETS exposures on airplanes during the era when smoking was permitted.[34] Smoking on planes is in a confined space in which the air is recirculated. The lead flight attendant in the case was Norma Broin, a lifetime nonsmoker who contracted lung cancer after flying for fourteen years with American Airlines. This class-action suit in Florida led to a substantial $349 million settlement with the defendant cigarette firms.[35]

This settlement, which was negotiated by the lawyers representing the case, was a much better deal for the attorneys than for the flight attendants. The plaintiffs seeking compensatory damages for their health harms received absolutely nothing. Rather, under the 1997 agreement negotiated by the attorneys, the cigarette industry would contribute $300 million to fund a foundation to study secondhand smoke.[36] The stewardesses with the health claims got none of this money. Their attorneys were less public spirited, as they negotiated $49 million in legal fees for their efforts. This imbalance in the financial terms negotiated by the lawyers representing the class led to justifiable public outrage by flight attendants and public interest groups, such as Public Citizen.[37] Unfortu-

Cartoon by Mike Keefe, from the Denver Post, *October 16, 1997. Reproduced by permission of dePIXion studios, inc.*

nately, efforts by the flight attendants to have the attorneys' sweetheart deal thrown out have been unsuccessful.[38]

The chief functions of any damages award are compensation and deterrence. In this instance there was no compensation of the victims, only a fee arrangement devised by the plaintiffs' lawyers to promote their own personal gain. Deterrence is largely irrelevant as well because smoking is already banned on all domestic flights. No additional incentives need to be provided. Moreover, the airlines (which controlled smoking policies on planes, not the cigarette companies) were not even involved in the suit. The main function of the case was to serve as a form of income redistribution from the cigarette industry to a group of lawyers who sold out their clients' financial interests for their own personal gain.

Thinking about Smoking Restrictions

The antismoking fervor has led to the support of a variety of initiatives that would dramatically restrict public smoking. The linchpin of those efforts has been the estimated health impact of ETS on nonsmokers. However, the existence of health effects has led many participants in the debate to lose sight of the competing interests involved.

Much of the scientific evidence concerning ETS is highly speculative. Existing studies focus only on exposure of other household members and fail to control adequately for household characteristics correlated with a smoking spouse that may also lead to risks of lung cancer and heart disease. This ambiguity does not mean that ETS does not pose risks. However, these risks are not large enough to be estimated reliably. Recent evidence indicates that even short-term ETS exposures do, however, have acute cardiovascular effects, indicating that ETS is a statistically significant coronary risk factor.[39] How these risks translate into health outcomes is not yet clear, but the concerns of nonsmokers should certainly be recognized as being legitimate. What is needed is a rational assessment of the risks, rather than an advocacy perspective from either side. Instead of focusing on worst-case scenarios, we should be seeking out the best available scientific evidence. Once this is done, we still may not know all the answers. Available scientific studies may not be conclusive, but that fact alone should not necessarily be a rationale for inaction. If there is a reason to believe there are risks, we should take protective measures based on our best estimate of these risks.

Regardless of which ETS risk estimates one employs, the ETS costs to society are clearly not infinite. Some sufficiently large costs attached to restrictions could potentially make some ETS restrictions not in society's best interest. Indeed, if we calculate the costs of ETS as well as the other insurance-related costs generated by smokers, cigarette smokers still pay their own way, given the taxes they pay for consuming the product. The financial merits of the case by themselves, even after monetizing the ETS costs, in no way justify banning all public smoking.

That is not to say that some form of smoking restrictions would not be desirable. Nonfinancial concerns are also relevant. However, when we examine the desirability of smoking regulations, we should recognize the competing effects such efforts have. Nonsmokers clearly benefit, though it is likely that the nuisance cost is more important than the health cost. Smokers lose a substantial benefit to their welfare by having their smoking activity restricted, and losses accrue to society in terms of forgone taxes. Companies suffer forgone profits. There are also direct costs of restrictions, such as the expense associated with setting aside smoking areas and the possible productivity loss from impeding smoking behavior. In many instances, the ideal outcome will be smoking restrictions that also recognize the legitimate interest in smokers' welfare by, for example, having smoking lounges rather than a complete ban.

The market is often well equipped to deal with such trade-offs by reflecting the competing costs and benefits of restricting smoking. Indeed, most enterprises in the United States have enacted smoking-related policies. OSHA cited the widespread prevalence of workplace restrictions when it formally abandoned its ETS regulatory proposal in 2001. Other regulations restricting smoking may be well founded. When formulating such policies, there is a need for reason and balance in recognition of the welfare consequences of such smoking restrictions, not only for nonsmokers but for smokers and society at large.

VII

RISK BELIEFS AND ADDICTION

A principal underpinning of smoking policies and smoking litigation is a belief that smokers are not making rational decisions. The two most salient concerns with respect to such judgments are whether smokers properly assess the risks of adverse health effects and whether they understand the difficulty of quitting smoking, which we will refer to as "addiction." For several decades, government policies have sought to promote risk awareness through hazard warnings and other information disclosure efforts. Nevertheless, much of the smoking litigation, including the state and federal claims, has been based on the claim that smokers are ignorant of the risks and have been unwittingly lured into hazardous smoking behavior.

This chapter examines these conjectures and finds they are without merit. The available evidence demonstrates that people are aware that smoking is in fact quite risky for one's health. Survey evidence with respect to risk beliefs for all available objective risk measures suggests that these risks are widely understood. This result in many respects is quite encouraging in that it suggests that people's own knowledge combined with vigorous dissemination of public information about smoking has been successful in creating smoking risk awareness.

Hazard Warnings and Smoking Risk Information

The most prominent sources of smoking information are the government mandated warnings. These warnings, which appear on cigarette packs and in cigarette advertising, were the result of legislation passed by Congress. Government agencies, such as the Federal Trade Commission, also provided input. The key issues for any warnings effort are the following. First, what are the information gaps in consumer knowledge?

Second, do the warnings address these shortcomings and lead people to have correct perceptions of the risk? In particular, do people underestimate or overestimate the risks of smoking after reading the warnings? Examination of the warnings language alone cannot address these issues.

Warnings policies by their very nature are directed at the entire market. Cigarette companies cannot target the few individuals who may claim that they have not received the warnings, because their identities are not known. Rather, the task is to convey the message to the public at large, as is appropriate for a mass-produced consumer product. For that reason, the focus of court cases on whether an individual plaintiff read and understood the warning is often misdirected.

The guiding principle for my analysis is that the objective of warnings should be to promote informed risk-taking behavior. We may not agree with smokers' choices, but what is important is that they make knowledgeable decisions for themselves. If people are fully cognizant of the risks of smoking, they should be permitted to make these risky choices in much the same way that we permit people to buy small cars, which pose greater accident risks to the occupants. This informed choice objective is different from an objective of reducing or eliminating smoking. Whether smoking will rise or will decline because of better information depends on whether people underassessed the risk initially.

The government-mandated warnings have undergone three discrete eras. These warnings periods are summarized in table 16. In 1965 Congress required that cigarette packages and advertising inform consumers that "Cigarette Smoking May Be Hazardous to Your Health."[1] Firms had to comply with this law beginning in 1966. Shortly thereafter, in 1969, Congress modified the warnings language to make it more declarative: "The Surgeon General Has Determined That Cigarette Smoking Is Dangerous to Your Health."[2] That law also provided legal protections to the industry against warnings-based suits. In 1984 Congress instituted a series of four rotating warnings regarding the health hazards of cigarettes, the benefits of quitting smoking, the risks to pregnant women, and the presence of carbon monoxide in cigarette smoke.[3] These rotating warnings are those now in place.

Cigarettes have few antecedents in the history of warnings. Moreover, the few warnings efforts that preceded cigarettes were for acute hazards that posed immediate and toxic risks. In 1927 Congress enacted the Federal Caustic Poison Act that for the first time required that a dozen extremely dangerous chemicals, such as hydrochloric acid and sulfuric acid be labeled "Poison." The first food and drug warnings began in 1938 with the Federal Food, Drug, and Cosmetic Act. Once again

Table 16 Cigarette Warning Content History

Warning Period	Warning Content[a]
1965	Caution: Cigarette Smoking May Be Hazardous to Your Health.
1969	Warning: The Surgeon General Has Determined That Cigarette Smoking Is Dangerous to Your Health.
1984	1. SURGEON GENERAL'S WARNING: Smoking Causes Lung Cancer, Heart Disease, Emphysema, and May Complicate Pregnancy.
	2. SURGEON GENERAL'S WARNING: Quitting Smoking Now Greatly Reduces Serious Risks to Your Health.
	3. SURGEON GENERAL'S WARNING: Smoking by Pregnant Women May Result in Fetal Injury, Premature Birth, and Low Birth Weight.
	4. SURGEON GENERAL'S WARNING: Cigarette Smoke Contains Carbon Monoxide.

[a]All warnings wording is specified by legislation. See 15 U.S.C. §§ 1331–1341 (1982) where in all cases the warnings language emerged from the legislative process.

the primary concern was with imminent hazards such as those arising from adulterated and misbranded products. Insecticides and herbicide labeling began in the following decade with the passage of the Federal Insecticide, Fungicide, and Rodenticide Act in 1947.[4] It was not until 1960 that over-the-counter drugs became a product over which there were federal rules for product labeling.[5] Also in 1960 Congress passed the Federal Hazardous Substance Labeling Act. Somewhat remarkably, this was the first legislation that specified the need to provide warnings for such hazards as flammability and radioactivity. The proper use of the human hazard signal words "DANGER," "WARNING," and "CAUTION" were also defined by this act.

This roster of efforts comprises the complete set of warnings efforts arising from federal legislation and government regulation before the advent of cigarette warnings. Up until that time, there were very few warnings requirements at all—nowhere near the level of warnings we now observe. Branding cigarettes as dangerous consequently was more of a distinction than it might appear today. The warnings efforts that did exist through 1960 were for dangerous poisons and other hazards that posed immediate hazards, unlike the longer-term risk of smoking. The earlier warnings also sought to prevent product misuse and inadvertent exposure, whereas cigarette warnings indicated that the product posed hazards even if used as intended by the manufacturer.

Warnings for many other products that are now an accepted part of our warnings landscape came after the enactment of the cigarette warnings requirement in 1965, for which compliance was to begin on January 1, 1966. Authority to regulate children's toys, including the possibility of warning, began with the Child Protection and Toy Safety Act of 1969. The creation of the health, safety, and environmental agencies in the 1970s led to a wide variety of other warnings efforts, such as for blasting caps, turpentine, small toy parts, and saccharin. The Occupational Safety and Health Act of 1970 created the Occupational Safety and Health Administration (OSHA), but it was not until 1983 that OSHA issued regulations governing the labeling of hazardous chemicals in the workplace. Even this seemingly obvious opportunity for a constructive warnings effort was the subject of internal political battles within Ronald Reagan's administration. The controversy over the regulatory proposal was ultimately resolved by my report in favor of the regulation prepared for the secretary of labor and the U.S. Office of Management and Budget, at the request of then Vice-President Bush.[6]

The 1980s was the "right-to-know" decade, as informational policies became a prominent policy tool. Warnings efforts began for products ranging from lawn mowers to alcoholic beverages, patterned after the landmark cigarette warnings policies.[7] We now take the widespread use of warnings for granted, but warnings for consumer products were a rarity when cigarette warnings began.

Hazard warnings are not the only source of information from the government. In 1964 the government issued a landmark report on the lung cancer risks of cigarettes. More than any other document, this report settled the smoking risk debate and concluded that there was in fact a substantial lung cancer risk from smoking. Beginning in 1967 the surgeon general issued annual reports on smoking risks, ranging from cardiovascular disease to nicotine addiction. While these reports are unlikely to be read by the citizenry at large, they do generate press coverage and provide an informational basis for public discussions of smoking risks.[8]

The media has been covering the hazards of smoking for decades, long before there were any official government reports on smoking. *Reader's Digest*, for example, published twelve articles on smoking health risks in the 1950s, seventeen in the 1960s, nineteen in the 1970s, and twenty-three in the 1980s.[9] The article count has been on the rise, reflecting the increased salience of the public controversy over smoking health risks.

These article counts also demonstrate that while the 1964 government report on smoking did a great deal to resolve the ongoing scientific debate over smoking, there was nevertheless awareness of a potential risk before the report was issued.

A June 1954 scientific study of smoking and lung cancer prepared for the American Cancer Society by Hammond and Horn was known to almost the entire American public. Indeed, in that year 90 percent of all respondents to a Gallup opinion poll responded "Yes" when asked whether they had "heard or read anything recently to the effect that cigarette smoking may be a cause of cancer of the lung."[10] Gallup poll results for 1999 indicate a comparable figure of 85 percent for that same question.

The leading U.S. public health officials also concluded that information regarding the risks of smoking had been communicated to the public. U.S. surgeon general, Dr. LeRoy Burney, testified in 1957 to a House of Representatives hearing on filter cigarettes:

> Our position is that we have informed the public through the excellent coverage of the press, radio, and TV. We have informed the official health agencies in the States who are responsible for this area, and we have informed the American Medical Association, recognizing that many people will go to their own physician for advice.[11]

Public receipt of smoking risk information is borne out in public opinion poll data from 1957. When asked, "Did you happen to hear or read about the recent report of the American Cancer Society reporting the results of a study on the effects of cigaret [sic] smoking?" 77 percent of the respondents said "Yes," with 82 percent of smokers answering "Yes."[12] The 77 percent general awareness of the American Cancer Society Study was so great that Dr. George Gallup pronounced it "a phenomenal figure in polling annals."[13]

Whether the advent of product warnings in 1966 would, in fact, provide new information to the public was not at all clear. Indeed, in the American Medical Association (AMA) letter of testimony to the FTC, AMA executive vice president, Dr. F. Blasingame, observed:

> With respect to cigarets, cautionary labeling cannot be anticipated to serve the public interest with any particular degree of success. The health hazards of excessive smoking have been well-publicized for more than 10 years and are common knowledge.
>
> Labeling will not alert even the young cigaret smoker to any risks of which he is not already aware.[14]

In his keynote address at the 1967 World Conference on Smoking and Health, U.S. Surgeon General William H. Stewart observed: "Today at least here in the United States, a substantial majority of the people have been exposed to the scientific evidence and have accepted it."[15]

These sentiments are echoed by Dr. Daniel Horn, who in his co-authored work with Dr. Cuyler Hammond documented the smoking linkage to ill health in their landmark 1954 report to the American Cancer Society. In his capacity as director of the National Clearinghouse for Smoking and Health, Dr. Horn concluded in 1968 that the smoking risk message was well known: "You could stand on the rooftop and shout 'smoking is dangerous' at the top of your lungs and you would not be telling anyone anything they did not already know."[16]

What, however, will be the effect of the ongoing debate that took place between the cigarette industry and public health officials on the risks of smoking? When the government and industry disagree, how will people assess the risks? This issue was of general concern to EPA in its pollution control efforts, and in Viscusi 1997a I presented empirical evidence on this issue. That study involved a field experiment in which hundreds of people participated. In each case, industry and government scientists disagreed about the cancer risks from pollution. The striking result is that in the presence of such disagreement between two different entities people adopted the worst-case estimate as their risk belief. In contrast, if two government scientists disagreed, people simply averaged the risk beliefs. These results suggest that people were likely to adopt the government risk estimates as being more credible.

Cigarette advertising also has drawn attention to the health risks. For almost the entire time during which today's smokers have been alive, there has been cigarette advertising in which mentions of the health properties of cigarettes have focused public attention on the risks. A 1935 Camel advertisement urged purchase of that brand since it was purportedly "milder."[17] Firms, such as the marketers of Kent cigarettes, advertised their effective filters with evidence of the harmful residues that were removed.[18] Other firms mentioned their lower tar level, where tar is a negative product characteristic that draws consumer attention to the product risks. Competitive advertising on the safety dimension became so fierce that in 1953 *Business Week* remarked that this advertising approach was not in the industry's interest: "Why has the industry persisted in this negative form of advertising even when, as tobacco growers and others complain, it hurts the trade by making people conscious that cigarettes may be harmful?"[19]

The continued advertising of low-tar and -nicotine cigarettes, as well as the development of "Light" and "UltraLight" variants of established brands such as Marlboro and Camel, suggests that marketing with an eye toward health concerns still draws consumer attention to the health consequences of smoking.

Smoking Risk Beliefs

National public opinion polls periodically report evidence of smoking risk awareness. By the 1970s, 90 percent of the public believed that smoking was "harmful," and the overwhelming majority linked smoking to lung cancer, throat cancer, and heart disease.[20] Similarly, when asked whether a particular product is not harmful, or somewhat/very harmful, almost the entire American public concludes that tobacco products are harmful—far more than for other product groups such as alcoholic beverages, food additives, fast food, and over-the-counter drugs.[21]

Such declarations of belief in product risks provide interesting background information but do not resolve the main matter of concern: Do people properly assess the risk? People may respond to a survey indicating that smoking is "harmful" and perhaps even "very harmful," but do smokers believe the risk is as great as scientists estimate? Simply knowing that people believe there is a potential for harm does not resolve the more fundamental issue of whether risk beliefs are too high or to low. Many people also believe that artificial sweeteners, candy, and dairy products are "harmful," but these products do not pose risks remotely similar to those associated with cigarettes. What people mean by "harmful" also varies from individual to individual. A question whether smoking is "risky" has no meaningful quantitative content because different smokers may have different threshold concepts as to what constitutes a risky product. College-educated workers, for example, are more likely to rate a job of given objective risk as being "dangerous" than are less well educated workers.[22]

Many Gallup polls have focused on specific diseases, and lung cancer has received the most scrutiny. Figure 3 sketches the trend of responses to the question of whether "smoking is one of the causes of lung cancer." The share of the population answering "Yes" was over 50 percent in 1949, rose to over 60 percent by 1970 and over 80 percent by 1980. What is also remarkable is that Gallup poll also recorded the percentage of people it termed "Undecided." These are people who may have heard something about the linkage but were not sure if in fact cigarettes caused lung cancer. Ever since the 1950s, at least 70 percent of the population answered "Yes" or "Undecided" to the lung cancer causation question. It is also noteworthy that by the 1990s, almost nobody was "Undecided."

Such opinion polls are interesting from a historical standpoint but

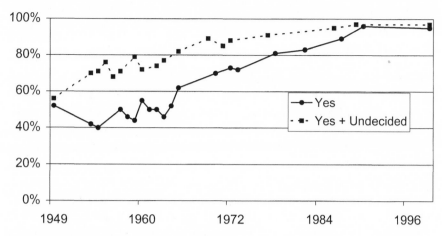

Figure 3 Gallup Poll responses to lung cancer causation question: "Do you think cigarette smoking is one of the causes of lung cancer?" Source: Gallup Surveys.

are not ideal. Does a probabilistic relationship between smoking and lung cancer qualify as a "cause"? How high must the probability be, more probable than not? One-half, or does any nonzero risk suffice?

In addition to these difficulties of interpretation, there is also the problem that it is difficult to get 100 percent awareness in any public opinion poll. Consider the following Gallup national poll results. Only 79 percent of respondents in 1999 stated that the earth revolves around the sun. In 1996 just 70 percent of the population could identify Al Gore as the vice-president of the United States, and only 62 percent of the population could identify Michael Jordan as the NBA M.V.P. and star of the Chicago Bulls basketball team. Recognition of stars of top rated television shows is similar, with 66 percent being able to identify Regis Philbin as the host of "Who Wants to Be a Millionaire?" (Gallup 2000) and 55 percent able to identify Jerry Seinfeld as the star of the TV show "Seinfeld" (Gallup 1996). Viewed in these terms, the smoking awareness figures are quite impressive.

Nevertheless, such questions do not resolve the real question of whether people fully understand the risks of smoking. To address these concerns, I have developed a series of objective risk measures in which respondents must give concrete answers to quantitative risk questions. Moreover, these questions address issues for which there is an available scientific reference point, making it possible to ascertain whether risk beliefs are accurate or err in a particular direction. For purposes of this assessment, I will use estimates based largely on studies reported by the U.S. surgeon general. Those risk estimates have received criticism for overstating the risk because they do not, for example, fully account for risk-related behavior of smokers other than smoking that affects their mortality and morbidity.[23] Nevertheless, there is no other salient risk reference point in the literature, so the evidence reported by the surgeon general will serve as my scientific reference point. I will take these estimates at face value without any adjustments for omitted factors such as the decrease in tar and nicotine levels since the much earlier era of smoking experience to which these studies pertain. Smoking is undeniably extremely risky to one's health, and ascertaining whether the public's risk beliefs accord with the risk estimates of the surgeon general is of independent interest, even if one prefers a different risk reference point.

This chapter will consider three broad classes of risk and four different surveys of U.S. risk beliefs. The three major risk components of smoking are lung cancer, total smoking mortality, and life expectancy loss due to smoking. The four surveys consist of a national 1985 survey, a regional 1991 survey, a national 1997 survey, and a 1998 survey in Massachusetts. All these surveys were undertaken as part of the cigarette litigation except for the 1991 survey that I undertook independently and without any industry funding or involvement. The other surveys were administered by national marketing firms (Audits and Surveys and Roper Starch), and respondents were not aware that the survey was funded by law firms representing the tobacco industry.[24] My estimates based on these surveys have appeared in numerous peer reviewed publications.

I first became aware of the 1985 smoking risk belief survey when I was asked to be a consultant on risk awareness and warnings to a law firm representing R. J. Reynolds. As part of my effort, I reviewed a compilation of studies that they had collected on risk beliefs, including the 1985 survey that a group of law firms had commissioned but not used. I was struck by the fact that the methodology of this survey, unlike that of other available surveys of risk belief, made it possible to make an objective assessment of the risk beliefs. In addition to analyzing the original survey data myself and discussing the survey with the survey research firm, I performed a series of independent analyses of alternative framings of questions in a 1991 survey that I undertook without any industry knowledge or support. This study bolstered and extended the 1985 results. The changes I made in 1991 became integrated in a 1997 national survey that was undertaken in response to the state attorneys general litigation. In 1998 I directed a modified version of the 1997 survey targeted solely at the Massachusetts population in connection with that state's lawsuit against the industry. These data provide a coherent and illuminating basis for assessing smokers' risk beliefs.

The interview mode was a random telephone survey, where the three marketing firm surveys used a random-digit dialing technique and then randomized the respondent based on who was present in the home. The survey was quite short. For example, the 1985 survey posed an open-ended question about the respondent's general attitude toward cigarettes, asked whether respondents had heard various statements about cigarettes, ascertained their lung cancer risk beliefs, and obtained demographic information on age and smoking status. Subsequent surveys expanded the risk and demographic questions.

One modification provided a test of the survey's validity. The 1998 survey put the question pertaining to what the respondent had heard about cigarettes after the risk perception question rather than before it. Some critics of my analysis have hypothesized that the questions on what the respondent had heard could affect the smoking risk belief responses.[25] This conjecture can be tested explicitly by altering the question order, placing the "Have you heard" question after the smoking risk belief question to determine if that made any differences. The 1998 survey altered the placement in this manner and found that the placement of this question was inconsequential.

Because the focus of the 1980s lawsuits against the cigarette industry was on lung cancer, the 1985 questions ascertained the lung cancer risk perceptions of the population. Unfortunately, the reports of the surgeon general give information on the total number of smoking-related illnesses and deaths, but not on the overall probability. Why the government does not provide probabilistic information remains a puzzle, if the objective of the policies is to raise probabilistic beliefs to the correct level. Empirical studies show that emphasis on the numerator of the probability without information on the denominator (i.e., the number of people exposed) will tend to boost public risk beliefs.[26] Using data from the surgeon general on the health consequences of smoking that was available in 1985, coupled with information on the size of the smoking population, I have estimated the lung cancer mortality risk of cigarettes to be 0.05–0.10, or 5–10 people out of 100 smokers will die from lung cancer because they smoke. My estimate of the risk is 0.06–0.13 using scientific studies for 1991 and thereafter.[27]

Eliciting meaningful probabilistic information in an interview is quite difficult. Interviewers face the practical task of getting people to think in probabilistic terms. This issue arose in a series of studies I ran on hazard warnings for the U.S. Environmental Protection Agency.[28] Those studies focused on hazards posed by chemicals and pesticides, not cigarettes. We found that providing respondents with a reference population denominator is a useful mechanism for dealing with probabilities and was superior to posing questions in terms of probabilities or fractions. The desirability of using a base population figure to enable people to think sensibly about risk frequencies is well documented in the psychology literature.[29] The denominator used in the smoking risk belief questions is 100 smokers. Specifically, the 1985 risk question was: "Among 100 smokers, how many of them do you think will get lung cancer because they smoke?" While the use of a denominator of 100 in the 1985 smoking risk survey undertaken for tobacco litigation was reasonable, I independently undertook tests of whether some other population reference point might be better understood. In my 1991 telephone survey, I also undertook a series of sensitivity tests using denominators of 1,000 and two million, which is the smoking population in the survey state, North Carolina.[30] Respondents in the telephone interviews invariably responded in percentage terms, which is supportive of use of the denominator of 100 smokers in the wording of the risk question.

Data from these surveys indicated that smokers were aware of the fatal lung cancer risks and the mortality risks of smoking.[31] This chapter expands on those studies with new survey evidence based on a national telephone survey of 1,013 respondents undertaken in February 1997,[32] and a 1998 survey in Massachusetts, of 1,002 respondents. After obtaining similar findings with a variety of samples and different risk belief questions, one can have more confidence in the results.

As the results in table 17 indicate, the findings for current smokers indicate a somewhat lower assessed lung cancer risk than for the population at large—0.37 versus 0.43 in 1985. However, each of these amounts dwarfs the previously discussed scientific estimates of the lung cancer mortality risk for that time period of .05–.10. An almost identical question wording appeared in the 1997 national survey, yielding responses that were a bit higher, as they rose to a level of 0.47 for the full sample and 0.40 for smokers. The scientific risk reference point at that time is a bit higher as well, as it is now .06–.13.

One question raised by these results is whether smokers are aware that the overwhelming majority of lung cancer victims die. More specifically, do people's estimates of lung cancer mortality also suggest substantial risk overestimation? The small-scale North Carolina study indicated lung cancer mortality risk beliefs of 0.38 for the full sample and 0.31 for smokers. These results, if anything, can be expected to understate the national risk perceptions because North Carolina is the leading tobacco-producing state in the nation. The 1998 results in table 17 for a larger Massachusetts sample indicate lung cancer mortality beliefs at roughly the same level as the 1997 lung cancer incidence question.

Because lung cancer was the first smoking risk to be highly publi-

Table 17 Summary of Smoking Risk Perception Results

Risk Question (Sample)	Full Sample	Current Smokers
Lung Cancer: Risk Probability Estimate		
Among 100 smokers, how many of them do you think will get lung cancer because they smoke? (U.S., 1985)	0.43	0.37
Among 100 smokers, how many of them do you think will die from lung cancer because they smoke? (NC, 1991)	0.38	0.31
Among 100 smokers, how many of them do you think will develop lung cancer *because* they smoke? (U.S., 1997)	0.47	0.40
Out of every 100 smokers, how many of them do you think will die from lung cancer *because* they smoke? (MA, 1998)	0.48	0.42
Total Mortality: Risk Probability Estimate		
Among 100 smokers, how many of them do you think will die from lung cancer, heart disease, throat cancer, and all other illnesses because they smoke? (NC, 1991)	0.54	0.47
Among 100 cigarette smokers, how many of them do you think will die from lung cancer, heart disease, throat cancer, or any illness *because* they smoke? (U.S., 1997)	0.50	0.42
And out of every 100 cigarette smokers, how many of them do you think will die from lung cancer, heart disease, throat cancer, or any other illness *because* they smoke? (MA, 1998)	0.54	0.46
Life Expectancy: Estimated Years Lost		
The average life expectancy for a 21-year-old male (female) is that he (she) would live another 53 (59) years. What do you believe the life expectancy is for the average male (female) smoker? (NC, 1991)	8.5 (males) 13.2 (females)	6.9 (males) 10.9 (females)
As you may know, an average 21-year-old male (female) would be expected to	10.1 (males) 14.8 (females)	7.9 (males) 12.3 (females)

(*continued*)

Table 17 *continued*

Risk Question (Sample)	Full Sample	Current Smokers
Life Expectancy: Estimated Years Lost		
live to the age of 73 (80). What do you think the life expectancy is for the average male (female) smoker? (U.S., 1997)		
As you may know, an average 21-year-old male (female) would be expected to live to the age of 73 (80). What do you think the life expectancy is for the average male (female) smoker? (MA, 1998)	10.1 (males) 15.9 (females)	8.6 (males) 13.2 (females)

Note: The sample sizes for the studies were 3,119 for the 1985 national survey; 206 for the 1991 North Carolina survey; 1,013 for the 1997 national survey; and 1,002 for the 1998 Massachusetts survey.

cized, one might hypothesize that this risk is overestimated, whereas other smoking risks are not. To address this issue, the 1991, 1997, and 1998 surveys all included a question that was a minor variation of the 1991 question wording: "Among 100 smokers, how many of them do you think will die from lung cancer, heart disease, throat cancer, and all other illnesses because they smoke?" As the findings in table 17 indicate, the answers exhibit little variation by year. The full sample of all respondents regards smoking-related mortality as roughly a 50-50 proposition, while smokers believe the mortality risk ranges from 0.42 to 0.47. Estimates based on statistics reported by the U.S. surgeon general indicate a risk of 0.18–0.36.[33] Estimates in the surgeon general's report are derived from analyses of the American Cancer Society's second Cancer Prevention Study. Subsequent studies have found that these estimates fall short on a number of dimensions. The sample itself was not nationally representative but was based on referrals of friends and relatives of American Cancer Society volunteers. The study included both self-reported data as well as proxy respondents who may not recall the other person's smoking history correctly. Moreover, statistical analyses of the data reported by the surgeon general control only for age. Other factors, such as alcohol use or occupational exposures are not recognized.

More recent estimates by scientific researchers at the Office on Smoking and Health of the Centers for Disease Control and other prominent health research institutions have focused instead on more recent nationally representative samples and have made an effort to control for some important risk factors in addition to age. These studies have found that the estimates by the surgeon general are 19 percent[34] to 40 percent[35] larger than those obtained using more representative data with more controls. Thus, my estimates of the overall mortality risk of smoking would be adjusted to a range of 0.15–0.30 if they are 19 percent too great and 0.13–0.26 if they are 40 percent too great. Although these more recent estimates constitute a more valid scientific reference point, to be conservative I will use the earlier surgeon general's estimates as the scientific reference point for assessing whether there is public underestimation of the risk.[36]

While these results indicate that the average risk beliefs are high, is there some major component of the population that has not absorbed the smoking message? The data in table 18 for the 1997 national population presents results that indicate universal understanding of smoking risks. These findings are representative of my other survey years as well.[37]

The overwhelming majority of the sample *overestimates* the lung cancer risks associated with smoking. Only 9 percent of current smokers believe that the lung cancer risk is below 0.05 and only 15 percent of current smokers believe that risk is below 0.10. These responses to the lung

Table 18 Lung Cancer and Death Risk Perceptions for Cigarette Smoking for the 1997 National Survey (percentages of respondents replying with particular risk levels)

Risk Range	Lung Cancer Risk[a]		Death Risk[b]	
	Full Sample (N=981)	Current Smokers (N=233)	Full Sample (N=982)	Current Smokers (N=234)
Risk < 0.05	5.5%	9.4%	4.0%	6.8%
0.05 ≤ Risk < 0.10	4.4%	5.6%	3.7%	5.6%
0.10 ≤ Risk < 0.20	9.2%	11.2%	8.1%	10.7%
0.20 ≤ Risk < 0.30	12.4%	13.7%	11.0%	11.5%
0.30 ≤ Risk < 0.40	8.5%	10.7%	7.8%	8.5%
0.40 ≤ Risk < 0.50	3.3%	3.4%	6.7%	7.7%
0.50 ≤ Risk < 0.60	21.2%	22.3%	19.2%	22.6%
0.60 ≤ Risk < 0.70	7.7%	5.2%	6.9%	7.3%
0.70 ≤ Risk < 0.80	10.9%	9.0%	11.9%	6.4%
0.80 ≤ Risk < 0.90	6.5%	2.1%	7.7%	2.6%
0.90 ≤ Risk < 1.00	5.7%	2.1%	7.2%	5.1%
Risk = 1.00	4.7%	5.2%	5.6%	5.1%
Mean risk	0.468	0.395	0.501	0.424

[a]Out of every 100 cigarette smokers, how many of them do you think will develop lung cancer *because* they smoke?
[b]Out of every 100 cigarette smokers, how many of them do you think will die from lung cancer, heart disease, throat cancer, or any other illness *because* they smoke?

cancer question could, however, be too great to the extent that respondents include other smoking risks as part of their response to the lung cancer risk assessment. As the findings in table 18 indicate, that there are no particular problem groups that are not as aware of the mortality risks associated with cigarettes. Only 23 percent of current smokers believe that the smoking-related mortality risk is below 0.20. Most smokers believe the mortality risk is quite high.

A salient question regarding whether smokers are informed is whether the message regarding the hazards of smoking has reached less well educated population groups. Better-educated people are less likely to smoke. To the extent that their nonsmoking status comes from knowledge of smoking risks attributable to their greater education, then one might be concerned about the need to broaden the smoking risk information effort to bring in a broader spectrum of society.

Table 19 breaks out each of the three risk perception variables according to a series of education groups for my 1997 national survey. At a broad level of aggregation are categories of respondents with less than college education or those with a college degree or more. These categories in turn are subdivided into narrower groupings. The findings are similar for all these risk measures. Quite simply, more education does not raise smoking risk beliefs and, in the case of lung cancer, may even lower risk beliefs by a small amount.

The reported risk beliefs for total mortality risks are perhaps most striking. These with less than a college education believe that the probability of a smoking-related death is 0.51, as compared to a virtually indistinguishable value of 0.50 for college graduates. Even high school dropouts have a mortality risk assessment of 0.54 so that the least well educated group in the sample exhibits no evidence of a smoking risk information deficit.

Knowledge of the hazards of smoking does not require extensive educational background. Warnings appear on cigarette packs and in cigarette advertising. The media has disseminated the message broadly, with all segments of society receiving the message. Education is, however, strongly related to lifetime wealth. Willingness to incur health risks diminishes as one's income level rises. Education is also correlated with social class factors and the propensity of one's peers and coworkers to smoke. The observed strong correlation of education and smoking rates needn't require any education-related information deficit, but can arise from differences in tastes and social acceptability.

Table 20 illustrates the extent to which risk assessments are insensitive to the kinds of basic smoking information included in various cigarette warnings and in national opinion polls. The various rows of the

Table 19 Risk Perceptions by Educational Level for 1997 Audits and Surveys Data

Educational Level	Number of Observations	Mean (Standard Error of Mean)		
		Perceived Lung Cancer Probability	Perceived Probability of Death	Perceived Expected Years of Life Lost
Full Sample				
Less than college	673	0.483	0.509	13.10
		(0.011)	(0.011)	(0.352)
Dropout before H.S. graduation	86	0.526	0.543	14.29
		(0.036)	(0.033)	(1.268)
High school diploma	337	0.482	0.498	12.92
		(0.016)	(0.016)	(0.517)
Some college	250	0.472	0.513	12.95
		(0.018)	(0.018)	(0.485)
College degree or more	302	0.446	0.497	11.49
		(0.016)	(0.017)	(0.385)
College degree	200	0.470	0.514	11.59
		(0.020)	(0.021)	(0.466)
Graduate school	102	0.398	0.462	11.31
		(0.027)	(0.027)	(0.683)
All respondents	975	0.472	0.505	12.60
		(0.009)	(0.009)	(0.271)
Males				
Less than college	309	0.472	0.492	10.65
		(0.017)	(0.017)	(0.479)
Dropout before H.S. graduation	40	0.512	0.545	9.97
		(0.052)	(0.048)	(1.483)
High school diploma	161	0.455	0.476	10.56
		(0.024)	(0.024)	(0.742)
Some college	108	0.483	0.498	11.01
		(0.027)	(0.026)	(0.613)
College degree or more	157	0.410	0.461	9.09
		(0.023)	(0.024)	(0.467)
College degree	109	0.441	0.475	9.67
		(0.028)	(0.029)	(0.576)
Graduate school	48	0.339	0.428	7.71
		(0.040)	(0.044)	(0.757)
All respondents	466	0.451	0.481	10.12
		(0.014)	(0.014)	(0.355)

(*continued*)

Table 19 *continued*

		Mean (Standard Error of Mean)		
Educational Level	**Number of Observations**	**Perceived Lung Cancer Probability**	**Perceived Probability of Death**	**Perceived Expected Years of Life Lost**
		Females		
Less than college	364	0.493	0.524	15.17
		(0.015)	(0.015)	(0.482)
Dropout before H.S. graduation	46	0.538	0.541	18.29
		(0.050)	(0.047)	(1.823)
High school diploma	176	0.506	0.519	15.05
		(0.022)	(0.021)	(0.682)
Some college	142	0.464	0.525	14.40
		(0.024)	(0.025)	(0.688)
College degree or more	145	0.484	0.534	14.05
		(0.022)	(0.022)	(0.544)
College degree	91	0.505	0.560	13.89
		(0.027)	(0.028)	(0.685)
Graduate school	54	0.448	0.491	14.31
		(0.037)	(0.033)	(0.902)
All respondents	509	0.490	0.527	14.84
		(0.013)	(0.012)	(0.377)

table correspond to the kinds of statements the person may have heard regarding smoking, ranging from "cigarette smoking will most likely shorten life" to defenses of cigarette smoking, such as "cigarette smoking is not bad for a person's health." The final entry of whether "cigarette smoking causes flat feet" is a question that will distinguish individuals who perhaps are either particularly ill-informed or are not giving reasoned responses to the survey questions. Virtually everyone in the sample—from 96 percent to 99 percent—had heard each of the two adverse statements regarding the risks of cigarettes. Moreover, one's smoking status did not affect whether one had heard either of these types of statements regarding cigarette risks. In contrast, roughly one-third of the sample had heard the various statements exonerating cigarettes of risk. Perhaps surprisingly, it is current smokers who exhibit the lowest fraction of people—22 percent—who had heard that "cigarette smoking is not bad for a person's health." Clearly, the hazards of smoking are not a secret and are not unknown to smokers themselves.

Table 20 Profile of Groups Who Have Heard Ideas about Cigarette Smoking in the 1997 National Survey

Fractions Who Have Heard Idea and Their Mean Mortality Risk Perception
(and Standard Error of Mean Risk)

	Full Sample		Current Smokers		Former Smokers		Nonsmokers	
	Heard	Risk	Heard	Risk	Heard	Risk	Heard	Risk
Cigarette smoking will most likely shorten life.	0.968	0.473 (0.009)	0.967	0.399 (0.019)	0.981	0.462 (0.019)	0.961	0.516 (0.013)
Cigarette smoking is dangerous to a person's health.	0.986	0.471 (0.009)	0.984	0.396 (0.018)	0.992	0.464 (0.019)	0.984	0.513 (0.013)
Cigarette smoking is bad for a person's health, but not dangerous.	0.361	0.454 (0.016)	0.329	0.388 (0.030)	0.327	0.413 (0.035)	0.397	0.499 (0.021)
Cigarette smoking is not bad for a person's health.	0.314	0.473 (0.017)	0.222	0.339 (0.037)	0.322	0.452 (0.034)	0.356	0.523 (0.021)
Cigarette smoking causes flat feet.	0.032	0.510 (0.052)	0.016	0.215 (0.076)	0.033	0.369 (0.091)	0.039	0.638 (0.057)

In addition to listing what fraction of the sample had heard the various ideas concerning cigarettes, the table lists the associated mortality risk perceptions conditional upon hearing the particular statement and falling into the sample group designated by the column heading. Thus, for the full sample who had heard that "cigarette smoking is not bad for a person's health," the risk value is the average mortality risk only for people who had heard this statement. People who have not heard it are excluded from this calculation. In every case, smokers have a lower risk assessment than the other groups, even though they have heard the same particular type of information. Nevertheless, the risk assessments are quite high for smokers, though not as great as for nonsmokers or for former smokers. To the extent that a lower assessed risk of smoking will lead one to be more willing to engage in smoking behavior, the lower risk beliefs of smokers are not unexpected.

The data on lung cancer perceptions and mortality risk beliefs capture discrete events pertaining to different health outcomes. What is missing is a demonstration that people understand the quantity of life at risk and not just whether they will get lung cancer or some other disease. If these ailments are believed to strike once one is already in a nursing home, then little will be lost compared to premature mortality in middle age.

More specifically, do people underestimate the life expectancy that will be lost due to smoking? If that is the case, then even an accurate assessment of the probability of premature mortality will lead to an inadequate assessment of the risk. To address this issue, the survey asked people life expectancy questions indicated in table 17. Although the wording of the question differs a bit by survey wave, the common theme of the approach is to first inform respondents of their gender-specific life expectancy at age twenty-one. This information prevents the question from serving as a test of respondent knowledge of both normal life expectancy and the effect of smoking on life expectancy. By presenting the normal life expectancy data, respondents could better isolate the marginal effect of smoking on life expectancy, which is the main matter of interest. The 1991 survey posed the question in terms of remaining life expectancy at age twenty-one, whereas the 1997 and 1998 surveys focused on the total life expectancy conditional upon the person's survival to age twenty-one. The substance of the questions is identical, but the framing is somewhat different.

The results in table 17 indicate a higher life expectancy loss assessed by the full sample than for smokers, and larger effects for females than for males. Among the smoking population, males assess the expected life expectancy loss as being from 6.9 to 8.6 years, and females assess it as 10.9–13.2 years.

Table 21 Respondents' Assessed Life-Expectancy Loss Due to Smoking in the 1997 National Survey (in years)

Sample	Mean (Standard Error of Mean)		
	Males	Females	Total
Full sample	10.1	14.8	12.6
	(0.4)	(0.4)	(0.3)
Current smokers	7.9	12.3	9.9
	(0.7)	(0.8)	(0.5)
Current nonsmokers	10.9	15.5	13.4
	(0.4)	(0.4)	(0.3)
Former smokers	9.6	14.8	12.3
	(0.6)	(0.7)	(0.5)
Lifelong nonsmokers	11.6	15.8	14.0
	(0.5)	(0.5)	(0.4)

Table 21 shows the difference, for various groups of respondents in the 1997 national survey, between the respondents' estimated life expectancy for a smoker and the average life expectancy. So, for example, male former smokers estimated that the average male smoker will live 9.6 fewer years than will the average nonsmoker. Overall, people believe that cigarette smoking leads to a life expectancy loss of 12.6 years. The assessed life expectancy loss by current smokers is somewhat less, ranging from 7.9 years for males to 12.3 years for females. Each of these life expectancy loss estimates is greater than the actual life expectancy loss. My estimates based on scientific estimates yielded a life expectancy loss in the vicinity of 3.6 to 7.2 years.[38] Some estimates now in literature suggest a point estimate of 6.6 years as the life expectancy loss.[39] Note that one's loss in life expectancy consists of the probability of dying from smoking at any given age multiplied by the corresponding length of life lost. It is not the loss in life expectancy conditional upon one's death. As in the case of the mortality risk probability assessments, the evidence suggests that smokers believe the risks to be lower than do nonsmokers, but they nevertheless *overestimate* the hazards associated with smoking.

The pertinent question concerning accurate beliefs is whether people's risk beliefs agree with scientific estimates, not whether smokers have risk beliefs as high as do nonsmokers. Figures 4, 5, and 6 compare the results for the perceived risks of smoking to the scientific estimates of the risks of 0.06–0.13 for lung cancer after 1991, and 0.18–0.36 for total mortality risk.[40]

In every instance, people overperceive the risks of smoking. This

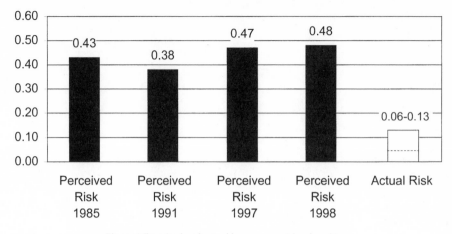

Figure 4 Perceived and actual lung cancer risks of smoking

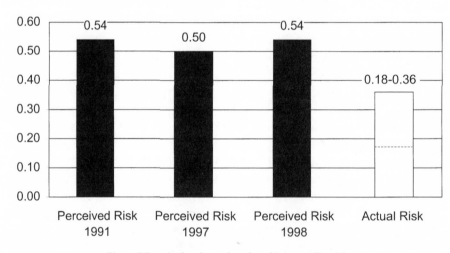

Figure 5 Perceived and actual total smoking mortality risks

tendency is greatest for lung cancer risks, which are the most highly publicized, but it is also true of total mortality risks and life expectancy loss. The risks of smoking, which are in fact considerable, are actually exaggerated in people's minds.

Survey evidence from other countries indicates similar overperception of smoking risks. Liu and Hsieh (1995) found that in Taiwan the general population believes the lung cancer risk of smoking to be 0.36, and smokers assess the risk to be 0.28. The evidence from Spain reported by Viscusi et al. (2000) indicates that the perceived risk of lung cancer from smoking is 0.50 for the entire population and 0.46 for smokers. These es-

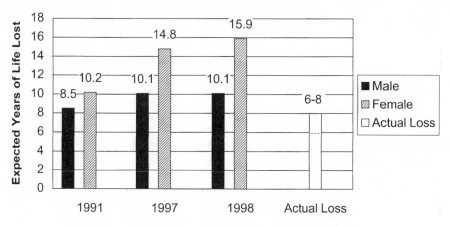

Figure 6 Perceived and actual life expectancy loss due to smoking

timates are in the same general range as my findings in the different surveys for the United States.

Possible Rejoinders

The overwhelming implication of these different sets of statistics is that people are generally aware of the hazards of smoking. As a consequence, it is unlikely that additional hazard warnings intended primarily to simply alert people to the general risk of smoking will have much additional effect. This does not imply that there is no informational role that the government can play. It does suggest, however, that a truly useful function needs to be more imaginative than a minor variation on past informational approaches.

How might one respond to this evidence suggesting that smokers understand the risks? The psychologist Paul Slovic, who served as a plaintiff's expert in the cigarette litigation, advanced four possible critiques of my smoking risk perception studies.[41] First, the fact that people perceive a probability of some adverse outcome does not imply that they understand the severity of the outcome. While this issue may be a problem in studies that simply ask if smoking is "risky," in my surveys the outcome is a well-defined severe health outcome including lung cancer, death, and life expectancy loss. Death and cancer are among the most highly valued and severe health consequences.

A second shortcoming that he suggests is that people may be subject to an optimism bias and not believe that the risks will actually affect them. Optimism bias will be discussed in detail below. I will simply re-mark here that such optimism is a matter of conjecture and has never been documented as affecting smoking behavior. Indeed, if people were truly over-optimistic regarding smoking risks, then having higher smok-ing risk beliefs would not discourage smoking, whereas in fact there is a strong relationship of this sort.[42]

Slovic's third criticism is that such risk questions may not address the repetitive and cumulative nature of the risk. However, the questions I use ask about lifetime mortality risks and life expectancy loss and consequently explicitly capture the long-term health consequences of smoking hazards. Long-term health consequences take on a particular significance when the risk from repeated exposure is not the same as the risk of individual exposures, scaled up appropriately. If there is some threshold below which there is no risk, then risks from repeated expo-sures may be quite different from the risk one would encounter from each cigarette multiplied by the number of cigarettes, taking into ac-count, of course, that one can die only once. Similar complications arise if there is a nonlinear dose-response relationship, in which case one must be especially careful to avoid hazard exposures at levels where the risk probability escalates steeply. It is these threshold and possible nonlinear aspects of repeated lifetime exposures that create the analytical interest in this phenomenon. Somewhat surprisingly, Slovic emphasizes the cu-mulative risk concern but does not grasp the importance of these distinc-tive dose-response characteristics. In his view, the risk of falling down stairs that one climbs repeatedly, with an identical probability of falling each time, is a cumulative risk. Thus Slovic's discussion of cumulative risks confuses two quite different concepts—a repetition of independent and identical risks over time versus a nonlinear dose-response relation-ship for repeated exposures to a particular hazard.

In Slovic's final criticism he hypothesizes that smokers do not un-derstand that smoking is addictive. Addiction is a quite different matter from whether smoking has a high probability of causing lung cancer, heart disease, or life expectancy loss. While these questions do not ad-dress addiction at all, other survey data discussed below are pertinent.

The original survey evidence offered by Slovic, based on a small-scale survey at a single high school, in no way addresses any of the four problems that he raises. Typical of the risk questions Slovic (1998) posed to evaluate the accuracy of risk beliefs was the following: "Every single cigarette causes a little bit of harm." Respondents could then indicate whether they strongly disagree, disagree, agree, strongly agree, or don't know. Unfortunately there is no correct answer to this question. Even the author did not know the "right" answer.

What is "a little bit of harm" and what health consequences meet that test? Consider my midpoint smoking mortality risk estimate of 0.26. If one smoked a pack every day throughout the year for forty years, the mortality risk per cigarette is under one in a million. Does a risk of this magnitude constitute a "little bit of harm," a lot of harm, or a negligible amount of harm?

Indeed, Slovic states that he does not even know the answer to the question of how much harm is "a little bit of harm."[43] Similarly, the qualitative questions posed by Slovic and others that ask people questions such as whether "there is really no risk at all for the first few years" and ask degrees of agreement with such statements do not permit one to make any precise judgments whatsoever regarding whether the person correctly perceives the risk.

On some of Slovic's measures, smokers and nonsmokers perform similarly. On others, smokers give somewhat lower risk assessments, though these results are sensitive to how one codes the different qualitative responses. Slovic's main test of whether smokers are informed is whether their risk belief responses are comparable to those of nonsmokers. However, even if it is true that smokers' risk awareness scores are lower, that comparison is irrelevant to the fundamental issue of whether smokers underassess the risk relative to its true level, not what nonsmokers think it is. For every one of my objective risk measures, responses by smokers in table 17 were below those of the full sample. These results do not imply that smokers underestimate risks. The appropriate policy concern is whether smokers understand the risk relative to an accurate scientific reference point, not relative to the views of nonsmokers. On that matter studies such as Slovic's are completely silent. By assumption, studies by such critics of smoking treat nonsmokers as making wise choices and smokers foolish ones. The task in their view is to give smokers the risk beliefs and other pertinent choice characteristics of nonsmokers.

The survey questions asked by researchers such as Slovic also do not provide an objective characterization of the health effects. Slovic's questions are particularly subject to his own first criticism of my smoking risk analyses, which is that people may not understand the severity of the consequences involved. Is "a little bit of harm" a more well-defined health effect than lung cancer, death, or life expectancy loss?

In an effort to challenge my results, Slovic (2001) reported his own survey findings in which he replicated my question pertaining to the lung cancer risk to 100 smokers. His results were even stronger than my own, as respondents aged twenty-three and over perceived the lung cancer risk as 0.49, while young respondents aged fourteen to twenty-two perceived the risk as even higher—0.60. These findings provide strong corroboration of my work.

Slovic (2001) focuses instead on a different approach to eliciting lung cancer risk beliefs in which respondents are asked how many out of 100 smokers would die from each of the following causes of death: automobile accidents, heart disease, stroke, lung cancer, and all other causes of death.

There are three problems with Slovic's methodology. First, cigarette smoking greatly increases the risk of heart disease and stroke as well as lung cancer. By giving people a list of causes of death, most of which are linked to smoking, Slovic has simply shifted some of the lung cancer risk answers to heart disease and stroke. If people respond that smokers will die of heart disease and stroke rather than lung cancer, does this prove that people don't understand that smoking is dangerous?

Second, what do the responses to his question imply about people's lung cancer risk beliefs? Even when faced with the cause-of-death list including stroke and heart disease, adult respondents assess the lung cancer risk to smokers as 0.24, and youths assess the risk as 0.28. Slovic emphasizes that these numbers are lower than when the lung cancer question is asked alone. This observation is irrelevant. What he fails to acknowledge is that even these risk beliefs indicate an overassessment of the risk as compared to the scientific estimates. Indeed, the responses greatly exceed even the upper bound of the lung cancer risk range, which is 0.13.

My third observation relates to the question wording for the cause-of-death list. As respondents assessed the number of smokers' deaths for each category, interviewers kept a running tally to make sure that the answers totaled 100. Given this constraint, items mentioned late in any list will tend to be undervalued. Randomization will reduce these ordering effects. The interviewers randomized the first three categories: automobile accidents, heart disease, and stroke. Somewhat surprisingly, they were given written instructions not to randomize the position of lung cancer, keeping it in the fourth position. This question framing will depress the lung cancer answers.

Given this effort to drive down people's estimates of their lung cancer risk beliefs, it is remarkable that these survey responses indicate a risk overassessment. What matters is not whether one can artificially depress responses for one of many smoking disease categories, but rather, do people understand that taking into account all major health consequences, smoking is dangerous? The answer is a resounding "Yes."

One study that did attempt to use a quantitative risk perception value relied upon a somewhat different question included in the U.S.

government's Health and Retirement Study. Respondents received no baseline information regarding normal life expectancy. They then confronted a life expectancy question that asked them to rate their chances of survival to age seventy-five, then to age eighty-five. There were consequently two key differences from my life expectancy question—the absence of normal reference point information and the use of a scale that is seemingly qualitative but actually has no well-defined meaning, particularly across respondents.[44]

Schoenbaum (1997) uses the results of this survey to suggest that heavy smokers overestimate their survival probability. Light smokers did not underestimate the risk in his study. Antismoking critics such as Hanson and Logue (1998) have touted these results as showing that smokers underestimate the risks. The Health and Retirement Study question used for the analysis is the following: "Using any number from zero to ten, what do you think are the chances that you will live to be 75 or more?" This question does not distinguish smoking risk effects per se. One must infer the incremental effect of smoking based on the difference between smokers' and nonsmokers' responses, attributing all the difference to smoking rather than factors correlated with smoking. Moreover, to be meaningful, both groups have to interpret the scale the same way and have the same understanding of normal life expectancy. This survey question compounds the respondent's understanding of normal survival rates with the incremental effect of smoking.[45]

In addition, the question wording does not elicit a well-specified probability, as compared to my questions in table 17. An indication of the inappropriateness of a probabilistic interpretation of the question is revealed by comparison of the assessed chance of living to age seventy-five with the respondents' rating of the chance of survival to age eighty-five, which were not reported by Schoenbaum (1997). Using the same ten-point scale, over one-third of all respondents in the Health and Retirement Study rated their chance of living to age eighty-five as being at least as great as or greater than the chance of living to age seventy-five. Quite a spectacular feat, because you have to make it to age seventy-five to have a shot at age eighty-five. In fact, for this sample the actual odds of living to age eighty-five are half as great as living to age seventy-five. These within-subject comparisons reveal inconsistencies indicating that people were not applying the ten-point scale the same way for the two survival questions. Even more dramatic anomalies exist in the survey results. For female respondents, the assessed probability of survival to the target age in the question *decreases* the closer the respondent gets to the target age, which is contrary to the facts. The responses consequently may reflect a qualitative sense of health status more than survival odds.

There is no reason to believe that the ten-point scale in the survey is a valid probability metric.[46]

The absence of normal life expectancy information in such questions presents even more of a problem, because respondents cannot reliably assess how their smoking status and lifestyle affect life expectancy without knowledge of what it should be for the average person. Knowledge of such information is likely to be correlated with educational status, which in turn is strongly correlated with smoking, thus biasing the results.

The importance of providing baseline life expectancy values is apparent even to the designated experts in the cigarette litigation. For example, consider the response of a risk awareness witness, Harvard law professor Jon Hanson, who cited Schoenbaum's work approvingly and who was a designated expert in the state of Washington lawsuit and in other lawsuits against the cigarette industry:

Q. If I asked you what you thought your probability was of living to 75, what would you answer?

A. I think I would answer, I don't have the vaguest sense—I don't have the vaguest sense of what my probability of living to age 75 is, except that it's—that's too strong. I think it's something greater than 20 percent. That's my own vague sense of how I were to answer a question put to me of that sort . . .

Q. And that's the best you could do?

A. I might be able to do better, but I would need more information about what are the actual expectations generally for white men, as you described me, and then I would want—

Q. Well, let me just make sure. You are a white man, aren't you?

A. Yes.[47]

Survival questions without life expectancy information are likely to leave other respondents clueless as well. Rather than rely on risk belief questions that test several aspects of knowledge jointly and never even focus respondents on the incremental effects of their smoking behavior, it is preferable to isolate the smoking–life expectancy linkage as my questions have done.

A final strand in the smoking perception literature pertains to the hypothesis that people may understand the risk to others but do not believe it will affect them. This is the notion that people say "it can't happen to me," even though they recognize a risk to others. Such a lack of personalization of the risk is called "optimism bias."

Claims that smokers ignore the risks to themselves are contradicted by survey questions that address that matter directly. Consider the responses to the Gallup poll question asked of smokers only: Do you think smoking is or is not harmful to your health?" The percentage of respondents answering "Yes" was 94 percent of the general public in 1987, 93 percent of smokers in 1990, and 90 percent of smokers in 1993. Indeed, that 1993 Gallup poll found that 65 percent of all smokers believed that smoking had already affected their health, and 78 percent believed that it was likely or very likely that they would have serious health problems from smoking if they continued to smoke.[48]

An empirical test of whether smoking risk beliefs have to do with risks to the individual and not simply risks to others is that the smoking risk assessments have a substantial effect on the smoking probability. If these hazards were only pertinent to others, not the respondent, they should not affect the respondent's smoking behavior. Based on my 1985 survey results, I found that if people understood the lung cancer risk of smoking accurately as opposed to overestimating it, the societal smoking rate would increase by 6.5–7.5 percent.[49]

In view of such survey results, how could one hypothesize that smokers do not, in fact, believe that the risks pertain to them? Much of the purported optimism bias effect can be traced to how the question is posed.

Typical of an optimism bias survey is to ask people whether they are above average, below average, or average drivers in terms of their safety.[50] Almost all respondents consider themselves to be above average or average. Not surprisingly, this result holds for almost every risk, not just driving or smoking.[51] Studies purporting to demonstrate the existence of optimism bias have addressed virtually all types of risk. Indeed, smoking has been a latecomer to the field. Some researchers have failed to find an optimism bias effect for smoking. Jenks (1992) set out to show that smokers were subject to optimism bias but did not find that this was the case. He concluded (p. 574): "Quite possibly, the information bombardment by the media has become so strong that it is now impossible to avoid the information or deny the health cost of smoking."

What, if anything, do such results tell us? These comparative risk questions in effect ask respondents to find fault with themselves. Who wants to admit that they are worse than average? When polled, virtually none of my students believe that they should receive a below average grade for the course.

In a study of consumer safety risks undertaken for the U.S. Environmental Protection Agency, Wesley Magat and I examined the optimism bias hypothesis for consumer hazards pertaining to the risk of child poisonings from household chemicals.[52] We wanted to determine for the federal government whether optimism bias responses to comparative questions carried over to risk-taking behavior. We found that very few respondents believed that the products they used posed above average child poisoning risks. If this apparent optimism bias were reflective of their risk beliefs, one would expect their risk-averting behavior to be lax just as the optimism bias proponents hypothesize that prospective smokers will be lured into smoking by an optimistic assessment of the risk. However, when faced with an opportunity to buy products posing less severe child poisoning risks, participants in the study responded with extremely large valuations for the safety improvements. Indeed, the amounts were far more than could be justified by the extent of the risk reduction. This coupling of optimism bias responses to a comparative risk question with extreme willingness to pay for modest safety improvements suggests that the comparative wording of the optimism bias questions elicits effects other than underestimation of the risks.

A similar example of the literature on risk optimism consists of the following results from a study done by Harvard Medical School researchers.[53] The survey data they analyzed asked respondents whether they had a higher than average risk, an average risk, or "about the same" risk of heart attack or cancer as others. The authors then matched the responses with smoking status. They found that 29 percent of current smokers believed that they had a higher risk of heart attack than average and 40 percent believed that they had a higher risk of cancer than average, which the authors viewed as indicating that people were not sufficiently aware of the risks to themselves.

In some respects interpreting these data is a matter of assessing whether the glass is half full or half empty. Judge Frank Easterbrook cited this study as providing evidence that there was risk awareness among smokers, as smokers as a group were significantly more likely to believe that they had an above average risk of either heart attack or cancer.[54]

My additional analysis of these survey data provides further evidence for smoker rationality. The medical researchers divided respondents into two groups—those who believed that their cancer or heart attack risk was average or below average and those who believed the risks were above average. Why did the authors pool the average and below average responses in their analysis, given that these were distinct survey responses? I performed an independent analysis of these responses, focusing on those who believed their risks were average or below average. Within these two categories smokers were significantly less likely to believe that their lung cancer or heart attack risks were below average. Smokers consequently are more likely to rate their risks as above average and are also less likely to rate the risks as being below average if they don't believe the risks are above average. In addition, analysis of the duration of smoking further strengthens this result, as additional amounts of smoking increase the likelihood that the person believes that the heart attack risk or cancer risk is above average and decrease the probability that it is below average. People who have given up smoking similarly have lower risk beliefs than do current smokers.

The only possible remaining problem area is that many smokers report that their cancer and heart attack risks are about the same as others'. Responses to survey questions indicating that one is average are often the norm because people do not want to find fault with themselves relative to the average person in the population. Over half of all the respondents to the survey believe that they face the same cancer risk as others, and half believe that they have the same risk of a heart attack. Indicating that the risk is the same as the average is also a convenient, time-saving response in survey contexts. Answering "average" to questions enables respondents to get through what was, in fact, an extremely long survey more quickly. For other questions asking about whether the person was average, the dominant response was often that the individual considered himself or herself to be average with respect to that dimension. For example, 49 percent of the sample thought that they worried about the same amount compared to a person in the same situation.[55] Moreover, answering other questions in the survey indicating an "average" or "about the same" response makes one more likely to respond "average" to the questions about heart disease or lung cancer, which is consistent with people using the average response category in situations where they do not want to spend the time drawing fine distinctions.

There is also the difficulty of how respondents might interpret what it means to be "about the same" in terms of risk. What is the comparison group? How much does one have to differ from the average amount to no longer be average? If your weight is currently average and you gain five pounds, are you no longer average? Ten pounds? Twenty pounds? What these questions don't do is ask respondents what the smoking attributable risk is in a manner that has a meaningful quantitative metric so that people can interpret the question in a sensible manner.

Optimism bias researchers have failed to find optimism bias effects for more meaningful question framings. Psychologists such as Paul Slovic who have asked adolescents to rate their personal risk from cigarettes on a seven-point scale obtain virtually the same responses when asking them to rate the risk to themselves from cigarettes as when asking them to rate the risk to peers from cigarettes. For both smokers and nonsmokers, there is no significant difference between the personal risk rating and the risk rating to one's peers.[56] Indeed, the point estimates of the risk assessment are actually higher for the risk to oneself than the risk to one's peers, contradicting the optimism hypothesis.

Two critiques of my risk perception work based on efforts by a plaintiff's expert in the tobacco cases appeared in Hanson and Logue 1998 and Hanson and Kysar 1999. These articles suggest that for a variety of reasons, the 1985 survey results have shortcomings, but neither article offers comparable survey evidence that would get the questions right. Why have these and other critics not published surveys indicating that people underestimate the risks of smoking? The reason is simple. No matter how you ask the question, any reasonable formulation of the survey question will show that people know about the riskiness of smoking.

Hanson and Logue observe that respondents often picked salient answers such as 5, 10, 25, or 50 lung cancer deaths out of 100. Whether doing so imparts a bias in any particular direction has not been demonstrated. If people round their lung cancer case estimate up from 4 to 5 and down from 6 to 5, then there is no bias in any particular direction. Such salient responses will lead to symmetric errors that cancel each other out.

Critiques of my work have focused almost exclusively on the 1985 lung cancer question. But the major strength of the survey evidence I have presented is that we obtain comparable results for a wide variety of questions, different health effects, different samples, and different time periods. The results are robust, as they should be. People know that smoking is dangerous.

But is there not a remaining informational gap that must be addressed? Do all smokers know that cigarette smoke contains benzene? Are people aware that some studies have linked smoking to pancreatic cancer? Surely such information gaps remain.

However, having knowledge of all the underlying science is not a prerequisite to sound decisions. What is needed is that people have a sufficiently high assessment of many adverse consequences of smoking to deter them from smoking to the same extent as if they knew the true risks of the adverse health effects. Research on people's risk beliefs regarding lung cancer, total mortality, and life expectancy loss due to smoking provides strong evidence of such awareness.

Perception of Risks of Addiction

Smoking is hard to quit. For years, the surgeon general of the United States designated the smoking habit as a problem of habituation rather than addiction. The 1964 landmark report on lung cancer of the U.S. Department of Health, Education, and Welfare explicitly designated smoking as a habit rather than an addiction: "The tobacco habit should be characterized as an habituation rather than an addiction."[57] Then, in 1988, U.S. Surgeon General C. Everett Koop designated the problem of quitting smoking as a problem of "addiction."[58] Philip Morris now refers to nicotine as a "drug."[59] Addiction involves more than accustomed consumption; it also entails psychoactive effects and withdrawal effects.[60] And as the surgeon general points out, there is also a strong relapse tendency.

Cigarettes have not moved from being a habit to an addiction because cigarettes have become more addictive. Cigarettes' average nicotine level has declined, making the difficulty of quitting presumably less.[61] Rather, the designation of the addictive character of cigarettes has become harsher as our understanding of addiction and the properties of cigarettes has evolved.

The distinction between addiction and habituation may be clear to the medical community. However, the public interpretation of addiction may be quite different. All "addictions" do not have equivalent consequences. Suppose, for example, that you were about to undergo surgery. Would you rather have as your surgeon a doctor who is "addicted" to cigarettes or one who is addicted to cocaine or heroin? Similarly, if you parked your car for the evening on a deserted city street, would you rather have to pass a few addicted cigarette smokers to get to your car or a few crack addicts? Regular cigarette smokers who, as a consequence, are "addicted" to cigarettes, simply do not generate the kinds of societal harms that are associated with drug addictions. Smokers continue to function as normal productive members of society.

The existence of costs of changing behavior is not unique to cigarettes or even to products known as habits or addictions. We incur transactions costs whenever we sell a house, switch jobs, or trade in a car. The fact that there are transactions costs to changing behavior does not imply that the original decisions were wrong or irrational. However, the existence of costs of change implies that we should be more careful in the original choice because there will be an economic penalty to changing our behavior.

Even if our behavior does not change and we are in effect "locked into" a less preferred course of action, this impediment to change does not imply that we will suffer unlimited losses. Suppose for example that there is a $4,000 cost of moving from one's current apartment to a more attractive apartment across town that charges the same rent. If the present value of the gains from the move exceed $4,000, moving will be attractive. Otherwise, it will not be. The maximum value of our welfare loss from this "addiction" is $4,000. In much the same way, the monetary equivalent of the costs of giving up smoking will establish an upper bound on the potential future welfare loss from continuing to smoke even if one would not choose to start smoking if that choice could be repeated. The costs of giving up cigarettes are real and consequential. Many people find it truly difficult to quit. But the fact that such costs exist does not imply that there are unbounded losses or that economic models are not pertinent.

Indeed, a recent economics literature has hypothesized that people may incur rational addictions,[62] that is, voluntary choice of behaviors they know will be addictive. At the time people initiate consumption of addictive goods, they may anticipate that their current consumption will increase their desire to consume more of the good in the future. Thus, there is anticipation of the addictive consequences, and people knowingly choose to incur those effects, according to those models of rational addiction.

Although the medical designation of cigarettes has changed from a habit to an addiction, in either case the basic thrust of the message is that quitting smoking is hard. Joni Hersch (1998) presents evidence that this aspect of smoking is well known. Hersch found that 13 percent of smokers polled regarding the difficulty of quitting indicated that smoking is addictive and 26 percent said that it is a habit, 57 percent indicated that it is both a habit and an addiction, and only 4 percent said that it was neither.[63] In a world of Smoke Enders, nicotine patches, and New Year's resolutions to give up smoking, who is truly ignorant of the difficulty of quitting smoking?

Nevertheless, changing smoking behavior is difficult, but not impossible. Millions of Americans have quit smoking—about half of all people who have ever been smokers.[64] Estimates for 1995 indicate that there are 47 million smokers and 44 million former smokers in the population.[65]

Whether addiction imposes losses depends in large part on whether smoking decisions are otherwise rational. Preferences matter as well. Presumably smokers have more of a "taste" for smoking behavior than do nonsmokers. Another pertinent preference component is people's attitude toward incurring health risks. Some people may be more unwilling than others to engage in activities that endanger their lives. As mentioned previously, there is evidence that smokers gravitate to other risky pursuits, in which case there will be a consistent pattern of trade-offs involving a willingness to incur health risks.

This issue has been the focus of a series of analyses by Joni Hersch and myself.[66] Many of the systematic differences between smokers and

Table 22 Risky Behaviors and Smoking Status

	Female (N=5,166)		Male (N=4,821)	
	Non-smokers	Smokers	Non-smokers	Smokers
Preventive behavior and attitudes[a]				
Seatbelt (%)	60.30	47.84	54.71	39.07
Check blood pressure (%)	82.25	78.94	70.11	65.31
Floss teeth (%)	32.04	26.09	22.70	13.67
More than average risk-taker				
(1–5)	2.08	2.20	2.57	2.68
Industry job risks				
Work loss rate (%)[b]	3.10	3.44	4.20	4.87
Restricted rate (%)[c]	3.63	4.03	4.84	5.50
Lost workdays per 100				
workers per year[d]	54.21	60.24	77.90	91.98
Own accidents[e]				
Accident at work (%)	2.43	3.57	4.49	6.52
Accident at work leading to				
work loss (%)	1.93	3.08	3.33	5.81
Any accident leading to work				
loss (%)	5.00	7.00	7.03	10.01
Accident at home (%)	2.73	3.43	1.50	2.71

Source: Hersch and Viscusi 1998. All differences between smokers and nonsmokers are statistically significant at the 95 percent confidence level except for home accidents for females.
[a]Percentage of the respondents who engage in the particular activity, and self-rated risk-taking on a scale of 1 to 5, where 5 indicates the highest degree of risk-taking.
[b]Percentage of respondents who have lost work due to injury.
[c]Percentage of respondents whose work has been restricted due to job injury.
[d]Average annual lost workdays per 100 workers in the respondent's industry.
[e]Percentage of respondents who experienced an accident in the past year.

nonsmokers are apparent in the data summarized in table 22. These differences remain even after using multivariate regression analysis that controls for a wide variety of demographic characteristics. Results appear on a gender-specific basis because of the potentially substantial differences in risk activities by gender.

The measures of preventive behavior and attitudes all indicate greater risk-taking by smokers. Smokers are less likely to use seat belts, check their blood pressure, or floss their teeth. They also consider themselves to be above-average risk-takers, though this scale is not as meaningful as is actual risky behavior. Perhaps the chief preventive activity in terms of risk consequences is use of seat belts. Sixteen percent fewer male smokers buckle up than male nonsmokers, with a 13 percent gap between female smokers and nonsmokers. Clearly, smoking is not the only risky aspect in their lives.

The personal accident pattern likewise shows consistent smoker-nonsmoker differences for each gender. Smokers choose to work in higher-risk jobs measured in terms of the work loss rate due to injury, the restricted days of work due to injury, or injury rate involving lost workdays. Once on these risky jobs, smokers are more likely to be injured on the job or to suffer an injury that leads to the loss of work. In Viscusi and Hersch 2001, we show that smokers are more prone to injuries at work than are nonsmokers even after controlling for the riskiness of the job as reflected in objective risk measures.

While incurring these job risks, smokers are of course engaged in a market transaction. Economists since Adam Smith have observed that workers on risky jobs will be paid more for extra risks. This compensation is hazard pay given to workers as part of their regular base wages before any accident occurs. Both smokers and nonsmokers will receive a compensating wage differential for bearing job risks. Firms with a greater average number of accidents will have to pay out more in hazard pay.

This theoretical hypothesis holds up in practice, but with a novel twist. Smokers and nonsmokers do get paid more for risky jobs than they would for riskless occupations. However, smokers get less extra hazard pay than do nonsmokers, even though they bear more risk. The difference arises because the rate at which smokers are compensated for injuries is so much lower than the rate at which nonsmokers are compensated. A useful measure of the rate of compensation is how much firms pay out in higher wages per injury at the firm. On average, firms pay out $39,000 in higher wages per injury to nonsmokers and only $20,000 per injury to smokers. Smokers presumably would prefer the combination of lower job risks and higher hazard pay received by nonsmokers. However, because smokers are more injury-prone on the job, firms in effect dock them some of their hazard compensation in recognition of the injury costs they generate.

Smokers' greater accident propensities are not restricted to work situations. As the bottom panel of table 22 indicates, smokers have greater rates of home accidents, particularly for male smokers, who have almost twice as many home accidents as do nonsmokers. Smokers bear greater health risks in a variety of arenas at home and at work.

This consistency across risk domains raises the question of whether smokers are making the same systematic mistakes across risk contexts. Hersch and Viscusi (1990) explored this issue using the original sample of employees from whom we elicited risk belief information. There was no evidence that the observed lower wage-risk trade-offs stemmed from underassessment of the job risks by smokers. Moreover, as was noted above for the smoking context, smokers have a lower assessment of the hazards of smoking than do nonsmokers, but their assessments are still substantial.

Another aspect of individual preferences is one's attitude toward the future. Are smokers myopic, and do they fail to place sufficient weight on the well-being of their future selves? Because smoking pleasures are immediate and smoking harms are deferred, the presence of temporal myopia could possibly generate more smoking behavior. In an environmental risk context, Harrell Chesson and I explored this issue as well and failed to find any greater proclivity of smokers to neglect their future selves.[67] Once again, such evidence is not conclusive, but it does provide a general indication that there is not evidence of rampant irrationality underlying people's decision to smoke.

Popular notions of addiction view cigarette smoking as being unresponsive to changes in price.[68] Dozens of studies have analyzed the demand for cigarettes.[69] These assessments have analyzed a wide variety of data sources over many different time periods. Not only is the demand for cigarettes a decreasing function of price, but the extent of price responsiveness is comparable to that of other consumer products. The principal summary measure of economic interest is the demand elasticity, that is, the percentage change in the quantity demanded of the good with respect to a 1 percent change in the price. For cigarettes the elasticity estimates cluster in the range of −0.4 to −0.7, meaning that a 10 percent increase in the price would lead to a 4–7 percent drop in the quantity purchased. These estimates are for the entire population, for which there is a broad consensus of price responsiveness. Unlike previous studies using less refined data, Hersch (2000) found that the price elasticities of demand for cigarettes for men and women were similar, and about −0.4 to −0.6. Interestingly, she also found that price effects are greatest for low-income smokers and matter little for high-income smokers, as one might expect. There is considerably more controversy over whether teenagers exhibit greater price responsiveness than do adults, as some studies suggest that this is the case and others fail to find any difference in price responsiveness.[70]

The key result from the standpoint of the addiction issue is that for the broad smoking population, including youths, price matters. But how does the price responsiveness compare with other products not normally associated with addiction and habituation? Is there evidence that consumers are more locked into their cigarette consumption and less responsive to price? Products with comparable or smaller price elasticities include: theater and opera (−0.18), toys (−0.30), jewelry and watches (−0.41), barbershops and beauty parlors (−0.20), stationery (−0.47), toiletries and preparations (−0.20), electricity (−0.13), water (−0.21), newspapers and magazines (−0.42), and legal services (−0.37).[71] As measured by short-run price responsiveness, people are no more addicted to cigarettes than they are to lawyers or the opera. The long-run price responsiveness of cigarette demand is much greater and is also comparable to that for many common consumer products. What we mean by addiction and why there is greater concern with addiction to drugs and cigarettes than to people's attachment to opera clearly goes beyond responses to price changes. However, these results are nevertheless useful in putting the character of what we mean by addiction in perspective.

Another index of the addictive or habit-forming character of cigarettes is how responsive people have been to smoking restrictions. As workplaces and public buildings have restricted smoking, we now witness groups of smokers huddled outside to smoke their occasional cigarette. Have these smokers also responded by cutting back on their cigarettes? The answer here, as well, is that the behavioral response has been substantial. As the convenience cost of smoking has risen, the extent of smoking has declined. These effects have largely been in terms of how much people smoke, not whether people smoke.

Hospital employees, for example, responded in a variety of ways to smoking restrictions.[72] A year after the smoking bans were implemented, hospital employees had almost twice as great a quit ratio as before the ban (i.e., .066 versus .038, where the ratio is defined as the number of former smokers divided by the number of "ever" smokers) as did their counterparts in the neighboring community. Those who did not quit reduced their smoking by an average of a cigarette a day. Evidence for a broader national sample indicates that smoking bans reduce the prevalence of cigarette smoking by 4.8–5.7 percentage points and cigarette consumption by 2.0–2.5 cigarettes per day.[73]

Decreased smoking is not just a phenomenon linked to smoking bans. Over time there has been a dramatic increase in the smoking quit rate and the number of former smokers. The ratio of former to current smokers rose from .32 in 1965 to .95 in 1998. This change has been particularly dramatic for better-educated groups, as the college-educated ratios of former to current smokers has risen from .97 to 2.2 over that same time period.[74]

The substantial quit rates and responsiveness to prices and smoking restrictions do not imply that quitting smoking is trivial. For many people, it is extremely difficult. However, this evidence of economic responsiveness is suggestive of the fact that quitting smoking is feasible and that there are bounds on the welfare costs associated with the costs of smoking habits or addictions.

What then are we to make of the fact that 68.2 percent of smokers say they would like to quit smoking?[75] It is difficult to assess what such questions are really picking up. Asking people if they would like to quit may lead respondents to seek approval by answering affirmatively. When asked such questions, people may be led by our strong antismoking environment to say they want to quit to deflect likely criticism of their smoking. Similar surveys show that many people would like to leave their spouse or their job,[76] and that the majority of the residents of Los Angeles would like to move somewhere else. Yet, they don't make these changes. Such quitting questions also may be capturing an underlying dissatisfaction with some attribute of the product or the relationship. In the case of cigarettes, people may in effect be saying that they wish that they could eliminate the product attribute—health risks. Yet, they nevertheless voluntarily choose to smoke their present brand rather than the test-marketed de-nicotined cigarette or the Premier or Eclipse— cigarettes that largely eliminated any cancer risk. Similarly, nicotine patches and nicotine gum provide alternative mechanisms for obtaining the nicotine without smoking. Ultimately, such quit-intention attitudinal questions tell us very little except that people are not generally pleased with all the attributes of cigarettes. Any interpretation of such subjective assessments beyond that is more problematic and less informative than the evidence of real economic behavior.

An intriguing test of the veracity of respondents' statements regarding their quit intentions is manifested in the disparity between intentions and actions found in a survey of Philadelphia parents.[77] Researchers asked 11,709 current smokers whether they would be interested in stopping smoking if a smokers' clinic could be arranged. Of this group, 4,775—or 41 percent of the entire sample—indicated that they would be interested in stopping smoking if such a program could be arranged. However, once the parents were offered the opportunity to attend a preliminary meeting about the clinic that was held at a convenient time, only 257 of them attended, which is but 5 percent of those who had expressed an interest in attending. When it came to actually making use of the clinic, only 150 actually did so, or 3 percent of those who said that they would, in fact, want to stop smoking if a smoking cessation clinic could be arranged. These results from a field experiment in Philadelphia bear out my principal hypothesis, which is that when smokers say that they would like to quit, that is not what they always mean.

A notable failure in smoking prevention efforts was the major intervention study funded by the National Cancer Institute known as COMMIT (Community Intervention Trial for Smoking Cessation).[78] This multimillion-dollar effort involved four years of intensive community intervention that would provide smokers with risk information, counseling by physicians, and aggressive antismoking efforts designed to foster quitting. At the time the study was launched, the researchers predicted dramatic gains in their battle against smoking. If only people were given the real facts and full institutional support for their attempts to quit, they would quit. The results indicate a complete failure of this effort. For the communities where the COMMIT intervention took place, the mean quit rate was 0.180 for heavy smokers and 0.306 for light-to-moderate smokers. For communities without the intervention, the quit rate was 0.187 for heavy smokers and 0.275 for light smokers. The absolute differences were modest. Heavy smokers, who were the principal target of the effort, were 1 percent less likely to quit in the COMMIT communities, and light-to-moderate smokers were 3 percent more likely to quit if exposed to COMMIT. Even this negligible effect disappears in my multivariate analysis of the data if one focuses only on U.S. communities rather than also including those in Canada.[79]

The lessons of the Philadelphia and COMMIT studies are twofold. First, statements of intentions to quit smoking should not necessarily be taken at face value. Such statements may be learned responses to deflect criticism in a strong antismoking environment. Second, increasing quitting behavior is not simply a matter of supplying missing information. Targeted aggressive campaigns and smoking cessation programs have failed almost completely.

The State of Current Knowledge

A dominant theme of the antismoking movement is the belief that smokers are ignorant of the risks. Presumably nonsmokers are privy to secret information about the hazards of smoking. Assuming that smokers do not share in the enormous amount of smoking risk information that has been disseminated (have they been locked in a cave?) bears no relation to reality. Smoking risks are without question the most highly publicized risks we face. Knowledge of the hazards of smoking is universal.

The result is that risk beliefs are too great, not too low. The general public and smokers believe that the hazards of smoking are much greater than scientists have estimated. These results hold true for lung cancer, mortality risks, and life expectancy loss. Indeed, when the FDA proposed that people be told that smokers face a one-in-three chance of premature death, I commented to the agency that such information could lower risk beliefs rather than raise them. The revised FDA regulatory proposal omitted this informational component.

There is no constructive role that can be played by warnings efforts that simply boost the overall smoking risk belief. The appropriate role of warnings policies is to foster accurate risk beliefs. Honest warnings efforts with respect to smoking risks would actually lead to lower risk beliefs for most people. Warnings of a general nature whose primary intent is to create a greater sense of general alarm serve no constructive function and should not be part of any responsible government policy. Honest communication of risks should be the foundation of all governmental information programs.

Warnings and other informational efforts can, however, serve a constructive function if they provide new information in a convincing manner. Exaggerated risk claims are not appropriate. However, if gaps in pertinent information regarding smoking risks can be identified, informational efforts to fill gaps can serve a constructive role.

Government officials consequently should turn to substantive concerns other than these salient risks of smoking. Are there other messages that we would like to convey, facts that are not yet understood? The evidence to date provides an optimistic projection of the likely effects of such policies. People can form smoking risk beliefs that are reflective of the hazards that have been communicated, and these beliefs do alter behavior. There is a real operational link between policies and smoking behavior. The task is to identify beneficial policy interventions that go beyond the generic message that smoking is dangerous, and that smoking is hard to quit. That fundamental message is already well understood.

YOUTH SMOKING: BEYOND JOE CAMEL

Joe Camel is now retired, but youth smoking continues to loom large as a policy concern. In no other area of cigarette policy is consensus more widespread than with respect to underage smoking. Neither the cigarette industry nor public health officials now support smoking by people under the age of eighteen. Purchase of cigarettes by those under eighteen is now illegal in the United States. There is also broad public support for measures to reduce youth smoking. This aspect of the public's concern has not been lost on political officials, many of whom use the youth smoking issue as the purported rationale for justifying many much broader interventions that go well beyond just targeting youths. Efforts to generate support for the various proposed national settlements of the cigarette litigation are among the most salient examples of how youth smoking concerns can be exploited to try to garner public support for policies with a quite different emphasis.

This chapter examines the character of the policy problems pertaining to youth smoking, which continue to confound policy analysts. In particular, it will explore the youth smoking issues and assess the various policy mechanisms that we have with which to address youth smoking. Is there, in fact, a youth smoking crisis, and, if so, is it new? To what extent can youth smoking be traced to the archvillain of the antismoking movement, Joe Camel, or to key determinants of smoking rates such as possibly inadequate risk beliefs? Are higher prices the answer? Unfortunately, many of the most widely espoused policy prescriptions appear to be ineffective.

Trends in Youth Smoking

Few people smoke their first cigarette as an adult. The overwhelming majority of smokers have smoked their first cigarette before age eighteen, sometimes much earlier. First of all we should determine how prevalent is youth smoking, whether there has been an increase in youth smoking rates, or whether we are perhaps just more sensitive now to youth smoking as an important policy concern.

Most public discussions of youth smoking rates focus solely on year-to-year trends, which can be misleading.[1] We hear that youth smoking is up. In recent years we have often witnessed claims that smoking rates for the last year for which we have data are higher than they were earlier. But how much smoking must one do to qualify as a "smoker" in such studies? Has youth smoking been steadily on the rise? When do random fluctuations become an alarming trend? And is the level of youth smoking in fact higher than its historical average?

Resolving these issues is a statistical matter that can be readily addressed. Table 23 reports two sets of data, each of which was gathered with supportive funds from the U.S. government. For concreteness, the measures in table 23 pertain to whether the respondent has reported smoking one or more cigarettes in the past month.[2] The smoking rates for twelfth-graders were 36.7 percent of that population in 1975. This percentage dropped to a low value of 27.8 percent by 1992. After that time, there was an alarming increase in smoking rates to 36.5 percent by 1997. Whereas high school seniors exhibit an upward trend in smoking rates in the 1990s, for twelve-to-seventeen-year-olds in the final column of table 23, smoking rates dropped until 1992 and have remained fairly steady thereafter. The very long term perspective is less bleak. High school seniors smoked less in 1996 than in 1975–79. The disappointing result is that, notwithstanding vigorous youth smoking policies, these smoking rates have not dropped substantially.

The level of youth smoking rates shown in table 23 is also perhaps disturbing in that these percentages appear to be higher than the publicized levels of adult smoking rates. However, such a comparison is misleading because the statistics for younger respondents only reflect whether the respondent has had a cigarette in the past thirty days. Youth is the time for trial and error, not when one is forty or fifty. Many youths are particularly likely to try a cigarette on an experimental basis or on an occasional basis during this time of their lives. A more informative statistic would be information focusing on regular or very recent smoking.

The Monitoring the Future survey reports such information in terms of whether the respondents smoked at least a half a pack of cigarettes per day.[3] The level of such smoking is much less than the thirty-day reported smoking rates. These statistics also indicate an upward trend, with 10.7 percent of twelfth-graders reporting such smoking

Table 23 Thirty-Day Prevalence of Cigarette Use by Teenagers, 1975–1996

Date	12th Graders (%)[a]	12–17 Year Olds (%)[b]
1975	36.7	data not available
1976	38.8	data not available
1977	38.4	data not available
1978	36.7	data not available
1979	34.4	data not available
1980	30.5	data not available
1981	29.4	data not available
1982	30.0	data not available
1983	30.3	data not available
1984	29.3	data not available
1985	30.1	29.4
1986	29.6	data not available
1987	29.4	data not available
1988	28.7	22.7
1989	28.6	data not available
1990	29.4	data not available
1991	28.3	20.9
1992	27.8	18.4
1993	29.9	18.5
1994	31.2	18.9
1995	33.5	20.2
1996	34.0	18.3
1997	36.5	19.9
1998	35.1	18.2
1999	34.6	15.9
2000	31.4	data not available

Note: % = percentage of respondents who reported smoking one or more cigarettes in the past month.
[a]Data from Monitoring the Future 2000, http://monitoringthefuture.org/data/00data.html#2000data-cigs.
[b]Data from Substance Abuse and Mental Health Services Administration (SAMHSA)1999, http://www.samhsa.gov/oas.

behavior in 1991, and 14.3 percent by 1997. This rate stabilized to a value of 11.3 by 2000. These smoking rates are about half of the smoking rates for adults, but nevertheless indicate that a substantial portion of the high school senior population does in fact smoke cigarettes on a regular basis. Moreover, the upward trend in smoking a half pack of cigarettes per day seems to be greater than that for more occasional cigarette use.

Smoking Restrictions

Purchasing cigarettes was not always illegal for youths. Some states for a long time had no restrictions.[4] By 1992, the age restrictions on cigarette purchase had been tightened in most states to require that the person be at least eighteen before purchasing cigarettes. Two states, Montana and New Mexico, had no restrictions whatsoever even by 1992, and Georgia retained seventeen as the age cutoff. By 1995 however, the minimum legal age for purchase was at least eighteen throughout the country.[5]

The legal smoking age data in table 24 is instructive in assessing some of the wrongful conduct allegations against the cigarette industry as well. The federal lawsuit and other litigation efforts have recently highlighted the alleged targeting of youths in marketing reports supplied to the cigarette industry. These studies purportedly indicate a marketing strategy that involved selling cigarettes to underage smokers. For example, marketing research studies frequently generate survey responses for particular age groups, such as age eighteen to twenty-four. In some cases, the cutoff is age sixteen. While such marketing efforts may be inconsistent with current age restrictions for smoking, they are quite consistent with the kinds of regulations that prevailed at the time when such marketing analyses were undertaken. Moreover, setting a precise age cutoff for exposure to advertising is, in fact, quite difficult.

Now that there is an age eighteen restriction, it is important that the cigarette industry not market cigarettes to underage smokers. Firms typically wish to attract younger consumers (within their legal consumer population set), because such consumers have the potential to use the product for a longer period of time than older consumers. In addition, they are less likely to have developed a long-term allegiance to a particular brand than are older consumers. Advertisements for cars, beer, and other consumer products generally show youthful consumers enjoying the particular product in question. Cigarette companies likewise will tend to use people just over the legal smoking age in their advertising. The Master Settlement Agreement imposes restrictions on ads to the underage population. In June 2000, tobacco firms eliminated advertising in a large number of adult-oriented publications because they also had a substantial youth readership. Philip Morris, the market leader, was the first to announce an ad ban. R. J. Reynolds executives, however, commented that while they wanted to restrict advertising to youths, they were also concerned with the competitive aspects of such restraints as well. Perhaps because of its different approach, R. J. Reynolds was sued in 2001 over advertising to youths, and Philip Morris was not. Whether

Table 24 Minimum Age for Legal Sale of Tobacco

State	1990	1992	State	1990	1992
Alabama	19	19	Montana	None	None
Alaska	16	19	Nebraska	18	18
Arizona	18	18	Nevada	18	18
Arkansas	18	18	New Hampshire	18	18
California	18	18	New Jersey	16	18
Colorado	18	18	New Mexico	None	None
Connecticut	16	18	New York	18	18
Delaware	17	18	North Carolina	17	18
District of Columbia	16	18	North Dakota	18	18
Florida	18	18	Ohio	18	18
Georgia	17	17	Oklahoma	18	18
Hawaii	18	18	Oregon	18	18
Idaho	18	18	Pennsylvania	16	21[b]
Illinois	18	18	Rhode Island	16	18
Indiana	18	18	South Carolina	18	18
Iowa	18	18	South Dakota	18	18
Kansas	18[a]	18	Tennessee	18	18
Kentucky	None	18	Texas	16	18
Louisiana	None	18	Utah	19	19
Maine	18	18	Vermont	17	18
Maryland	16	18	Virginia	16	18
Massachusetts	18	18	Washington	18	18
Michigan	18	18	West Virginia	18	18
Minnesota	18	18	Wisconsin	None	18
Mississippi	18	18	Wyoming	None	18
Missouri	18	18			

Sources: The 1990 regulations are from U.S. Department of Health and Human Services, Public Health Service, Centers for Disease Control 1990, table 4, p. 71. The 1992 regulations are from U.S. Department of Health and Human Services, Public Health Service, National Institutes of Health 1993, appendix B, table 2, pp. 113–14.
[a]Minimum age applies only to cigarettes.
[b]Minimum age for smokeless tobacco is 18.

firms should avoid advertising to younger, but legal, smoking populations altogether is more problematic. The solution is not to eliminate all such advertising, which would lead to severe anticompetitive effects.

Unfortunately, the state regulations that have been promulgated to date appear not to have been particularly influential in affecting youth smoking. A detailed analysis by Joni Hersch explored a variety of such regulatory policies and found that they are not as powerful as were factors such as parental concern with children smoking. Hersch (1998) found that the two methods states used in dealing with violations of minimum age restrictions for purchase were penalties for purchase and imposition of sanctions on retailers. However, she found that few states imposed penalties on the minors who actually purchased cigarettes or possessed cigarettes, whereas one might have expected states to levy penalties analogous to those imposed for illegal purchase and possession of drugs. As for retailers, the sanctions for initial violations typically are quite small. While some states provide for stronger sanctions, there is no conclusive evidence about the strength of enforcement.

Hersch found that differences among states in these regulations are not consequential. On the basis of the responses of a sample population aged fifteen to twenty, it seems that the difficulty that minors face in purchasing tobacco products is not viewed as being much different for the more restrictive states compared to the less restrictive states. However, smokers in this age range are significantly more likely to view purchases as being difficult in the more restrictive states than are nonsmokers, perhaps because they have tried to purchase cigarettes more often. Nevertheless, only one-fourth of smokers in the restrictive states view cigarettes as being difficult to purchase even though they are minors.

Hersch's next finding is even more disturbing. One might have thought that if an underage youth thought that cigarettes were difficult to purchase, they would be less likely to smoke. However, people who consider the purchase of cigarettes to be difficult are actually more likely to purchase tobacco than are those who do not view the sanctions as posing a problem in obtaining cigarettes. Causality may be difficult to sort out. It is unlikely that making cigarettes difficult to purchase increases youth smoking. A more plausible explanation is that people who smoke often, and consequently attempt to make such purchases more frequently, may be more aware of the barriers to purchase that do exist.

The minimum age of legal purchase also has no apparent effect on smoking rates in the state where these ages vary in the manner indicated in table 24. The failure of the minimum age restriction to be influential is particularly surprising because one might have thought that the states with high age limits also would have a tougher enforcement mechanism as well. Age restrictions, however, have yielded no apparent effects.

Asking young respondents questions about how hard it is to purchase cigarettes may not be the best barometer. The best measure of the reality of youth access to cigarettes is to examine where they get the cigarettes that they smoke as opposed to asking them whether they think it is easy for them to purchase cigarettes. Such statements with respect to ease of purchase may be misleading. Surveys do not precisely define what "easy" means in terms of degree of difficulty. Moreover, many of the responses are tainted by nonsmoking youths indicating that it is easy to get cigarettes even though this is something that they may have never attempted.

Data from the 1998 school-based youth survey in California indicates that the retail outlets appear to be the source of very few cigarettes smoked by youths.[6] That survey asked youths what was the source of their last cigarette. For eighth-graders, only 8 percent indicated that they bought them themselves, and for tenth-graders, only 10 percent indicated that they bought them themselves. Thus, 90 percent of respondents indicated that they had gotten their last cigarette by means other than purchasing them at a retail establishment.

Where, then, did they get their cigarettes? The dominant response for the source of the last cigarette smoked is that a friend gave them to them, which was the case for 54 percent of tenth-graders and 42 percent of eighth-graders. A friend buying them cigarettes also plays an important role for 9 percent of tenth-graders and 7 percent of eighth-graders. Getting cigarettes from a family member is the source for 7 percent of tenth-graders and 10 percent of eighth-graders. Taking cigarettes from a person without permission is the source of cigarettes of 18 percent of the eighth-grade respondents and 9 percent of the tenth-grade respondents. Other cigarette sources include getting cigarettes from other people besides family and friends, having a family member buy them cigarettes, and stealing them from a store, each of which accounts for a very small portion of the sources of cigarettes.

These statistics indicate a much different picture of the source of cigarettes than one might glean from reading the popular press. The weak link is not retail establishments. The evidence that indicates little difference across states with respect to crackdowns on retail establishments may simply be a reflection of the fact that for the most part buying cigarettes from retail establishments is not that easy for underage smokers. Thus, boosting the enforcement of such prohibitions against purchase may make little difference.

What would, for example, be the percentage effect of eliminating, as a source of cigarettes, purchases from retail establishments by the smokers themselves? At least 90 percent of the respondents would still report obtaining cigarettes because they did so from a source other than a retail establishment. There might, of course, be some kind of cascade effect whereby cigarettes obtained from friends would not have been purchased by these friends had the prohibition against retail sales to underage smokers been enforced more vigorously. However, if there had been such more vigorous enforcement, one would also expect youths to adapt to some extent by obtaining cigarettes from other sources. Asking older friends or older cigarette smokers they might meet to make the purchase has become an increasingly common means for evading the restrictions.

The fundamental importance of family concern with smoking that is borne out in broader studies of the determinants of youth smoking is borne out in these statistics as well. Obtaining cigarettes from family members or having family members buy them cigarettes was as important a source of cigarettes to the respondents as was retail purchases. Enforcing restrictions on retail purchase of cigarettes vigorously is clearly desirable. However, it is important to recognize that emphasizing this policy approach is likely to make only a negligible dent in youth smoking. Even with fully effective prohibitions against retail sales to youths, the effect on youth smoking rates would be minimal.

Popular Explanations That Don't Seem to Be the Answer

What then is the cause of youth smoking? The most convenient answer in recent years has been to blame Joe Camel, the advertising symbol for Camel cigarettes. Joe Camel was created by a marketing firm in 1987 to celebrate the ninety-seventh birthday of the promotion of the Camel cigarette brand, produced by R. J. Reynolds. The impetus for developing Joe Camel was in fact to target potential younger smokers, who at the time were predominantly smoking Marlboros. Since Camel cigarettes was a very old brand, it had also developed an older consumer base. The company was attempting to broaden the demographic appeal of Camel cigarettes to include younger consumers. In many respects, Camel cigarettes were in a similar position to that of venerable car companies such as Cadillac, Buick, and the recently retired Oldsmobile brand, which sell almost exclusively to consumers over the age of sixty. Ideally, producers of such products want to reach younger age groups, both to expand the market and to develop a customer base for the longer term. These concerns are not unique to the cigarette industry. Indeed, almost all television advertisers are concerned with having a sufficiently young demographic mix for the programming in which they place their ads.

The Joe Camel imagery was that of a roguish character who would be appealing to younger age groups. The target market was eighteen-to-twenty-four-year-old smokers. Joe Camel was publicly unveiled in 1988, launching the highly successful Joe Camel campaign. Soon thereafter, Joe Camel had become a villain in the eyes of the antismoking movement, in large part because these ads were successful in repositioning the brand and bolstering its sales. The introduction of female camel friends for Joe provoked further outcry from antismoking groups. To antismoking groups, Joe Camel had become the Saddam Hussein of cigarettes. Joe Camel was the visible target of their crusade. By personifying the evils of cigarettes, Joe Camel became a clear-cut enemy who, once destroyed, would solve the youth smoking problem.

Joe Camel was retired voluntarily by R. J. Reynolds in 1997, producing obituaries in business sections of newspapers and commentaries by public officials. President Clinton stated: "We must put tobacco ads like Joe Camel out of our children's reach forever."[7] The president's chief domestic policy advisor, Bruce Reed, also rejoiced at Joe Camel's demise, observing: "Joe Camel is dead. . . . He had it coming."[8] The secretary of the Department of Health and Human Services, Donna Shalala, also expressed pleasure: "I'm very happy to say goodbye to Joe Camel."[9] Senator Edward Kennedy joined in the chorus as his press release on the death of Joe Camel proclaimed: "Joe Camel died young—and so will vast numbers of children who started smoking because of R. J. Reynolds' cynical advertising."[10]

Was Joe Camel really the culprit responsible for youth smoking? The statistics presented in table 23 fail to jump up in 1988, which was the first year Joe Camel strutted onto the advertising scene. Indeed, youth smoking rates from 1975 to 1987 were equal to or higher than the smoking rates in subsequent years, and smoking rates for high school seniors declined in 1988 and 1989. There is no apparent link between the advent of Joe Camel in 1988 and the rise in youth smoking in 1993. Joe Camel has since been retired, but there have been no reports of plummeting youth smoking rates throughout the country.

The case against Joe Camel, which was subsequently dropped by the Federal Trade Commission, was based largely on studies suggesting that there was widespread recognition of the Joe Camel brand logo among young children.[11] Companies traditionally argue that the main role of advertising is to affect brand choice rather than product use, whereas some antismoking groups were concerned that youths might be affected in starting to smoke as well. Did Camels, in fact, take over the youth smoking market? Marlboros remained the dominant brand smoked by youths, not Camels. Consider data from 1993: Marlboro had 61 percent of the market share, as almost two out of every three cigarettes smoked by youths was a Marlboro. Newports came in second with a 13 percent market share, much of which was among black smokers. Camels ranked third among brands chosen by youths, with a 12.8 percent market share.[12] The targeting of Joe Camel, rather than the venerable Marlboro cowboy, seems to bear no relationship whatsoever to the smoking patterns of the underage group of policy concern. The advantage of Joe

Camel as the target of the antismoking movement was that Joe Camel was a relatively recent figure whose presence more closely coincided with the surge in public efforts to control smoking, whereas the Marlboro cowboy had been riding the range for decades.

The more interesting statistical test is whether the Joe Camel campaign led to a surge in youth smoking of Camels. Available data suggest that in the 1990s Camel sales to youths were declining, not rising. In 1993, 13 percent of youths reported that they smoked Camels, and in 1998 only 10 percent smoked Camels.[13] Neither the level of Camel smoking nor the trend in Camel smoking is consistent with Joe Camel being responsible for the youth smoking problem.

Another possibility is that there is a lack of adequate regulation of youth smoking. People cannot buy cigarettes now unless they can prove that they are age eighteen. However, as was discussed above, this was not always the case. The data for 1990 are particularly instructive, as there were then six states that had no age requirements whatsoever for the purchase of cigarettes. Many states had age requirements beginning at sixteen or seventeen, and only two states had age requirements of at least age nineteen before one could purchase cigarettes legally. This quite different regulatory environment emerged after the birth of Joe Camel. Within today's regulatory environment, it may be surprising that R. J. Reynolds sought to target eighteen- to twenty-year-olds with its Joe Camel campaign. There is also the chance that seventeen-year-olds would see such ads as well. But it was not so long ago that regulations in many states did permit the legal sale of tobacco to younger age groups.

If Joe Camel is not the cause of youth smoking, could it be perhaps instead that youths do not adequately understand the dangers of smoking? This explanation too does not seem to be persuasive. Indeed, youths appear to be even more concerned with hazards of smoking than are adults. They have been raised in a much stronger antismoking environment. In particular, evidence from the 1985 national survey that is the counterpart of the lung cancer risk belief results I discussed earlier indicate that respondents aged sixteen to twenty-one believe that the lung cancer probability from smoking is 0.49, and even current smokers in this age group believe that the lung cancer probability is 0.45. These estimates are somewhat higher than they are for the population more generally, for which the full sample estimates the risk at 0.43 and current smokers estimate it at 0.37.[14] The risks of smoking are not hidden from teens. Indeed, the age-related pattern of risk perceptions is quite consistent with what one would expect given the changing informational context. People in the younger age groups have the highest risk perceptions, and people in the oldest age groups have lower risk beliefs.

More qualitative measures of risk awareness also suggest that there is substantial awareness of smoking risks. The Monitoring the Future study also asked twelfth-graders whether they thought people exposed themselves to a "great risk" of harming themselves physically or in other ways from smoking. Although "great risk" is not defined, and certainly has many deficiencies as a risk measure, presumably it should have a similar interpretation by a particular respondent considering different questions. Thus, such questions cannot be used to assess if risk beliefs exceed true risk levels, but they may be useful in indicating relative risk beliefs, albeit imperfectly. The percentage of respondents regarding smoking one or more packs of cigarettes per day as a great risk was relatively stable from 69.4 percent to 73.1 percent between 1991 and 2000. By comparison, it is noteworthy that in 2000, only 48.4 percent of respondents viewed taking crack cocaine once or twice as a great risk, 34.3 percent of respondents viewed taking LSD once or twice as being a great risk, 23.4 percent believe that smoking marijuana occasionally was a great risk, and 64.7 percent viewed taking cocaine powder occasionally as a great risk.[15] Cigarette smoking consequently is viewed as being on a par with the hazards of many much more potent and illegal drugs. Moreover, it is noteworthy that over two-thirds of all young respondents view cigarettes in this manner. More qualitative evidence from the Monitoring the Future study tells much the same story. Students seem quite aware that smoking is risky, and this belief has grown over time. The percentage who believe smoking a pack or more a day holds great risk increased from 56 percent in 1976 to 69 percent in 1991. In 1991, 72 percent of these seniors considered smoking a dirty habit, 74 percent preferred to date nonsmokers, and 61 percent believed that becoming a smoker reflects poor judgment.[16]

Another hypothesis offered by some commentators is that adolescent youth smoking arises from an optimistic bias that affects risk beliefs. However, this theory is not consistent even with the literature on optimism. Consider in particular the results of a poll of high school students regarding the risks of various personal activities on a seven-point scale.[17] As I indicated in the discussion of risk perception data, more generally, such qualitative scales are not as valid as the objective risk measures I have used, but they are among the soundest measures used in the optimism bias literature. Respondents first rated the risk of cigarettes to themselves. In particular, respondents rated the risk of cigarettes as follows: "If you did this activity, to what extent do you believe that you would be personally at risk of getting hurt or getting sick? (1 = very much at risk; 7 = not at all at risk)." People who smoked cigarettes rated their personal risk at 4.3, whereas those who did not smoke rated their personal risk at 2.1. Each respondent also rated the risk of cigarettes to their peers: "If some other person your age engaged in this activity, to what extent do you believe that he/she would be at risk of getting hurt or getting sick? (1 = very much at risk; 7 = not at all at risk)." Smokers rated the risk to peers at 4.4 and nonsmokers rated it at 2.2. Because a lower score indicates a higher risk, for both smokers and nonsmokers, risks to oneself are rated higher than the risk to one's peers, though the differences in responses are not significantly different.

For decades, the dominant view has been that the youth smoking problem was the result of social influences. If only policies could alter these influences, youth smoking rates would decline. To test this widely held theory, forty school districts in the state of Washington participated in an ambitious study utilizing a smoking prevention program designed by the National Cancer Institute, following guidelines established by the Centers for Disease Control and Prevention. The result was that there was no significant effect of the experimental interventions as compared to the control school districts.[18] These extremely negative results from an ambitious and carefully controlled study consequently appear to rule out another possible avenue for influencing youth smoking.

Factors That Could Be Influential

What are the main factors that do affect youth smoking? Hersch (1998) found that restrictions on smoking in the home appear to be especially influential. Just as parental interest is important in affecting whether children do their homework, it also appears to play a major role in affecting youth smoking behavior. Recall too the California survey results that family members are as important a source of cigarettes as retail establishments. In Hersch's study, to be classified as a smoker the respondent had to have smoked at least 100 cigarettes in his or her lifetime and at least one cigarette in the last thirty days. Hersch finds that teens who live in homes where smoking is not permitted have smoking rates one-third to one-half the size of the smoking rates of teens who live in households where smoking is permitted. For those aged fifteen to twenty in houses where smoking is allowed, white females have smoking rates of 25.4 percent, white males have smoking rates of 24.8 percent, nonwhite females 11.5 percent, and nonwhite males 14.3 percent. The smoking rates are dramatically lower for each of these groups in households where smoking is not allowed. White females have smoking rates of 7.4 percent, white males have smoking rates of 10.8 percent, nonwhite females 3.0 percent, and nonwhite males 4.0 percent. Potential gains from involving parents in the underage smoking decision are enormous.

Many of the concrete proposals for reducing youth smoking have focused on price mechanisms, arguing that if prices of cigarettes are increased, the demand for cigarettes by youths will decline because cigarettes have become more expensive. This relationship for youth smoking is not qualitatively different than that for the rest of the population, in that there is price sensitivity in the expected direction.

What has particularly caught the interest of policy makers is whether there is especially great sensitivity on the part of youths to the higher prices of cigarettes. Because youths have smaller total budgets than their adult counterparts, one might hypothesize that shifts in price would affect cigarette consumption more for younger smokers than for older smokers.[19] Some studies suggest that youth may be particularly responsive to prices and that the effect may be on the order of a 10 percent price increase leading to a 14 percent drop in the quantity of cigarettes purchased by youths.[20] Other estimates suggest that smoking participation among high school seniors is responsive to price, with an elasticity of about −0.7, but that younger teens are not price sensitive.[21] DeCicca, Kenkel, and Mathios (2000) found that minority youth were more price sensitive than were white youths. Other estimates fail to indicate any differential responsiveness of youths to prices, thus calling into question the efficacy of raising prices to discourage youth smoking in a differential manner, especially since most youths don't buy cigarettes.[22] If there is no differential price sensitivity of youths, then higher prices will discourage smoking among smokers of all age groups, not simply the target age group of concern.

A second concern with respect to the role of prices is the nature of their effect on smoking. Do higher prices influence whether one smokes at all, or is the influence with respect to the total number of cigarettes smoked? Econometric evidence suggests that the price sensitivity is important both with respect to the quantity of cigarettes as well as the discrete choice of whether one chooses to become a smoker.[23]

Irrespective of whether adults and underage smokers respond differently, there is also the more fundamental economic question of whether tax policy is too blunt an instrument to be used to address youth smoking. If underage smokers constituted a large percentage of the consumer base for cigarettes, then prices would be a sensible mechanism for discouraging smoking among this group. A detailed study of the rate of underage smoking was a 1990 analysis of the annual consumption of cigarettes consumed by those aged eight to seventeen, which in that time period included states for which underage smoking was legal.[24] In terms of total cigarette sales, the estimate is that 0.95 billion packs of the 24.35 billion packs of cigarettes sold were purchased by youths aged eight to seventeen—or under 4 percent. Another national survey yielded estimates of the total number of cigarette packs sold illegally in 1991 to cigarette smokers aged twelve to eighteen.[25] That study focused on illegal purchase, not total cigarette consumption. Overall, 255.7 million packs of cigarettes were sold illegally to minors annually. This figure is lower than the overall consumption statistics because in many states it was legal to purchase cigarettes before the age of eighteen in 1991, which was the year of the survey. These estimates imply that 1 percent of all cigarettes sold were sold to those between the ages of twelve and eighteen.

These statistics suggest that youth smoking and underage smoking is but a very small fraction of the total amount of cigarettes purchased in the United States. Policies that raise the price of cigarettes for all consumers, not just for underage youths, will consequently impose economic penalties that fall almost entirely on people for whom it is legal to smoke. If the objective is to discourage youth smoking in particular, more refined policy instruments than simply raising the overall price of cigarettes would appear to be more effective.

Even if raising the price of cigarettes is not especially effective in discouraging youth smoking, one might nevertheless argue that good is being accomplished by discouraging smoking among adults. However, that is a quite different rationale than using the youth smoking effect as the principal justification for the policy. Whether one wishes to impose economic penalties on adult smokers depends on whether higher prices are needed to promote efficient choices among adults. The evidence presented in the previous chapters suggests that one would be hard pressed to develop a strong economic rationale for penalizing adult smokers.

Policies That Seem to Matter

Although purchase restrictions and higher prices may not be especially effective in reducing youth smoking, they may nevertheless have some beneficial effect, particularly if the purchasing restrictions are enforced. Thus, these efforts could be part of an overall policy to decrease youth smoking. However, there are other policy tools that also might be utilized, such as informational campaigns targeted to the youth audience.

One effort that has received considerable attention has been the Florida antismoking program. Some experts have credited this effort with reducing smoking rates by at least 10 percent.[26] This effort featured what was designated a TRUTH Campaign in which youths developed antismoking ads that had a rebellious tone and were intended to be effective in reaching the youth market. Some observers describe these ads as "in-your-face anti-smoking ads" that "have an MTV edge with some very dark humor."[27] The short-term results of this advertising campaign may have been substantial, as teen smoking rates declined in Florida from 1998 to 1999, where this decrease was the largest drop in the country and the state's largest drop in more than twenty years.[28]

Efforts to slash this funding from the Florida legislature, however, suggests that the edgy character of the advertising campaign may have, in fact, been too controversial and offensive to certain segments of the population. In any case, the task for any antismoking campaign for youths is not simply to discourage smoking, but to provide information that the teenage viewers of the ad will regard as honest and informative. Shrill ads that undermine official credibility do a disservice to warnings efforts in general. The criterion for effective warnings that they provide new information in a convincing manner need not be discarded in our zeal to discourage youth smoking. Honest communication of information that educates the public remains the guiding principle. Distorting facts for a good cause or smearing either a product or an industry ultimately will undermine the government's credibility more generally. These principles should continue to guide the underlying content of the ads, which one can then film in a manner that will catch the attention of the recipients, if that is believed to be necessary.

California also has a vigorous advertising campaign with respect to cigarettes, funded by California Proposition 99. This advertising campaign includes billboards, television ads, and extensive information distributed by nonprofit organizations. Much of this effort is concerned with the dangers of secondhand smoke. However, the campaign as a whole also is related to youth smoking. The penetration rate of these ads in creating awareness of smoking risks and the hazards of environmental tobacco smoke is almost universal. Thus, the ads have been effective in reaching their target audience with the smoking risk message.

Notwithstanding the aggressive advertising campaign and the substantial knowledge concerning cigarettes, teen smoking has not declined. Teen smoking rates in California remained relatively steady over the five-year period through 1996, whereas adult smoking rates fell over that same period.[29] However, given the rise in teen smoking nationally in table 23, this performance is not necessarily a failure.

One much discussed potential danger of antismoking campaigns is that they might glamorize smoking as being a rebellious activity. On balance, however, it seems to be the case that cigarette smoking is not viewed favorably by youths. Consider, for example, the responses in 2000 of twelfth-graders in the University of Michigan Monitoring the Future study.[30] Respondents were asked whether they disapprove or strongly disapprove of "People who smoke one or more packs of cigarettes per day." A striking 70.1 percent of all twelfth-grade respondents indicated disapproval. The percentages disapproving for students in younger grades is even higher, as there is 76.7 percent disapproval among tenth-graders and 81.9 percent disapproval among eighth-graders. It is also noteworthy that in each case the disapproval ratings for cigarette smokers exceed that for people who smoke marijuana occasionally. These high disapproval ratings when coupled with the substantial risk awareness information suggests that the weak link in youth smoking policies is not a failure to communicate the risk to the broad majority of underage smokers.

While it is too early to declare that any particular tobacco informational campaign is the ideal model for reducing youth smoking, there is considerable benefit to adopting the general strategy of running various experiments across different states, learning about their differing effectiveness, and choosing the campaigns that appear to be the most effective. Because a policy objective is to eliminate underage smoking altogether, reduction in youth smoking rates as a result of the informational campaign is certainly one legitimate measure of the efficacy of these programs. However, an additional concern is that these informational campaigns educate the consumers rather than simply discourage smoking behavior. Negative campaigns that lack legitimacy in the eyes of the public will potentially undermine antismoking efforts in the longer run and can compromise the credibility of governmental informational campaigns more generally.

There is also potential for rebellious responses to ads that attempt to browbeat youths into not smoking. It is quite common now for commentators to observe that antismoking campaigns can potentially glamorize smoking and enshrine it as a symbol of teenage rebellion, thus encouraging smoking behavior. Whether there is such a mechanism at work has long been much debated. However, such controversies can readily be resolved by proper policy assessments that determine the net effect of the antismoking campaigns on youth smoking rates in different states and by identifying those that appear to be most effective on balance.

Developing a Youth Smoking Policy

Some components of any sensible policy to decrease underage smoking are clear-cut. Age restrictions on the purchase of cigarettes represent an important component. Ensuring that these restrictions be enforced vigorously is essential, but will have only a modest effect on youth smoking rates. Informational campaigns also may be effective, particularly if they are tailored to youths. However, in designing such campaigns, one should not lose sight of the fundamental criterion that should be met by all sound informational efforts: They should educate consumers in an honest and informative way rather than simply attempting to deter them from consuming a product, through negative ads. Such efforts will undermine the credibility of informational campaigns, imposing a cost on informational efforts of all kinds, not simply those directed at cigarettes. In such informational campaigns, the credibility of the government should not be sacrificed in our zeal to deter youth smoking.

Perhaps the most important influence that has been identified in assessments of youth smoking is the role of parents. Households that permit smoking in the home are much more conducive to underage smoking than those that do not. To the extent that parental smoking rates decline over time and efforts are made to restrict exposures to environmental tobacco smoke in the home, then there will also be additional benefits in terms of decreases in youth smoking rates. Vigilance in limiting access to family members' cigarettes is a neglected but important concern as well.

In many respects, however, the problem of youth smoking is not entirely dissimilar to the problems facing smoking policy more generally. At present, a major danger with respect to youth smoking is the purchase of bidis. Bidis are thin cigarettes popular in India, which cost about $2 a pack.[31] These cigarettes are not marketed by major U.S. tobacco firms and, as a consequence, are not subject to the same kinds of penalties and regulations. Youths find these cigarettes attractive because of their low price, which is below that of conventional cigarettes. In addition, they are available in over a dozen flavors, such as strawberry, chocolate, and vanilla.

Unlike conventional cigarettes, bidis are hand-rolled and are unfiltered. The wrapping is of tenu leaves, which are less permeable than cigarette paper and consequently lead the smoker to inhale more deeply. While bidis are not exempt from taxes or the surgeon general's warning, surveys of bidis sold to minors indicate that they often lack the tax stamp. Moreover, in the overwhelming majority of cases they fail to include a health warning about the dangers of cigarettes. Bidis are also sold in different outlets than conventional cigarettes, such as head shops and some natural food stores, which may be more lax about sales to minors.

The emergence of bidis is unlikely to be a unique event in cigarette

CHAPTER EIGHT

marketing. The costs imposed by the Master Settlement Agreement have increased the prices of conventional cigarettes marketed by major U.S. companies. One would anticipate that there would be additional entry of alternative cigarette products. These new entrants will undercut the prices of conventional cigarettes and may also sacrifice product quality. Consumers will also know less about the hazards of such cigarettes and may be lulled into believing that alternatives to conventional cigarettes such as bidis are, in fact, natural safe alternatives to conventional cigarettes.

To prevent such errors in consumer choice, the cornerstone of any government policy in this area should be to promote competition with respect to product safety. Rating of comparative risks of cigarettes and alternatives to cigarettes will enable consumers to make sounder judgments with respect to their cigarette consumption. Companies will also compete on the safety dimension, leading to a reduction in the health costs of cigarettes that can be achieved by exploiting the enormous potential of market forces.

IX

PROMOTING SAFER CIGARETTES

Recent developments in the national smoking debate herald the emergence of a more aggressive regulatory regime. Activities through the courts, legislation, and regulatory policy will all affect the nature of cigarettes and their marketing. The government has several available methods to regulate risky products. The first form of regulation is providing information—either by providing hazard warnings or restricting advertising. This has been the dominant policy approach.

A second form of regulation is to alter the character of the product itself. Health and safety standard regulations mandate various kinds of safety improvements. For example, regulatory agencies have specified the height and dimensions of handrails in the workplace,[1] have mandated the installation of seatbelts and airbags in cars,[2] and required the use of flame retardants on children's pajamas.[3] In contrast, the government has never subjected cigarettes to similar kinds of technological requirements aimed at promoting safety. There has been, for example, no effort to require filters on cigarettes or even to identify, apart from tar and nicotine information, which cigarettes are safer. In stark contrast to its approach to other dangerous products, the government has inexplicably discouraged safety improvements for cigarettes.

The most extreme form of regulation is to ban a product altogether. Currently, over one in five of U.S. adults continue to smoke.[4] Although it is feasible to limit the age at which people can buy cigarettes and the kinds of cigarettes that are sold, it seems unlikely that a complete ban would be fully effective.[5] Moreover, even the antismoking critics have not claimed that the market failure is so great that a complete ban is necessary. There have been occasional calls for an end to smoking and a smoke-free society, but there has been no major effort to achieve this outcome through a ban.

What is needed now is a regulatory effort that goes beyond the warning message and promotes cigarette safety in much the same way that other government agencies use health and safety regulations to foster safety of products, jobs, and the environment. Policies to date have not utilized this opportunity to reduce risk. Rather than stimulating safety innovations, the FDA and the surgeon general have taken an adversarial position and have discouraged the promotion of safer cigarettes, focusing instead on eliminating smoking behavior. This chapter advocates a regulatory policy shift, advocating two new broad kinds of policies to promote greater safety in cigarettes, just as the government fosters greater safety in motor vehicles and in the workplace.

First, the government should develop a comprehensive rating system to indicate the hazards associated with different cigarettes to assist consumers in being able to match their cigarettes with their risk preferences. Such an aggressive comparative risk information policy would exploit the market forces reflected in the greatest shift in smoking behavior in the past half century—the decrease in the average tar level of cigarettes. Consumer demand for safer cigarette products is clearly substantial, and the government could develop a safety rating system that would truly inform consumers of risk characteristics of cigarettes in a manner that goes beyond the current tar and nicotine ratings.

Second, the government should encourage technological advancements in cigarette design that reduce either their nicotine content or other health hazards of cigarettes. These technological advancements may be quite radical and may substantially change the character of the cigarette, as in the case of the Premier cigarette and Eclipse cigarette developed by R. J. Reynolds. Manipulations of a product's character through safety devices is a well-established regulatory approach. Questions will of course remain as to how safe the results of such advances are, compared with cigarettes currently marketed, given the way people may smoke such cigarettes. The FDA should assume a leadership role both by encouraging advancements in cigarette safety by rating the comparative riskiness of products that reflect these new safer designs, and by promoting rather than discouraging consumer purchase of such safer cigarettes.

Underlying this regulatory proposal is a general assumption that the objective of government policy should be to promote informed consumer risk-taking. Giving people safer options to choose from can only be welfare-enhancing, providing that the government also establishes a mechanism to assess and communicate the product risks. Informed choice requires that consumers understand not only the overall hazardousness of smoking, but also the relative risks of different smoking choices. Moving to this constructive approach requires that the FDA abandon its current anti-industry stance. Promotion of informed choice recognizes that adult consumers have a right to smoke and to incur the associated risks, provided that society has not banned smoking altogether. Expanding the range of consumer choice by encouraging the introduction of safer cigarette designs would be consistent with such an appropriate recognition of consumers' rights to make the product choices that are reflective of their preferences.

Do We Need More Warnings?

A major theme of this chapter is that assessing the adequacy of consumer information involves much more than simply asking whether consumers are aware that smoking is risky. Even if there is widespread knowledge of the health risks of smoking, there nevertheless may be a constructive role for government action. To make ideal choices among the cigarettes available for purchase and to create incentives for cigarette companies to provide the kinds of cigarettes that are most in line with consumer preferences, consumers will require much more refined information than simply a general awareness of the hazards of smoking. People ideally should be able to determine the comparative risks of different smoking options.

Targets of Regulatory Opportunity

To get a sense of the potential opportunities for beneficial informational cigarette regulation it is helpful to analyze the manner in which cigarette regulations have affected smoking behavior to date. A useful starting point is to analyze the trends in cigarette consumption over time shown in figure 7. The solid line represents the number of cigarettes consumed per capita over the last half century. The dotted line represents the per capita cigarette consumption adjusted for the level of tar in the cigarettes. The tar rating for cigarettes is a widely publicized single summary statistic that is indicative of the chemical hazards in the cigarette.[6]

The trend in smoking consumption has been consistently downward since the mid-1970s. As indicated in figure 7, from the mid-1960s to the mid-1970s, per capita consumption was flat—and per capita consumption actually *rose* significantly from 1944 to 1964. Thus, the major effect of the initial wave of cigarette warnings and public information about smoking was to flatten the growth in cigarette consumption, rather than to reverse the trend and generate a decline in the level of per

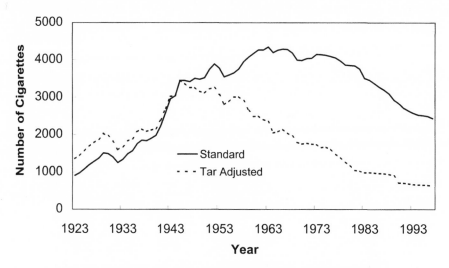

Figure 7 Per capita cigarette consumption in the United States (1923–1997)

capita cigarette consumption. Because of the contemporaneous nature of warnings policies and other cigarette information, studies have not been able to disentangle these influences statistically. By the mid-1990s, per capita cigarette consumption had declined from its peak but was not substantially below its level of fifty years earlier.

The trend for tar-adjusted cigarette consumption in figure 7 reflects a much starker shift in cigarette smoking behavior. Whereas cigarettes average 46.1 mg tar per cigarette in 1944, by 1994 the average tar level in cigarettes was 12 mg. The tar-adjusted per capita consumption weights the per capita consumption figures by the tar level in that year relative to its 1944 level. If one were to assume for simplicity that the risk of cigarettes is linearly related to the tar level, then over this fifty-year period the risk of cigarettes would have declined by almost three-fourths.

The dramatic decline in the tar-adjusted per capita consumption of cigarettes reflects an apparent desire on the part of smokers to better match the riskiness of cigarettes with their own preferences. To the extent that smokers are responding to health concerns, they have done so primarily by choosing lower-tar cigarettes.[7]

A particularly dramatic decline in average tar levels occurred from 1957 to 1960. This period, which has been designated as the "Great Tar Derby," was one in which the cigarette companies competed in terms of their tar levels.[8] Cigarette companies' advertisements touted the lower tar levels of their brands as compared to that of other brands. Kent cigarettes, for example, claimed that they had "significantly less tar and nicotine than any other filter brand." The Marlboro ad declared: "Today's Marlboro—22% less tar, 34% less nicotine." Duke cigarettes touted the fact that their product offered the "lowest tar of all lo-tar cigarettes."[9]

As a result, during this very short period of the Great Tar Derby, the average tar and nicotine levels of cigarettes purchased by consumers was one-third lower than it was before.[10] Competition on the part of cigarette companies with respect to the safety dimension of their product elicited a substantial consumer response. Unfortunately, this progress was not permanent. The Federal Trade Commission (FTC) did not embrace the low-tar competition and instead negotiated an industry agreement to ban tar and nicotine advertising in 1960. Although the official rationale for this action remains unclear,[11] it played an obstructionist role by discouraging the provision of safety-related information for cigarettes to consumers and by impeding the public's ability to choose lower-tar cigarettes. The U.S. surgeon general also weighed in, making a recommendation that people not smoke low-tar cigarettes. This policy statement reflected the continuing opposition of the surgeon general to all safer cigarette policies. The exclusive emphasis was on eliminating smoking altogether. Due in part to the pressure exerted by the American Cancer Society to reverse this ill-conceived policy of suppressing tar and nicotine information,[12] the FTC relented and ultimately permitted tar and nicotine advertising. The initial step was the publication of tar and nicotine levels by the FTC in 1967, and, by 1991, a new voluntary industry agreement required cigarette companies to disclose their tar and nicotine levels.

A final noteworthy pattern in figure 7 is the flattening of the tar-adjusted cigarette consumption levels in the 1990s. The rise of generic and budget brand cigarettes, and their associated high tar levels,[13] led to a flattening of the decline in tar-adjusted consumption amounts. This phenomenon highlights a potential danger of regulating cigarettes in a way that would make cigarette brands indistinguishable.[14] All cigarettes are not equally risky. Suppose, for example, that we adopted the proposal to suppress cigarette advertising and brand identification. Consumers will presumably have less brand attachment and focus more on the price than the quality dimension of cigarettes. If that were the case, then lower-priced cigarettes would become relatively more attractive. If these cigarettes also tended to have higher associated tar and nicotine levels, as is the case with current generic cigarettes, then the effect of such a policy could be to increase rather than decrease the risks of smoking.

A similar pattern is exhibited by smokers' choice of filter cigarettes. In much the same way that smokers switched to low-tar cigarettes to reduce their hazards, there has also been a movement toward filter ciga-

CHAPTER NINE

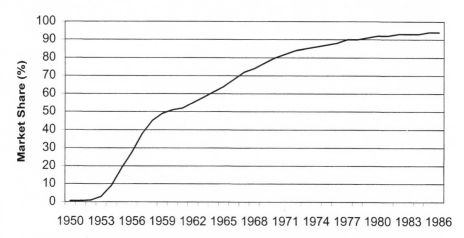

Figure 8 Trend in purchase of filter cigarettes. Source: U.S. Department of Health and Human Services 1989a.

rettes in order to decrease the tar levels consumed. The evidence with respect to filter cigarettes is particularly striking.[15] As figure 8 indicates, filter cigarettes have taken over the cigarette market. In 1952 only 1 percent of all cigarettes sold in the United States were filter cigarettes. Shortly thereafter, prominent scientific studies began to link smoking with cancer. The public's response was to seek a safer cigarette. By 1959, the filter cigarette market share figure had jumped to 49 percent. By 1985, 94 percent of all cigarettes sold had filters, as these became the dominant cigarette in the U.S. cigarette market. Indeed, the decline of venerable brands such as Pall Mall and the rise of brands such as Winston and Marlboro is attributable in large part to the presence of filters on some of these other brands.

The trends for the adoption of filter cigarettes also parallel those for tar in that there appear to be no discrete changes in the trend with the advent of the warnings. In 1965 when Congress passed legislation requiring warnings, the cigarette consumption and the tar levels of consumption were fairly flat, and the percentage of consumers choosing filter cigarettes rose from 61 percent in 1964 to only 64 percent in 1965. The 4 percent increase in 1966 when warnings were universally adopted is also consistent with the existing trend. Similarly, the next warnings era that began in 1969 was associated with an additional 3 percent rise in filter cigarette usage, which is identical to the increase experienced from 1967 to 1968. The advent of the rotating warnings in 1984 was accompanied by no change in filter cigarette usage, which remained constant at 93 percent.

The data on changes in tar levels, filter cigarette usage, and per capita cigarette consumption all provide a consistent pattern in which there has been increased attention to the health-related properties of cigarettes. Consumers have ultimately responded by smoking fewer cigarettes, but more importantly, they have attempted to change the kinds of cigarettes they smoke, focusing on filter cigarettes and low-tar cigarettes. These market responses suggest that consumers would also take advantage of government efforts to foster additional safety competition with respect to cigarette characteristics.

Underlying this discussion is an implicit assumption that smokers now attempt to match the kind of cigarettes they purchase with their concern for the health hazards of cigarettes. Available evidence indicates that such matching does in fact occur. Overall, 87.1 percent of people who smoke low-tar cigarettes (≤ 3 mg tar/cigarette) express concerns about the health consequences of smoking.[16] In contrast, only 54.8 percent of those who smoke the high-tar cigarettes (≥ 21 mg tar/cigarette) express health concerns.[17]

It would be potentially very useful if the government were to provide risk ratings for cigarettes. Current tar and nicotine ratings provide partial information, but this information is neither complete nor conclusive. For example, do people tend to inhale lower-tar cigarettes more deeply, thus altering their risk characteristics?[18] If so, how much does this affect the reduced risk? The answers to such questions cannot be obtained simply by assessing a product's tar rating.

Asking the individual consumer to resolve such scientific issues is unreasonable. Trial and error with different kinds of cigarettes may be instructive with respect to immediate health effects, such as shortness of breath, but does not provide comprehensive information. The government could play a potentially productive role in gathering and disseminating the research regarding the health hazards of cigarettes. The government could accomplish this by funding its own central research effort, thus avoiding the duplicative efforts of the research by each individual cigarette company. This effort could be financed by cigarette taxes. In addition, governmental research would presumably have more credibility than privately funded research, concerning which some might be skeptical of the role of the private vested interests.

Another possible governmental role might be to establish standards and to review the scientific research undertaken by the cigarette industry. Testing new brands and their health consequences presumably would be the responsibility of the cigarette industry itself, in much the same way that pharmaceutical companies have responsibility for testing the implications of new pharmaceutical formulations. In the case of prescription drugs, the FDA has established testing guidelines that pharmaceutical companies must adhere to as part of the testing process. The FDA then reviews these test results and mandates additional study if necessary.[19] In much the same way, the FDA could establish guidelines for testing alternative cigarette products and rating their safety. As with any valid scientific procedure, the results of such tests should be replicable so that other scientists who undertook the same kinds of tests in conformance with the FDA guidelines would generate analogous results. The FDA could also establish a peer review process for its testing to ensure its scientific credibility.

The Cigarette Safety Policy Record

The FDA could play a highly productive role by rating the comparative safety of cigarettes, thus providing consumers with information that would enable them to better match a product's risk characteristics with their own preferences. One could envision a rating system that captured not only the risk characteristics of cigarettes, but also additional factors, such as the implications of how different kinds of cigarettes are smoked, if that is in fact a consequential concern. In this manner, the FDA could publish comparative risk ratings for cigarettes that would enable consumers to assess the relative riskiness of their choices.

This kind of informational function has a substantial history in other areas. Point-of-purchase displays in supermarkets, for example, are often helpful to consumers in their choice of products based on their nutritional value. A noteworthy characteristic of such information is that comparative information about the bad attributes, such as salt or fat content, may have a greater effect on consumer choice than does information about positive attributes, such as vitamins.[20] Thus, consumers often use the comparative information to target aspects of a product that they wish to avoid. Comparative risk ratings of cigarettes would highlight the health hazards of cigarettes, thus providing the kind of information that would be particularly useful to health-conscious consumers.

Cigarettes differ greatly in their tar and nicotine content, as is indicated by the ratings for ten leading brands presented in table 25. Even within particular brands there is substantial heterogeneity. Marlboro, for example, comes in several varieties shown in table 26. The tar and nicotine levels range from 5 mg in tar and 0.5 mg in nicotine to 16 mg in tar and 1.2 mg in nicotine.[21] In much the same way as point-of-purchase

Table 25 Tar and Nicotine Ratings for Cigarettes: Ratings for the Top Ten Cigarette Brands in the United States

Rank	Brand	Market Share 1996	Nicotine[a]	Tar[b]	CO Content[c]
1	Marlboro	32.3%	1.1	15	14
2	Newport	6.1%	1.4	18	19
3	Doral	5.9%	.8	13	16
4	GPC	5.8%	.9	4	15
5	Winston	5.3%	1.2	16	17
6	Basic	4.8%	1.1	15	16
7	Camel	4.6%	1.4	18	20
8	Salem	3.6%	1.4	17	19
9	Kool	3.6%	1.2	16	16
10	Virginia Slims	2.4%	1.1	14	12
	All other	25.6%			
	Total cigarettes sold (in billions)	381.77			

Source: Federal Trade Commission, "'Tar,' Nicotine, and Carbon Monoxide of the Smoke of 1206 Varieties of Domestic Cigarettes for the Year 1994," FTC file #962 3099, July 15, 1997, http://www.ftc.gov/os/1997/9707/.
[a]Nicotine in milligrams per cigarette.
[b]Total particulate matter in milligrams per cigarette less nicotine and water.
[c]Carbon monoxide in milligrams per cigarette.

supermarket displays foster better consumer choices based on nutritional information, posting a tar and nicotine distribution for cigarettes could assist consumers in making choices regarding cigarette safety.

The cigarette ratings remain based on the Cambridge Testing Method, approved by the Federal Trade Commission in 1966, which utilizes machine testing to simulate smoking behavior. The FTC updates this testing procedure periodically, as it did in 1980 due to technological advances in carbon monoxide and nicotine measurement.[22] The testing improvements made by the FTC ideally will also reflect how deeply a person inhales, which in turn may affect the amount of tar and nicotine ingested. The FTC continues to revise these procedures.[23]

Evidence of the risks of different types of cigarettes is not as well developed as one would like but is nevertheless suggestive of significant risk differences. Lower-tar products are in fact less risky, especially with respect to lung cancer.[24] Moreover, smokers of filter cigarettes have a 20 percent lower risk of cancer than smokers of nonfilter cigarettes. This estimate is a net effect that fully accounts for any compensating behavior, such as the manner of smoking.

Table 26 Tar and Nicotine Ratings for Different Marlboro Cigarettes

Size	Filtered	Pack	Type	Nicotine[a]	Tar[b]	CO Content[c]
100	yes	hard		0.5	5	7
King	yes	hard	ultra-light	0.5	5	7
100	yes	hard	light	0.8	10	12
100	yes	soft	light	0.8	10	12
King	yes	hard	light	0.8	10	12
King	yes	hard	medium	0.8	11	12
King	yes	soft	light	0.8	10	11
King	yes	soft	25 pkg, light	0.8	10	11
King	yes	soft	medium	0.9	11	12
100	yes	hard	medium	1.0	13	12
100	yes	soft	medium	1.0	12	13
King	yes	hard		1.1	16	14
King	yes	soft		1.1	16	15
King	yes	soft	25 pkg	1.1	15	14
100	yes	soft	Gold pkg	1.1	15	14
100	yes	soft	Red pkg	1.1	15	15
100	yes	hard	Gold pkg	1.2	15	15
100	yes	hard	Red pkg	1.2	16	15

Source: Federal Trade Commission, "'Tar,' Nicotine, and Carbon Monoxide of the Smoke of 1206 Varieties of Domestic Cigarettes for the Year 1994," FTC file #962 3099, July 15, 1997, http://www.ftc.gov/os/1997/9707/.
[a]Nicotine in milligrams per cigarette.
[b]Total particulate matter in milligrams per cigarette less nicotine and water.
[c]Carbon monoxide in milligrams per cigarette.

The informational strategy could consist of three components. First, post at the point of purchase comparative ratings of a group of cigarettes across a broad spectrum of cigarette tar and nicotine levels. Consumers would then be able to assess the different riskiness of cigarette brands by seeing where their cigarettes might fall within the distribution. Second, make available a readily accessible reference listing of tar and nicotine levels of all cigarette brands both at the point of purchase and on the Internet. This listing would include all brands, whereas the first component above would focus on a representative selection of the range of choices. Third, require all cigarettes to list the tar and nicotine levels on each pack and in each ad. As scientific knowledge becomes refined, tar and nicotine levels might be supplanted by other, possibly more comprehensive, risk measures. Thus, ideally, the measures should seek to characterize the overall riskiness and type of risks.

Providing comparative risk information for cigarettes is not, however, the same as simply listing the chemical composition of cigarettes. Knowing that cigarettes contain, for example, arsenic, formaldehyde, or other chemicals would not be particularly instructive even to a cancer specialist, without knowledge of the quantities of these chemicals in the cigarette smoke. To maximize usefulness, therefore, the information should not require the consumer to make the risk assessment based on the chemical list, but should instead provide an overall risk rating that summarizes the risk implications in a manner that can be understood. Such a risk rating need not be a single summary statistic. It may prove useful, for example, to have risk indices on multiple dimensions, such as cancer, heart disease, respiratory ailments, and the difficulty of quitting. The degree of diverse forms of information one should provide will, of course, be limited by information processing capabilities. Field tests to determine the most effective warning approach will be useful in this regard.

Formulating the risk information in such a manner also can eliminate some of the current distractions over cigarette additives. Massachusetts introduced the first tobacco disclosure law in the nation known as Chapter 234 of the Massachusetts General Laws. That law required companies to submit annual reports listing the toxic ingredients in cigarettes.[25] The tobacco industry claimed that this law would violate trade secrets and challenged the law in court. On November 13, 1998, the First Circuit U.S. Court of Appeals refused to lift the preliminary injunction that had been granted.[26] Thus, the state was prevented from forcing the ingredient disclosures.

Cigarette companies, however, have already begun to respond to the policy concern of ingredient disclosure efforts by offering additive-free cigarettes, such as a Winston cigarette that contains no additives.[27] As indicated by the tar and nicotine ratings in table 25, Winston is not an especially safe cigarette on these risk dimensions. Does this concern over additives make sense from the standpoint of risk policy? In terms of the overall risk, concern over additives is akin to asking whether the car that ran you over also had lead paint on it. Cigarette smoking is a tremendously risky activity even for cigarettes without flavor enhancers or other artificial additives. The states' disclosure efforts are misdirected. The warnings effort should focus consumers' attention on the overall product riskiness rather than on potential distractions that could distort consumers' risk beliefs.

The controversy over cigarette additives reflects the inherent inconsistency of many antismoking efforts. Efforts by the Massachusetts legislature and others to force disclosure of cigarette additives led to the marketing of additive-free Winstons. Antismoking groups then objected that they believed marketing additive-free cigarettes could mislead consumers into thinking that additive-free cigarettes were safer. But if the additives were not more dangerous, why did the state seek to require their disclosure? In response to these pressures, Winston ads now include a disclaimer disavowing that their cigarettes are safer. Indeed, the FTC filed a complaint against R. J. Reynolds for simply advertising that Winston did not include additives. The outcome was that future Winston ads would include the statement: "No additives in our tobacco does NOT mean a safer cigarette."[28] The industry is consequently subjected to often inconsistent policies pertaining to potential dangers of cigarette additives, which are often included to affect flavor or the tobacco burn rate. Antismoking critics seek to have it both ways—apparently claiming that additives are risky while not allowing a company that does not include additives to point out that excluding additives should then reduce the product's riskiness. The problem is that particular risks of cigarettes should not be singled out. What is needed is an overall risk-rating scheme for cigarettes.

The current restrictive environment greatly limits the ability of tobacco companies to tout their safety-related properties. Consider the "No Bull. No Boundaries." ad campaign for Winston cigarettes, which are free of the additives that have been the target of mandatory disclosure legislation.[29] The ad consisted of a multipage magazine insert that begins with page 1 announcing the Winston Racing Nation campaign, which was an auto-racing-related contest. Pages 2 and 3 were visible jointly and featured the surgeon general's quitting smoking warning (black type against white background) on the left-hand page along with a single sentence of ad text (for example, "We are united by freedom and a passion for racing."). The left page also gave the toll-free number for entering the contest and the age twenty-one or over restriction for participating in the contest. There was no other text on the right, on page 3, other than "No additives in our cigarette does NOT mean a safer cigarette," which was a boxed warning in white type against a red background. Page 4 repeated the surgeon general's warning along with a photo and a single statement unrelated to smoking risks (for example, "We are free to be ourselves."), and page 5 repeated the no-additive disclaimer. Page 6 repeated both the surgeon general's warning and the no-additive disclaimer so that consumers would never miss the disclaimer if they opened out the fold-out page 7 to obtain the contest entry details. The final page of the insert repeated the warning and the disclaimer and provided the FTC tar and nicotine rating.

This advertising insert consequently provided both the surgeon general's warning and the no-additive disclaimer four times each. However, nowhere in this campaign did R. J. Reynolds ever mention that the cigarette had no chemical additives in an affirmative manner, much less tout this characteristic as a safety benefit. The ad instead was completely defensive in highlighting that there were no safety benefits from having no additives. But if there are no safety benefits from eliminating chemical additives, legislative efforts and pressures by state and federal agencies to compel ingredient disclosure should be abandoned. If there are safety benefits or if we believe that consumers should have the right to choose even if there are no demonstrable benefits, disclosures should be encouraged. Market competition would then promote the elimination of additives as firms would compete on that dimension. At present, we set standards for labeling of organic produce and the disclosure of food additives such as BHT even though there are often no proven significant health benefits from altering consumption choices on the basis of this information. While the scientific evidence is still evolving, we nevertheless wish to provide people with information so that they can make choices in line with their individual preferences. In much the same way, the government should set standards for what it means for cigarettes to be "additive free" or safe on other dimensions and encourage companies to promote informed choice regarding these attributes, rather than silence these efforts or require defensive disclosures that undermine the potential role of competition on the safety dimension.

The current concern over additives is a needless distraction. Smoking is very risky, and the presence of additives does not alter that basic property. What is needed is a comprehensive risk rating for cigarettes that summarizes the overall riskiness of each brand. Isolating particular risks, irrespective of their magnitude, is not useful. Attempting to generate consumer alarm about particular additives may lead cigarette consumers to switch brands, but is this a good outcome? Winston has tar levels of 16 mg and nicotine levels of 1.2 mg—far in excess of many lighter cigarettes that contain additives.[30]

Additive-free Winstons are not the only cigarettes that have confronted the difficulties of conveying the benefits of their product attributes. Carlton is in a similar quandary with respect to tar and nicotine levels. This cigarette has extremely attractive scores on these dimensions, as Carlton 100s have only 1 mg tar and 0.1 mg nicotine. By comparison, regular Marlboros have 16 mg tar and 1.1 mg nicotine. Tar and nicotine levels are the safety dimensions that the government selects and for which it specifies the testing approach. Yet, for fear of making unsubstantiated safety claims that may lead to government sanctions, the company's 1999 ad touts the tar and nicotine levels but then disavows that they have any significance.

The ad declares:

1 mg. Isn't it time you started thinking about number one? Think Carlton. With 1 mg tar. It's the Ultra Ultra Light.

Brown and Williamson then disavows any safety claims being made on behalf of the product:

1 mg "tar," 0.1 mg nicotine average per cigarette by FTC method. Actual tar and nicotine deliveries will vary based on how you hold and smoke your cigarette. It is not our intention to suggest that a 1 mg. "tar" cigarette is any safer than other cigarettes.[31]

Of course these cigarettes are safer than the average Marlboro and other similar cigarettes. The current regulatory regime puts companies in a preposterous position. Either the tar and nicotine levels are correlated with cigarette risks, which they surely are, or they are not. If the government is unwilling to permit firms to make comparative safety claims based on these risk dimensions, then it should establish new risk measures that can serve as a reliable guide to product risk. Such measures can also take into account whether people smoke such cigarettes differently, such as inhaling more deeply or covering up the side air vents as they smoke. Such compensating behavior affects risks but does not alter the fact that there are real differences in product riskiness.

There is a general sense that current policies often flail about, with no clear guiding principle other than criticizing the cigarette industry. A sounder approach is to focus concern on the level of the product's risk and to quantify the risk as much as possible. Consumers will profit from knowing that the absolute total risk of a cigarette brand is at a particular level. Scare tactics that focus on the presence of ammonia or flavor enhancers are intended to create alarm rather than a sound understanding of the overall product risks and health consequences.

Rating the comparative risks of cigarettes is, to a large extent, simply an extension of the current informational approach administered by the Federal Trade Commission. Conceivably the FDA could also take the lead in fostering much more ambitious changes in the character of cigarettes. In much the same way as health, safety, and environmental regulations require safer plant and equipment and safer products,[32] the FDA likewise could take actions that promote the design of safer cigarettes.

Consider the two traditional risk components of cigarettes—tar and nicotine. In the case of nicotine, which is closely related to the difficulty of quitting smoking, Philip Morris introduced several nicotine-free cigarettes that were test-marketed in 1991.[33] The brand names included Next, Merit-Free, and Benson and Hedges de-nic. Rather than welcome these products, antismoking groups petitioned the FDA to take broader action against cigarettes by designating nicotine as a drug and by initiating a broader range of regulatory actions against cigarettes.[34] Philip Morris also lost $350 million on an attempt in 1989 to market cigarettes stripped of their nicotine by a process similar to that used to make decaffeinated coffee.[35] Other companies such as Safer Smokes in Atlanta had plans to announce the "Bravo" cigarettes made from lettuce.[36] The safety of lettuce as compared to tobacco has not been assessed in a reliable manner.

The cigarette industry has made several attempts to manufacture "safer cigarettes" or smoking devices. Perhaps the greatest technological innovation affecting cigarettes was the development of the Premier cigarette by R. J. Reynolds.[37] The Premier, which was subsequently tested and marketed in a new design under the brand name Eclipse, did not burn tobacco.[38] Rather, in its initial design the smoker would light a carbon tip at the end of the cigarette. This tip in turn would heat a capsule filled with porous beads coated with tobacco extract (this aluminum capsule was eliminated in the Eclipse design). In the case of both the Premier and Eclipse, the vapor then traveled through tobacco papers to release even more tobacco flavor.[39]

Notwithstanding the technological sophistication of the new design, the Premier closely resembled conventional cigarettes in many respects. It had the external appearance of a cigarette; the individual would smoke the cigarette in the same fashion and would hold it in the same manner. The Premier also delivered the nicotine level associated with conventional cigarettes. There was, however, one dramatic change. Since it did not burn tobacco, the Premier caused less adverse biological activity than do other cigarettes.[40] Carbon monoxide risks remained, but the mainstream and sidestream smoke condensates were all less genotoxic than those of reference cigarettes.[41]

The Premier and Eclipse did, however, lack other valued product attributes. They did not offer as good a taste in the view of most consumers. Smokers often characterized the taste with various expletives. In addition, smokers could not flick their ashes, as no ash was formed. Some people also had difficulty in determining when the cigarettes were out. However, the ability to experience the effects of nicotine was not noticeably impaired, and consumers could experience much of the act of smoking in terms of the physical activity.

The Premier and Eclipse cigarette experience does, however, indicate that taste and other product attributes matter. Smoking is not simply a means of satisfying a nicotine addiction, as some suggest. Smoking parallels many other consumption activities in that consumers enjoy many aspects of the product, not just the nicotine. Over time one would expect that cigarette companies would refine the taste and other attributes, particularly if a major market for the newly designed product emerged. The relentless opposition of the U.S. surgeon general to a safer cigarette policy approach has certainly not helped promote these alternative designs.

Marketing this "safer" cigarette was a nontrivial task since cigarette companies are not permitted to make health claims on behalf of their product.[42] The Premier packaging, for which I served as a hazard warnings consultant in the label design, referred to the "cleaner smoke," which was not a health claim but a reference to its overall smokeless character. The company did not make any explicit health claims on behalf of the product. The brochure attached to the cigarette pack described its characteristics as follows:

> Premier is the first cigarette you smoke by *heating tobacco—not burning it.*
>
> It's a breakthrough that changes the very composition of cigarette smoke—substantially reducing many of the controversial compounds found in the smoke of tobacco-burning cigarettes. Those that remain include carbon monoxide, but the amount of carbon monoxide is no greater than in the best-selling "lights."
>
> What it all comes down to is a cleaner smoke—for you and everyone around you.[43]

One can view cigarettes in abstract terms, as embodying a number of characteristics. Many of these characteristics remained under the new design of the Premier. One principal characteristic that was affected was that there was a less desirable taste associated with the cigarettes, but this effect differed depending on whether the cigarette was of the regular or menthol variety. In addition, there was no burning of tobacco, thus eliminating all risks associated with that particular process.[44]

Product changes of other kinds continue to emerge, with no clear guidance from the government regarding their desirability. Philip Morris, for example, test-marketed a cigarette with paper that was less likely to ignite certain fabrics.[45] This product development could potentially reduce fire safety risks of the product, an important concern for smokers and nonsmokers alike. An innovation with seemingly adverse implications for safety is the packing of greater concentrations of tobacco in the Doral cigarette.[46] What we mean by a cigarette in terms of total tobacco smoked and the character of the tobacco may vary greatly, creating a great opportunity for the government in rating risks and promoting safety.

Rather than embracing positive innovations such as the Premier, the reaction was marked by an attitude of suspicion and distrust. Just as the surgeon general opposed low-tar cigarettes, the 1989 U.S. surgeon general's report voiced these official concerns about the new product:

> The marketing of a variety of alternative nicotine delivery systems has heightened concern within the public health community about the future of nicotine addiction. The most prominent development in this regard was the 1988 test marketing by a major cigarette producer of a nicotine delivery device having the external appearance of a cigarette and being promoted as "the cleaner smoke."[47]

To criticize this innovation because it was not the same as not smoking at all is to miss the fundamental contribution of this product. All products consist of multiple attributes, some of which affect risk aspects of the product and others of which affect other aspects of consumer demand. The Premier cigarette did not increase nicotine, one of the major risk components linked to concerns of habituation and addiction. Rather, the cigarette only manipulated two attributes, taste and cancer risk. Premier largely eliminated the cancer risk, and the main price paid was a decrease in the taste provided to consumers. The Eclipse cigarette was reported to be better in this regard than the Premier. For smokers who claim that they smoke because they need to do something with their hands, they enjoy the act of smoking, or they enjoy the effect of the nicotine, this product would meet these objectives. For smokers for whom taste is an essential concern, this new product would not be as attractive as conventional cigarettes.

Other alternative cigarette mechanisms have also emerged. Philip Morris in fact test-marketed the puff-activated lighter in 1997 in an attempt to reduce the amount of sidestream smoke emitted. This device, known as the Accord cigarette, enables smokers to smoke cigarettes in discrete puffs and to eliminate sidestream smoke between puffs. Unlike the Premier cigarette, the smoke taste is unaffected. The degree of environmental tobacco smoke emitted is substantially less with this product. The fire risk would be reduced as well. Nevertheless, antitobacco forces hammered it, without acknowledging any of the risk reduction benefits: "Critics say the device demonstrates the lengths to which the tobacco industry will go to make a dangerous addiction more socially acceptable."[48] One critic even speculated that "children might be able to use the device to conceal smoking from parents."[49] Such speculative fears appear to be desperate attempts to undermine the product, not reasoned concerns. Use of the Accord requires a battery recharger for the battery-powered smoking system and involves a startup cost of $50. The product will be less financially attractive to children and will involve more paraphernalia than conventional cigarettes.

CHAPTER NINE

Other companies are exploring the use of tobacco leaves with a lower tar content as a way to reduce the risk. Brown and Williamson Tobacco Corporation, the third largest cigarette company in the United States, is developing a cigarette made from tobacco with lower levels of nitrosamines, a dangerous carcinogen in tobacco smoke.[50] Clove cigarettes with much less well understood risk properties are also making inroads. If safer designs are promoted, or at least not discouraged, by the government and purchased by consumers, companies will have a financial incentive to improve the product.

In the absence of official support from the public health community, R. J. Reynolds commissioned a wide range of medical studies to document the greater safety of the Premier cigarette. An advisory committee convened by the Emory University School of Medicine provided oversight of a series of studies assessing the hazards of the Premier cigarette. The compilation of these studies documents the safety characteristics of the product. As viewed by this committee, the cigarette design achieved the stated objectives:

- To simplify the chemical composition of mainstream and sidestream smoke emitted by the new cigarette.
- To minimize the biological activity of the mainstream and sidestream smoke emitted by the new cigarette.
- To achieve significant reduction of environmental tobacco smoke from the new cigarette.[51]

The committee commended these objectives and concluded that they have been substantially achieved through the research and development program, as represented by the information presented to the committee for review.

One of the many studies commissioned as part of this review involved the intake of tobacco smoke by animals. These tests supported the greater safety of the new cigarettes: "Although the studies were only of ninety-day duration they did clearly demonstrate the decrease in adverse biological activity from the new cigarette when compared to effects induced by smoke from reference cigarettes."[52]

The committee's review of a study focusing on the presence of mutagens in human urine was similarly positive:

> It agreed that the urine mutagenicity results showed a significant difference between persons smoking reference or new cigarettes, and no difference between nonsmokers and smokers of the new cigarette. The Committee also agreed with the conclusion that, as assessed subjectively by nonsmokers, there is a substantial reduction in the irritant properties of Environmental Tobacco Smoke produced by the new cigarette compared to that of reference cigarettes.[53]

Finally, the report addressed the potential toxicity of the ingredients in the new cigarette, and it concluded, once again, that the evidence favorably supported the safety of the new cigarette design: "The information presented states that the new cigarette is manufactured from components having little or no toxicity."[54]

The carbon monoxide risks remained, so this product was not entirely risk-free. Moreover, these studies, even though undertaken by highly reputable medical researchers, could not resolve all scientific issues.[55] It is in this regard that the FDA could undertake a fundamental policy role. Rather than having a company commission a medical school to oversee a set of studies, the FDA could outline which types of studies might be useful for making any precise inferences regarding a product's safety. In the case of new cigarette designs, such as the Premier, a two-step approach might be desirable. First, the company could commission a series of studies such as they did on the Premier, and then the FDA could review the results of these studies. On the basis of this review, the FDA could establish guidelines for additional research that would need to be undertaken in order to draw sufficiently precise conclusions regarding the safety of the product.

The results of these studies in turn could be a part of the comparative risk rating of cigarettes and alternative cigarette designs. Thus, the safety of cigarettes—including nonconventional cigarettes—could be included in the ratings system. Rather than simply rating the tar and nicotine levels of cigarettes, the system would need to include other attributes as well. For example, pertinent dimensions might be the following: cancer risk, carbon monoxide, environmental tobacco smoke, and nicotine. One could easily envision other sets of attributes that could be described to consumers to assist in their choice.[56] Rating along multiple attributes is essential. Some alternative cigarette designs may increase the carbon dioxide risk but decrease the cancer risk. Thus, the cigarettes are much safer overall but not necessarily on all dimensions.

Ideally, it would be helpful to undertake field experiments to determine how the provision of different kinds of information affects consumer risk beliefs and choices. The general spirit of these studies would be similar to those that I have undertaken with several former colleagues at Duke University.[57] We undertook these studies for the U.S. Environmental Protection Agency to provide them with guidance for the labeling of pesticides and hazardous chemicals. What we found is that the structure and the format of the information greatly affected people's ability to process the hazard warning.[58] Content is consequently not the sole concern. Moreover, providing too much information can potentially be detrimental in that it can distract consumers' attention from the basic message, creating problems of information overload.[59]

Oversimplifications, such as claiming that consumers cannot process hazard warning information, are certainly not correct. Similarly, the other extreme, at which one might hypothesize that consumers perfectly process all information given to them and act upon this information, also is not true. However, there does exist a wide body of scientific literature regarding the design of hazard warnings.[60] Through appropriately designed experimental tests of alternative warning approaches it is possible to ascertain which structures of information work and which do not. Before embarking on a new risk-rating policy for cigarettes, it would be valuable to undertake such experimental studies so that we can better design the safety rating system to optimize its efficacy.

A Constructive Role for Government Policy

The most essential change that I am proposing in FDA policy is that it undertake a constructive role in fostering technological innovations to promote cigarette safety. Such a stance would require a shift in the attitude of the FDA toward the industry. The current policy reflects an anticigarette stance like that of the avowed quest for a smoke-free society by the year 2000.[61] This kind of arbitrary absolute objective is unachievable, and in fact it was not realized. What can be done, however, is to reduce the hazards associated with smoking.

Adopting a stance that promotes the consumption of safer cigarettes will exploit perhaps the most powerful force in markets—the role of consumer choice. This century has witnessed a decline in many of the risks we face: motor-vehicle accident death rates are down, jobs are safer, home accidents are down, and environmental hazards are diminishing as well.[62] As we become richer, we value our health more. As a consequence, the increased affluence of the United States and its citizenry will increase the demand over time for safer cigarette products.

The dramatic reduction in cigarette tar levels reflected in figure 7 illustrates the potential impact of market forces. There has been a substantial downturn in the tar levels of cigarettes as consumers have sought safer cigarette options. Likewise, filtered cigarettes now dominate the market. Technological devices such as the Premier cigarette would simply exploit the consumer demand for safer products by matching safer cigarettes with the preferences of consumers who seek to reduce the risks of cigarettes.

Perhaps one source of reluctance to such an approach is that it is not as uncompromising as taking a strict antismoking policy. However, the objective of any government policy ideally should be to promote the health and welfare of the citizenry, not simply to restrict cigarette smoking per se. The current policy approach of failing to promote safer cigarettes in effect is using death as the principal deterrent to reduce smoking rates. While it is true that some people may choose to smoke safer cigarettes rather than give up smoking altogether, the government should not be in the role of restricting technological devices that enhance safety and reduce the truly substantial risks of smoking. Government cigarette regulation could potentially do more to promote smokers' health by being more supportive of such innovations than it has been to date.

Somewhat incredulously, the pending federal lawsuit against the industry claims that it is the industry, not the government, that has conspired to suppress safety innovations. Such allegations are the opposite of the truth and are driven by the prospect of obtaining treble damages based on these legal claims rather than the reality of cigarette marketing. At almost every turn, the federal government has failed to promote safer cigarettes and, in many instances, has sought to undermine these products. Indeed, the same federal suit that attacks the companies for suppressing safety innovations also seeks to find the companies liable for ads for low-tar cigarettes.

This litigation-driven hypocrisy should be abandoned. At present, companies cannot make risk-related product claims without risking governmental sanctions. Without being able to communicate such information, companies will never be able to convey facts about comparative cigarette risks adequately to the public. The government must end this informational blackout by establishing a rational risk rating system for cigarettes.

The idea of fostering safer cigarette designs is novel. Such a function has never been a component of the official antismoking efforts on the part of U.S. government agencies. This absence of a strong interest in technological improvements to enhance cigarette safety is in striking contrast to the regulatory approach that exists elsewhere throughout the health, safety, and environmental establishment. By expanding the range of policy tools that are being used to address the hazards of smoking, this effort would not only enhance the well-being of smokers, who will be able to make informed choices from an improved and expanded menu of options, but it will also lead to potentially dramatic improvements in our national health.

X

LESSONS FROM THE TOBACCO DEAL

For years the tobacco industry was the target of a succession of individual lawsuits. It fended off these assaults with an unblemished record of success. If any lawsuits were to be successful, one might have expected that it would be those involving individual plaintiffs. In these cases there were identifiable people who had contracted tobacco-related illnesses. The underlying impetus for these suits was not to recover abstract financial costs to a governmental entity, though sometimes individual medical expenses associated with tobacco-related illnesses entered the picture. The more fundamental concern was that these individuals had experienced irreversible losses to their health and well-being as a result of their cigarette smoking.

Somewhat surprisingly, it was not these concrete cases of individual welfare losses that led to the initial tobacco industry payouts. Rather, it was a series of lawsuits by state governments that reversed the legal fortunes of the tobacco industry. These suits were not about individual health at all. Only money. The welfare of smokers never arose as an explicit concern in any of these state lawsuits; the battle over tobacco had been reduced to an accounting exercise in which the states sought to reclaim financial costs associated with cigarettes.

That states could even be making such a claim was surprising. Such claims for compensation had never been made against any product. Did such suits even have standing in the courts? When this litigation first arose, there was considerable doubt as to whether such suits had any legal basis. Moreover, the underlying mathematics of the consequences of smoking were not in the states' favor. On a societal basis, the net cost savings from cigarettes ranges from $0.29 to $0.32 per pack depending on the adjustments one makes for tar content. These cost savings are in addition to the excise taxes on cigarettes of $0.56 per pack at the time of the litigation. If one were to add the health costs associated with environmental tobacco smoke to the tally, it would offset much of the financial cost savings associated with cigarettes other than excise taxes if one uses the high estimates of these risks. However, these environmental tobacco smoke costs are not financial in character, but are comprised almost entirely of health-care losses in terms of the reduced individual welfare caused by illness. The financial costs of secondhand smoke are minimal; the environmental tobacco smoke effects were not part of any of the states' claims.

Notwithstanding this overall cost structure, the states nevertheless filed suits, singling out the particular cost components that increased as a result of smoking. The focal point of the litigation was on state-related Medicaid costs, including both the state and federal share. Even with this piecemeal approach, the cigarette industry potentially could have waged a successful battle. The courts might have found that such suits lacked a firm legal basis. Or the courts might have recognized any of the cost savings associated with excise taxes, reduced pension costs, or reduced nursing care costs. Having the courts recognize any one of these three cost savings components would have sufficed to eliminate any net social costs of cigarettes for the states. In some states, such as the state of Washington, preliminary rulings were in the industry's favor.

The cigarette industry's decision to propose a comprehensive settlement of all the litigation before it had ever lost a single state case proved to be an enormous error in judgment. The proposed national settlement fell through, and along with it disappeared the protections the draft settlement offered for the industry in the future, including limitations on class actions and punitive damages against the industry. What emerged instead was a far less satisfactory series of settlements with four individual states, followed by a comprehensive settlement for the remaining forty-six states. The total price tag for the industry that had avoided legal payouts for decades was $243 billion—and this included only the payout to the states, not the plaintiffs' legal fees as well. Because most of this amount would be financed through additional per-pack cigarette tax levied in the future, the viability of the industry is not threatened by the settlement. Smokers will be picking up most of the tab.

In several ways, these events were breakthroughs in litigation history. First, an industry that had long resisted settlements of any kind had now paid off a record-breaking damages amount. Second, the settlement imposed regulations on industry conduct as well as payments that were tantamount to an excise tax. Fiscal policy and regulatory policy were no longer the province of legislatures and the regulatory agencies. Third, the landmark character of the litigation that sought to impose health insurance costs of its products on the producer was never adequately tested in court but nevertheless has given rise to a whole new wave of litigation for other risky products.

A fundamental question raised by this litigation, and particularly by the role of the state and federal government in these suits, is whether liability should serve as a substitute for government regulation and taxation. If governmental entities find that cigarettes impose costs on society, excise taxes should be set appropriately, thus avoiding the costs of litigation. Moreover, explicit government regulations that emerge through the legislative process or through rulemaking by federal government agencies can reflect the technical expertise of these agencies as well as the public interest.

Government regulations that are tacked on to negotiated settlements for which the main purpose is simply to obtain money from the industry have not gone through the kind of analytical process of evaluation that is the norm for any other major federal policies. The existing rulemaking process for federal regulations requires that agencies explore a variety of alternative types of policy intervention, and assess their benefits and costs. There are also detailed mechanisms to ensure that there is adequate opportunity for public input on tax policy. None of this careful examination and public input occurred with the regulatory and tax policy proposals that emerged as part of the state settlement. Despite the rhetoric that the tobacco industry funds transferred to the states were needed to defray health-care costs and to fund tobacco education efforts, the monies have gone elsewhere.

The settlement and the disbursement of billions of dollars did not end the litigation, as the industry apparently hoped, but fueled it on a variety of fronts. The federal government weighed in, seeking its hundreds of billions of dollars in compensation. Asbestos trust funds, labor unions, Blue Cross Blue Shield, and other institutions also sought a piece of the action. Plaintiffs' suits and class actions gained new life, as plaintiffs' attorneys could wage multimillion-dollar court battles, and they were also armed with reams of documents obtained as part of the litigation.

The emergence of a rash of cigarette-related cases was not restricted to the United States. Other countries no doubt reasoned that if the industry was willing to pay off billions without any adverse verdict against it, why should they not also reap these windfall gains? Canadian provinces filed similar suits, which thus far have been unsuccessful.[1] In England there are now "excess tar" cases. The tobacco industry is now dispatching legal teams to South America and elsewhere to fend off the worldwide wave of litigation that was stimulated by the payoff. Chinese attorneys are contemplating similar claims.

Moreover, because of the failure to enact the Proposed Resolution, with its caps on punitive damages and protection against class actions, the cigarette industry became increasingly vulnerable. A Los Angeles jury levied a $3 billion punitive damages award in an individual smoker case. Even though this verdict was reduced by an appellate judge to $100 million, it nevertheless represents a tremendous rate of payoff for an individual case, particularly given that there are hundreds of thousands of such individual smokers who die from smoking-related diseases every year. A Florida jury awarded $145 billion in punitive damages in a Florida class-action case.[2] What the settlement did was to give rise to an overwhelming wave of future litigation without the legal protections that the tobacco industry had sought to include to fend off such efforts.

Perhaps the most salient consequence was the effect on the industry's image. Casual observers might assume that the tobacco industry is guilty on a large number of fronts if they are agreeing to settlement amounts of this magnitude. People might think, without knowing any details of the cases, that the payment of damages in the hundreds of billions of dollars surely must have been accompanied by equally outrageous wrongful acts. What the public does not appreciate is that the risks of litigation and unpredictable court outcomes often lead innocent parties to settle. Moreover, the dollar price tag of the settlement overstates how much harm it does to the industry. Payments are over twenty-five years and are equivalent to an excise tax that will largely be borne by cigarette smokers. Nevertheless, the settlement created an environment in which the facts of cases will not matter so much as the public's sense that the industry has done something so harmful that it warranted record-setting payoffs.

If the jury then finds the cigarette industry liable in future cases, the multibillion-dollar payout will establish a psychological anchor for future awards. Juries will tend to think in terms of much bigger award levels in the wake of the state settlement amount than they would have earlier, wholly apart from what reasonable damages might be. Indeed, in 1999 there was a $4.9 billion verdict against General Motors in a California case involving burn injuries suffered by six occupants of a Chevrolet Malibu, of which only $100 million was for compensatory damages. Undoubtedly jurors awarded $4.8 billion in punitive damages rather than a figure in the millions because the cigarette settlement led them to think in terms of billions rather than millions of dollars. The $3 billion individual cigarette case award and the $145 billion class-action award reflect similar anchoring effects. Billion-dollar verdicts had been almost unprecedented except for rare catastrophes such as the Exxon Valdez oil spill. The anchoring effects of the cigarette settlement consequently may have broad ramifications well beyond the cigarette industry.

Unfortunately, the cigarette litigation experience is not a single misguided venture. The regulation-through-litigation route is now viewed more generally as a financial cash cow. The gun industry was the next to come under fire, with the argument being that the absence of safety devices on guns and the manner of gun distribution created health-care cost externalities for society at large. Lead paint also became a target, as the state of Rhode Island recruited a veteran of the tobacco wars to launch a tobacco-style suit against manufacturers of lead paint, which is no longer even sold in this country. The state of Rhode Island and the city of St. Louis have filed similar lawsuits against the paint industry, charging that lead in paint imposes health-care costs arising from children's eating lead paint chips. As in the case of cigarettes and guns, the litigation target is a highly regulated industry. Indeed, lead has not been used in any interior or exterior house paint sold in the United States for decades.

A principal attorney from the tobacco cases, Dickie Scruggs, has since turned his attentions to the health care system. In much the same way as he organized statewide suits against the cigarette industry, in 1999 he became the main attorney in a health-care class-action group called the "REPAIR Team." By January 2000, this group had filed almost two dozen suits alleging that HMOs were guilty of racketeering and other violations, just as was alleged in the cigarette cases. In this instance, Scruggs has sought to duplicate the tobacco litigation formula from the Proposed Resolution by advocating that legislation resolve the suits, including provisions to pay off the attorneys involved in the litigation.[3]

The parallels with tobacco litigation included the funding of the payments through a new insurance premium tax akin to the tobacco tax surcharge in the proposed tobacco bills. Patients in the future would pay for the cost of his efforts through higher premiums just as smokers pay for the costs of the settlement through higher excise taxes per pack. As Scruggs put it, to "see how this would work, take a look at the McCain tobacco litigation. It's a provision very similar to what I'm proposing."[4] However, whereas a tobacco tax discourages use of tobacco, which poses risks to one's health, a tax on HMO premiums will discourage utilization of health care, which presumably will discourage people from getting the care that enhances one's health. Scruggs also has predicted that this litigation would bankrupt most or all managed care providers—an outcome that has not yet been experienced by firms in the tobacco industry.[5]

Whether this litigation will top Scruggs's personal tobacco winnings estimated to be as high as $900 million,[6] which he termed a "bonanza,"[7] is not clear. What is evident is that there will be efforts to replicate the highly lucrative tobacco experience and that the attorneys' fees from that litigation will finance these efforts. The failure of the tobacco cases to be played out in court with a definitive legal resolution consequently has left the legal status of such suits murky.

The regulation-by-litigation approach also has led to the award of the largest attorneys' fees in history. Lawyers involved in the case have become billionaires, and some lawyers who did very little or were only tangentially involved became multimillionaires. What is striking about these amounts is not only their record-setting magnitude, but the fact that they were not linked in any way to the amount of effort or the probability of the suit's success.

The nature of the legal fee arrangements also calls for aggressive reform. Why can't such litigation be handled in-house? If it is necessary to use counsel other than those who are in-house, there should be a competitive and open bidding process for this effort. If private attorneys are needed, they should be compensated fairly for their time. Public disclosure of these arrangements before the litigation should be mandatory to prevent abuses such as rewarding former campaign supporters or friends with lucrative sweetheart deals. Payment of the attorneys can be through hourly billings or a contingency fee approach in which there is a cap to avoid the windfall gains that were reaped in the tobacco litigation.

Those who will ultimately pay for the cost of these deals will be the citizenry at large. Separating the legal fees from the payout disguises their effect and hides it from public view. However, the economic reality is that the larger the share that goes to lawyers, the smaller will be the share that will benefit the citizens. Should states choose to continue to pursue regulation through litigation and bypass the legitimate governmental processes to regulate and tax products, the legal arrangements for such litigation should at least comply with minimal ethical standards.

For decades the main thrust of governmental policy has been informational in character. In all likelihood, warnings will continue to have a prominent role so long as cigarettes remain a legally marketed product. Information can potentially alter people's choices on a decentralized basis by providing them with a sounder basis for decision. However, current tobacco education efforts have gone astray from this original education mandate. Unlike the on-product warnings, many of these initiatives are not designed to inform consumers, but simply to smear the tobacco industry. Thus, they are not tobacco education efforts so much as they are antitobacco ads. However, my past work, as well as that in the broader literature on hazard warnings, indicates that to be successful, any warnings or informational policy must provide new information in a convincing manner. There is broad awareness among the smoking population of the risks involved with smoking itself, and there is considerable overestimation of the hazards posed by environmental tobacco smoke. What is needed is an informational effort that focuses on the shortcomings in information rather than on what consumers already know.

It is for this reason that I propose that we target our informational efforts at providing comparative risk information. What are the different risks posed by different types of cigarettes? If more underlying science is needed to obtain better information on these risks, that can be financed through excise taxes on cigarettes. Through a legislative expansion of the FDA's authority over cigarettes, that agency could monitor and administrate all such safety testing. To date, governmental policy has failed to exploit the powerful forces of the market to the extent that is feasible. The most overwhelming change in cigarette consumption over the past half century has been the dramatic drop in the tar levels of cigarettes, as consumers have sought to consume cigarettes that pose lower risks to their health. The government has at times banned the dissemination of tar and nicotine information, discouraged the provision of such information, and belittled industry attempts to develop safer cigarettes such as the Premier cigarette that represented a landmark safety breakthrough.

Rather than adopting an anticigarette stance, the government should focus its policy on promoting the welfare of its citizens. By enabling smokers to choose safer cigarettes that are more in line with their risk preferences, government policy will promote consumer welfare and individual health. Indeed, as society becomes more affluent, we will value individual health relatively more than we do now, and, as a consequence, cigarette-smoking rates will continue to decline. Providing risk information and fostering market competition in the development of safe cigarettes will accelerate this decline and promote individual health, while at the same time respecting individual choice.

NOTES

Chapter One

1. Sir Walter Raleigh engaged in a heated exchange with the King of England on the dangers of tobacco, and in 1642 Pope Urban II threatened smokers with excommunication. Tate (1989) provides a historical overview of U.S. smoking knowledge and policies. Even in the nineteenth century there was a strong antismoking effort in the United States.

2. Regulation of smoking behavior before people become adults is not, however, an intrusive form of paternalism. Many states have long imposed age restrictions on smoking, and these are now national in character.

3. In the 2001 case of *Richard Boeken v. Philip Morris, International House of Pancakes,* Case No. 226593 Superior Court of the State of California for the County of Los Angeles, the complaint filed March 16, 2000, stated, in allegation 71, "they engaged in 'scorched earth' litigation tactics." Presumably, however, both plaintiffs and defendants make decisions intended to increase their chance of winning the case and reducing litigation costs. Because tobacco companies face a myriad of such suits, their incentives are enhanced.

4. Charles W. Wolfram, "What Will the Tobacco Fees Set in Motion?" *National Law Journal,* December 23, 1998–January 4, 1999, p. A25, notes the $8.2 billion in fees for three states with separate settlements: Florida, Mississippi, and Texas. Estimates of fees for the forty-six states participating in the global settlement range from $10 billion to $30 billion. See Barry Meyer, "The Spoils of Tobacco Wars," *New York Times,* December 23, 1998, p. C1.

5. U.S. Chamber of Commerce press release, March 14, 2001, "Chamber Targets Excessive Legal Fees: Files 21 FOIA Requests on Tobacco Settlements."

6. "Rout of the New Evil Empire," *The Economist,* November 6, 1999, p. 30.

7. John Gibeant, "Getting Burned," *ABA Journal,* September 1998, pp. 42–51. Florida's Governor Lawton Chiles is being quoted. When asked how his private attorneys waging the state's tobacco suit were hired, his response was "I don't care."

8. David E. Rosenbaum, "Everyone Wants to Do Something about Tobacco, but Few Agree on What," *New York Times,* March 11, 1998, p. A14.

9. While the cover headline was "Lawyers from Hell," the article had a somewhat different title. See Joseph Nocera, "Fatal Litigation," *Fortune,* October 16, 1995, pp. 60–82. I was deposed by attorneys from O'Quinn's firm in the claim filed by the state of Texas against the tobacco industry.

10. One of these suits involving Daniel Becnel Jr. was *William Barnes et al. v. The American Tobacco Company, Inc., et al.* (U.S. District Court for the Eastern District of Pennsylvania, Civil Action No. 96CV-5903). This class action for medical monitoring damages in Pennsylvania was dismissed.

11. Although Dickie Scruggs reaped $1.2 billion in legal fees for his law firm, his personal take has been estimated as $400 million. See Adam Cohen, "Are Lawyers Running America?" *Time*, July 17, 2000, pp. 22–27.

12. "Killer Lawyers," *Forbes*, May 14, 2001, pp. 128–45.

13. For a description of Johnnie Cochran's class action, see Gordon Fairclough, "Tobacco Makers Face Suit Alleging Ads Targeted Children," *Wall Street Journal*, May 24, 2001, p. B14.

14. Schwartz (1999, 2000) examines many of the legal issues underlying such prospective litigation.

15. This discussion is based on the following sources: "Judge Halves Henley Damages to $25.6 Million," *Mealey's Litigation Report: Tobacco*, vol. 12, no. 24 (April 15, 1999); "PM Appeal Brief Attacks $25 Million Punitive Award in CA Suit," *Tobacco Industry Litigation Reporter*, vol. 15, no. 2 (December 27, 1999), p. 8; "California Lung Cancer Case Goes to Trial," *Greensboro News and Record*, January 13, 2000, p. B8; "Nation in Brief," *Atlanta Constitution*, February 10, 1999, p. 10A; and Bruce Frankel, Lyndon Stambler, and Ron Arias, "Facing Death, Patricia Henley Wins a Ground Breaking Judgment against the Tobacco Company—$51 Million," *People*, April 12, 1999, p. 97.

16. See Schwartz 1999, 559, for discussion of the stock market effects. Litigation risks also depressed the value of cigarette industry stocks by billions of dollars, though by far less than the actual settlement value. See Bulow and Klemperer 1998, 335, for the press comments on market valuations. Evans, Ringel, and Stech (1999) provide a series of thorough empirical tests of the stock market effects of a variety of salient litigation events.

17. See Sunstein, Kahneman, and Schkade 1998.

18. The case was *Dawn Apostolou, Administratrix of the Estate of Bonnie Apostolou v. The American Tobacco Company, et al.* (Supreme Court of the State of New York, Kings County, Index No. 34734/00).

19. Statements below are based on the deposition of Richard Boeken, December 18–19, 2000, in *Richard Boeken v. Philip Morris* (Superior Court of the Sate of California for the City of Los Angeles, Case No. 226593).

20. See James Sterngold, "A Jury Awards a Smoker with Lung Cancer $3 Billion from Philip Morris," *New York Times*, June 7, 2001, p. A14; Robert Jablon, "Jury Gives Lifelong Smoker $3B," Associated Press, June 7, 2001; Tom Vanden Brook, "Jury Orders Philip Morris to Pay Record $3B to Ill Smoker," *USA Today*, June 7, 2001, p. 5A.

21. See Final Judgment and Amended Omnibus Order, *Howard A. Engle, M.D., et al., Plaintiffs, v. R. J. Reynolds Tobacco, et al., Defendants* (Circuit Court of the Eleventh Judicial District, Dade County, Florida, Case No. 94-08 273 CA-22). Also see "Florida Judge Enters Judgment in Engle, Allows $145 Billion Punitive Damages Award," Bureau of National Affairs, *Product Liability*, vol. 28, no. 44 (November 13, 2000), pp. 1022–24. For discussion of the cigarette industry verdict, see Marc Kaufman, "Tobacco Suit Award: $145 Billion; FLA Jury Hands Industry Major Setback," *Washington Post*, July 15, 2000, p. A1.

22. Philip Morris contributed an additional $1.2 billion that will be returned to the company if its appeal is successful. See Gordon Fairclough, "Buying 'Insurance,' Tobacco Firms Agree to Pay $709 Million into Escrow Account," *Wall Street Journal*, May 8, 2001, p. A3. Also see "Florida Ruling Delays Payments to Smokers, Pending Appeals," *New York Times*, May 8, 2001, p. A16.

23. These anchoring effects are analogous to those found by Hastie, Schkade, and Payne (1999).

24. See Andrew Pollack, "$4.9 Billion Jury Verdict in G.M. Fuel Tank Case: Penalty Highlights Cracks in Legal System," *New York Times*, July 10, 1999, p. A7, and Ann W.

O'Neill et al., "G.M. Ordered to Pay $4.9 Billion in Crash Verdict Liability," *Los Angeles Times*, July 10, 1999, p. A1.

25. See Kessler 2001, 393, for a very brief sketch of his radical proposal.

Chapter Two

1. The "Proposed Resolution" was released "for settlement discussion purposes only, 6/20/97 3:00 p.m." The full text appears in Fox, Lightwood, and Glantz 1999, app. F, p. A-46.

2. See Schwartz 2000 for additional and broader discussion of these issues.

3. Schwartz (2000) provides a review of the pertinent cases.

4. See *State v. Philip Morris, Inc.* (577 N.W. 2d 401 [Iowa 1998]).

5. Matthew Cooper, "Tolls on Tobacco Road," *Newsweek*, June 22, 1998, p. 27.

6. Barry Meier, "First Brother-in-Law Has Tobacco Talks Role," *New York Times*, April 23, 1997, p. 21.

7. The shifting of the tax to smokers is a consequence of the respective elasticities of supply and demand for cigarettes. The long-run supply elasticity for tobacco products is very high.

8. Supreme Court of the United States, *Food and Drug Administration et al. v. Brown and Williamson Tobacco Corporation et al.*, certiorari to the United States Court of Appeals for the Fourth Circuit, no. 98-1152; argued December 1, 1999; decided March 21, 2000.

9. See Merrill 1998 and Sunstein 1998 for opposing viewpoints on this litigation.

10. See Viscusi and Magat 1987 and Magat and Viscusi 1992 for examples of this research.

11. Adler and Pittle (1984) provide such a critical assessment.

12. My own deposition for the state of Florida case took place after it was clear that there would be some form of negotiated settlement.

13. PR Newswire Association, Inc., December 11, 1998, "Tobacco Fee Arbitration Panel Announces First Decisions," p. 9, accessed from Lexis-Nexis.

14. See Susan Page and Jessica Lee, "Clinton Wants a $1.50 a Pack Cigarette Hike," *USA Today*, September 17, 1997, p. 84.

15. See Jeffrey Taylor, "Clinton Plans about Tobacco Dismay States," *Wall Street Journal*, January 9, 1998, p. A18.

16. See Barry Meier, "Tobacco Bill Being Offered by Kennedy," *New York Times*, November 10, 1997, p. 20.

17. See David Greising, Susan Garland, and Richard Dunham, "Now Big Tobacco Is Eager to Please," *Business Week*, February 16, 1998, p. 34.

18. See Taylor, "Clinton Plans."

19. Jackie Calmes and David Rogers, "Clinton's Tobacco-Based Budget Puts GOP in Hot Spot," *Wall Street Journal*, January 16, 1998, p. A16.

20. Ibid.

21. Chris Black, "Tobacco Industry Shifts on Nicotine," *Boston Globe*, January 30, 1998, p. A8.

22. "Senators Jockey on Tobacco Agreement," *New York Times*, February 1998, p. A20.

23. Greising, Garland, and Dunham, "Now Big Tobacco Is Eager to Please."

24. The McCain bill had the short title, as introduced, Universal Tobacco Settlement Act (S1415, 105th Congress, 1st Session in the Senate of the United States).

25. Jeffrey Taylor, "RJR's Chief Says Tobacco Deal Is Dead," *Wall Street Journal*, April 9, 1998, p. 83.

26. "McCain Readies New Legislation for Markup; Bill Will Lead to Bankruptcies, Industry Says," *BNA Product Liability Daily*, March 27, 1998, pp. 11–12.

27. Saundra Torry and Ceci Connolly, "Panel's Tobacco Struggle Was Only Round One Senators Warn," *Washington Post*, April 4, 1998, p. A4.

28. "Votes In Congress," *Washington Post*, April 5, 1998, p. A6.

29. "Commerce Committee Passes $506 Billion Tobacco Bill Opposed by Industry," *Mealey's Litigation Report: Tobacco*, vol. 11, no. 23 (April 2, 1998).

30. John Schwartz, "Tobacco Firms Say They'd Rather Fight," *Washington Post*, April 9, 1998, p. A1.

31. David E. Rosenbaum "Cigarette Makers Quit Negotiations on Tobacco Bill," *New York Times*, April 9, 1998, p. A1.

32. Torry and Connolly, "Only Round One."

33. Alison Mitchell, "For Tobacco, A Big Gamble," *New York Times*, April 10, 1998, p. A1.

34. John Schwartz, "GOP Panel Disputes Tobacco Bill's Price," *Washington Post*, May 11, 1998, p. A4.

35. "Significant Events in Fight against Tobacco," *Seattle Times*, June 18, 1998, p. A22.

36. "Senate Kills Tobacco Legislation; Democrats Say Fight Will Continue," *BNA Product Liability Daily*, June 19, 1998, pp. 15–16.

37. Helen Dewar, "McCain Winning by Losing? GOP Love-Him-Or-Hate-Him Senator Keeps Fighting Uphill," *Washington Post*, October 13, 1999, p. 86.

Chapter Three

1. This market has a strong highly elastic long-run supply, with demand elasticity from -0.4 to -1.0. The result is that consumers bear the brunt of the tax.

2. The dates of the state settlements were as follows: Mississippi. July 2, 1997; Florida, August 25, 1997; Texas, January 9, 1998; and Minnesota, May 8, 1998. Mississippi later received an additional $550 million after the Master Settlement Agreement was adopted. All settlement information can be found at www.library.ucsf.edu/tobacco/litigation.

3. It should also be noted that the Tobacco Institute served a general educational role as well by, for example, issuing its annual volume, *The Tax Burden on Tobacco*, which consists of over 200 pages of detailed data on cigarette sales, taxes, and prices. This report has served as a resource for numerous economic studies of the tobacco industry, including many estimates presented in this book. The final edition of the report bore an appropriately funereal black cover.

4. The statistics in this paragraph are from Philip Morris Companies, Inc., *1996 Year End Financial Fact Sheet*, spring 1997.

5. Several union cases have since either been thrown out or, in the case of the Ohio Ironworkers Union, led to a jury verdict in favor of the industry.

6. Insurance Information Institute 1998, 28.

7. Tobacco Institute 1998, 1.

8. John Bacon et al., "Jury Awards Ex-Smoker $51.5 Million in Tobacco Suit," *USA Today*, February 11, 1999, p. 3A.

9. "Judge Halves Henley Damages to $25.6 Million," *Mealey's Litigation Report: Tobacco*, vol. 12, no. 24 (April 15, 1999).

10. Barry Meier, "Punitive Damages Added in Smoking Verdict Case," *New York Times*, October 28, 2000, p. A14. What was especially noteworthy is that the plaintiff, Leslie Whitely, did not even begin smoking until after warnings were in place. Given the legal protections the law gave to cigarette companies in the post-1969 warnings era, this verdict was particularly surprising.

11. *Mealey's Litigation Report: Tobacco*, vol. 13, no. 2 (May 20, 1999); and Patrick McMa-

hon, "Family Wins Tobacco Suite: Jury Awards $81 Million in Death of Oregon Smoker," *USA Today*, March 31, 1999, p. 11A.

12. See "Report of the Task Force on Tobacco Litigation Submitted to Governor James and Attorney General Sessions by the Task Force on Tobacco Litigation Chaired by William Pryor, Jr., Deputy Attorney General," October 2, 1996, which is reprinted in the *Cumberland Law Review*, vol. 27, no. 2 (1997), pp. 575–652; see p. 583 of this article for the statement quoted. (Deputy Attorney General William Pryor was appointed attorney general to Alabama in 1997 to fill a vacancy and was elected to the post in 1998; most of the suit and all of the settlement negotiations occurred while he was attorney general.)

13. Master Settlement Agreement, November 1998, section 2, www.library.ucsf.edu / tobacco / litigation.

14. A useful summary of these statistics appears in Ann David, "Antitobacco Lawyers Get $775 Million: Panel in Massachusetts Case Signals End of Paydays in Excess of $1 Billion," *Wall Street Journal*, July 30, 1999, p. A3.

15. For these statistics and other data on the legal fees see Milo Geyelin, "Fat Legal Fees in Tobacco Cases Face Challenge," *Wall Street Journal*, June 16, 1999, pp. B1 and B6.

16. Alison Frankel, "After the Smoke Cleared," *American Lawyer*, January–February 1999, p. 48.

17. Mireya Navarro, "After Tobacco Settlement, Florida Battles Its Lawyers," *New York Times*, October 5, 1997, p. 10.

18. Saundra Torry, "Huge Fees for Anti-Tobacco Lawyers; Cigarette Firms Call Record $8 Billion Award 'Outrageous,'" *Washington Post*, December 12, 1998, p. A1.

19. Ibid.

20. Suein L. Hwang, "Plaintiffs' Attorneys for Texas Request $25 Billion Fee Award in Tobacco Case," *Wall Street Journal*, December 8, 1998, p. B11.

21. Richard Weekly, "Texans Deserve Better Answers on Tobacco Legal Fees," *Houston Chronicle*, January 14, 1999, p. A29.

22. Budget of the United States Government, Fiscal Year 2000, p. 941, 3USC 102.

23. Holman W. Jenkins, "Secret Lives of the Tobacco Arbitrators," *Wall Street Journal*, December 23, 1998, p. A15.

24. "Mass. Governor Moves to Cap Attorney Fees in Tobacco Cases," *Mealey's Litigation Report: Tobacco*, vol. 11, no. 21 (March 5, 1998).

25. Ibid., and Brian MacQuarrie, "Lawyers Await Tobacco Case Fees," *Boston Globe*, June 27, 1999, p. B1.

26. Frank Phillips and Brian MacQuarrie, "Law Firms Get $775 Million in Massachusetts Tobacco Suit," *Boston Globe*, July 30, 1999, p. A1.

27. Torry, "Huge Fees."

28. Tim Carvell, "Counsel for the Plaintiff," *Fortune*, September 29, 1997, p. 107.

29. Richard A. Oppel Jr., "Scrutinized, Lawyer Takes Far Lower Tobacco Fee," *New York Times*, May 7, 1999, p. A16; and "Texas Hearing Today on Houston Attorney's $260 Million Fee," *Mealey's Litigation Report: Tobacco*, vol. 13, no. 1 (May 6, 1999).

30. Mark Wolski, "Tobacco: Minnesota Court Upholds Attorneys' Fee, Sanctions Objectors to Pay Arrangement," *BNA Product Liability Daily*, November 25, 1998.

31. "Louisiana Outside Counsel Awarded $575 Million as Percentage of Settlement," *Mealey's Litigation Report: Tobacco*, vol. 13, no. 19 (February 3, 2000).

32. U.S. Chamber of Commerce Press Release, March 14, 2001, "Chamber Targets Excessive Legal Fees: Files 21 FOIA Requests on Tobacco Settlements."

33. See James Wooton, "'Litigation Bonds' Are a Risky Investment," *Wall Street Journal*, March 14, 2001, p. A22; and www.uschamber.com.

34. Leslie Wayne, "Trial Lawyers Pour Money into Democrats' Chests," *New York Times*, March 23, 2000, pp. A1 and A24.

35. Linda Kleindienst et al., "Squabbling Starts over Tobacco Cash," *Orlando Sentinel*, August 27, 1997, p. A1.

36. *USA Today*, May 19, 1999, pp. 15 and 16, and "Across the USA: News from Every State," p. 25A.

37. "Anti-Smoking Message Right on Target," *Detroit News*, June 24, 1999, p. A15.

38. National Conference of State Legislatures, reprinted in *USA Today*, "Spending the Settlement," November 22, 1999, p. 4A.

39. Richard Perez-Pena, "Pataki Wants Tobacco Cash to Ease Debt," *New York Times*, January 27, 1999, p. 1.

40. Barry Meier, "Tobacco Windfall Begins Tug-of-War among Lawmakers," *New York Times*, January 10, 1999, p. A1.

41. "The Local Review: Tobacco Funds to Be Used for Sidewalks, Parks," *Los Angeles Times Home Edition*, June 16, 1998, p. 4.

42. Rene Sanchez, "L.A. Eyes Tobacco Windfall to Pay Police Corruption Liabilities," *Washington Post*, February 18, 2000, p. A04.

43. Associated Press, "Impasse Ended, Bills Passed by Legislature," *New York Times*, June 15, 1999, p. B6.

44. Greg Moore, "Tobacco Companies to Sponsor State Drug Prevention Program," *Charleston Gazette*, June 3, 1999, p. 1A.

45. "Midwest Bond-Watch," *Bond Buyer*, May 12, 1999, p. 20.

46. Meier, "Tug-of-War among Lawmakers."

47. National Conference of State Legislatures, reprinted in *USA Today*, "Spending the Settlement," November 22, 1999, p. 4A.

48. Associated Press, "Tobacco Cash 'Free for All' Worries Some," Durham, NC, *Herald-Sun*, April 17, 1999, p. B3.

49. See Greg Winter, "State Officials Are Faulted on Anti-Tobacco Program," *New York Times*, January 11, 2001, p. A20.

50. Michael Janofsky, "Little of Settlement Money Is Spent on Tobacco Control," *New York Times*, August 11, 2001, p. A9.

51. Associated Press, "Letter: Fight Tobacco Suit," Durham, NC, *Herald-Sun*, August 8, 1999, p. A1.

52. "North Carolina Acts to Protect Tobacco Companies," *New York Times*, April 6, 2000, p. A20.

53. Wendy Koch, "Tobacco Firms Catch a Break for Time Being; Fla. Bill Ensures Industry Can Appeal Jury's Verdict," *USA Today*, May 8, 2000, p. 6A.

54. As the syndicated columnist Dave Barry observed regarding the federal suit:

> The Justice Department is charging that for many years, the tobacco industry, on purpose, did not tell people that cigarettes were bad for them. To cite just one blatant example, on numerous documented occasions during the 1950s and 1960s, R. J. Reynolds deliberately failed to run an advertising campaign using the slogan: Winston Tastes Good, and Gives You Lung Cancer!
>
> As a result of this type of clever deception, the Justice Department contends, smokers did not realize that cigarettes were hazardous. This is undoubtedly true of a certain type of smoker; namely, the type of smoker whose brain has been removed with a melon scoop. Everybody else has known for decades that cigarettes are unhealthy. I have known many smokers, and I have never heard one say: "You know why I stick these unnatural wads of chemically processed tobacco into my mouth, set them on fire and suck hot gases deep into my lungs? Because I sin-

cerely believe it poses no health risk!" ("Cold Turkey," *Washington Post Magazine,*
October 31, 1999, p. W28.)

55. Richard Oppel Jr., "Rhode Island Sues Makers of Lead Paint," *New York Times,* October 14, 1999, p. A18; David Segal and Amy Goldstein, "Tobacco Lawyers Aim at HMOs;
Slew of Suits Expected to Test Law Protecting Managed Care," *Washington Post,* October 1,
1999, p. E01; Barry Meier, "The World; It Just Looks Like a Smoking Gun," *New York Times,*
December 12, 1999, p. 6.

Chapter Four

1. Richard Perez-Pena, "Health Insurance Proposal Puts Pataki at Odds with Most Republican Leaders," *New York Times,* December 26, 1999, section 1, p. 40.

2. See Tate 1989.

3. These assessments are based on the calculations presented by Fullerton and Rogers
(1993, 74). Their measure of the severity of taxation is the ratio of taxes paid to the value of
gross purchases minus taxes paid. Based on this statistic, the implied tax rate nationwide
in 1984 for tobacco is 0.79, for alcohol it is 0.73, for gasoline it is 0.26, for utilities it is 0.04,
and for automobiles it is 0.06.

4. See the Centers for Disease Control's Web site for documentation of the 24 percent
figure: http://www.cdc.gov/tobacco/research_data/adults_prev/tab_3.htm.

5. These and other tax statistics reported in this paragraph are drawn from Tobacco Institute 1998.

6. This percentage of the cigarette tax share is drawn from p. 5 of Tobacco Institute
1998.

7. The statistics on regressivity discussed below are for 1990 and are reported in Viscusi 1995a, 58–60.

8. Federal Trade Commission, "'Tar,' Nicotine, and Carbon Monoxide of the Smoke of
1206 Varieties of Domestic Cigarettes for the Year 1994," July 15, 1997, FTC file #962 3099,
http://www.ftc.gov/os/1997/9707/.

9. U.S. Department of Health and Human Services 1989a, 665. See also the FTC Web
site, http://www.ftc.gov.

10. Evidence in support of the linearity of the dose-response relationship appears in International Agency for Research on Cancer 1985.

11. For discussion of the zero or minimal risks posed by low levels of carcinogens, see
Ames and Gold 1993.

12. Viscusi 1998b.

13. See Paul Meller, "New Effort at Curbing Tobacco Ads in Europe," *New York Times,*
May 31, 2001, p. W1.

14. See Manning et al. 1989, 1991.

15. See Hersch and Viscusi 1990, 1998, and Viscusi and Hersch 2001.

16. An identical assumption is made by Manning et al. (1991) and Gravelle and Zimmerman (1994).

17. Risks of low-birthweight babies due to smoking appear to be linearly related to
mother's nicotine level. See Elland et al. 1996. Evans, Ringel, and Stech (1999) provide a
detailed economic analysis of this potentially important cost component. Such costs include both internal costs to the smoker's family as well as external costs.

18. This table updates my estimates in Viscusi 1995a to 1995 data, as described in Viscusi 1999c. See those two articles for methodological details and data sources.

19. See Manning et al. 1991 for the base estimates.

20. An identical assumption is made by Manning et al. (1991) and by Gravelle and Zimmerman (1994).

21. Manning et al. 1989, 1991.

22. Tobacco Institute 1998.

23. Barendregt, Bonneux, and Vandermaas 1997.

24. See Arthur D. Little International, Inc., "Public Finance Balance of Smoking in the Czech Republic," Report to Philip Morris CR a.s., November 28, 2000.

25. See Laura Mansnerus, "Tobacco on Trial; Making a Case for Death," *New York Times*, May 5, 1996, section 4, Week in Review, p. 1. The attorney representing Philip Morris observed: "We didn't create this analysis, and we didn't go to court to assert it."

Chapter Five

1. Among the first states that filed these suits were Arizona, Connecticut, Florida, Hawaii, Iowa, Illinois, Indiana, Kansas, Louisiana, Maryland, Massachusetts, Minnesota, Mississippi, New Jersey, New York, Oklahoma, Texas, Utah, Washington, West Virginia, and Wisconsin. Several cities also filed suits as well, as did Puerto Rico, Guam, the Marshall Islands, and other government entities. Seven tribal suits and five taxpayer suits had also been filed by mid-1998. A detailed review appears in the *Seattle Times*, "Significant Events in Fight Against Tobacco," June 18, 1998, p. A22. See the Complaint for Damages and Injunctive and Declaratory Relief, *U.S.A. v. Philip Morris et al.*, Case Number 1:99 CVO 2496, 9/22/1999, p. 4.

2. Larry Rohter, "Florida Is Primed to Take Cigarette Makers to Court," *International Herald Tribune*, May 28, 1994.

3. "Maryland Senate Votes to Ease Tobacco Lawsuit Rules," *Liability Week*, JR Publishing, Inc., vol. 12, no. 15 (April 13, 1998).

4. Remarks by Judge Stephen Williams at U.S. Chamber of Commerce Conference on Liability and Regulation, Washington, D.C., February 23, 2000.

5. See *Memorandum in Support of the State's Motion for Ruling in Limine, or, Alternatively, for Partial Summary Judgement*, in re Moore, Attorney General ex Rel., State of Mississippi Tobacco Litigation (Cause No. 94-1429), August 11, 1995.

6. From Greg Gordon, "Government Seeks a Share of Tobacco Settlement Money; The Government Is Entitled to a Share of the Finds, Clinton Says, to Ensure It's Used Properly," *Minneapolis Star Tribune*, May 5, 1999, p. 10A; Senator Bob Graham of Florida characterized the federal intrusion as that of "a parent" helping them spend the money.

7. Not all states' estimates are subject to this error. The economists performing the estimates for Massachusetts did this calculation correctly, recognizing the shorter life expectancy. See Cutler, Epstein, et al. 2000.

8. The State of Minnesota, State of Minnesota Court, County of Ramsey, Second Judicial District, Second Amendment Complaint, Court File No. C1-94-8565.

9. The details discussed below are based on the Complaint for Damages and Injunctive and Declaratory Relief, *U.S.A. v. Philip Morris et al.*, September 22, 1999 (hereafter federal complaint).

10. Ibid.

11. See page 4 of the federal complaint.

12. See Racketeering Act No. 36 in the federal complaint.

13. This advertisement is Racketeering Act No. 39 in the federal complaint.

14. This text is Racketeering Act No. 37 in the federal complaint.

15. This is Racketeering Act No. 47 in the federal complaint.

16. This is Racketeering Act No. 48 in the federal complaint.

17. See Racketeering Act No. 1 cited in the federal complaint.

18. State of Mississippi, *Memorandum,* pp. 3, 21, 23.

19. Barry Meier, "The World; It Just Looks Like a Smoking Gun," *New York Times*, December 12, 1999, p. 6.

20. David Segal and Amy Goldstein, "Tobacco Lawyers Aim at HMOs; Slew of Suits Expected to Test Law Protecting Managed Care," *Washington Post*, October 1, 1999, p. E01.

21. It should be emphasized, however, that my tally will consider only insurance, pension costs, tax consequences, fires, and related factors. There may be broader economic consequences as well. These are discussed in Tollison and Wagner 1988.

22. State of Mississippi *Memorandum,* p. 2.

23. The estimates in the third section update the results reported in Manning et al. 1989, 1991.

24. In particular, the factors for each state include Medicaid financing rates, the percent of residents receiving Medicaid, medical care costs per recipient, costs of uncompensated community hospital care, state population levels, the number of state employees and their earnings, the percent of the population in nursing homes, state and federal pension costs, earnings tax rates, and a variety of other influences. See Viscusi 1995a, 1999c, for more details on the calculations.

25. For a contrasting view suggesting that the settlement was efficiency-enhancing, see Cutler, Gruber, et al. 2000.

26. See Viscusi 1995a.

27. This state excise tax for 1995 is weighted by the number of packs and is not a simple average.

28. My testimony on cost matters focused only on the importance of taking a lifetime cost approach and assessing what the medical costs would have been but for the alleged wrongful conduct. I never presented any of my cost estimates in litigation.

Chapter Six

1. The Veterans Administration Medical Center in Kentucky instituted a total smoking ban, as did other hospitals and medical facilities. An estimated 75 percent of the VA's patients were smokers, in part because of the demographic profile of the patient mix and the fact that Kentucky is a major tobacco stronghold. Many patients weathered rain and snow in order to smoke.

2. "Nation's Toughest Smoking Ban Is Adopted," *New York Times*, December 13, 2000, p. A22.

3. The Gallup poll statistics are from Viscusi 1992b.

4. For a more comprehensive review of the differences in the risks, see Huber, Brockie, and Mahajan 1993.

5. The California Environmental Protection Agency (1997) recently reviewed the health effects of ETS as well, but these estimates draw upon the EPA estimates for lung cancer and the Steenland estimates for heart disease, as discussed below.

6. A 95 percent confidence level one-tailed test is equivalent to a 90 percent confidence level two-tailed test. The appropriate confidence level to be applied can be a matter of statistical debate depending on one's theoretical assumptions.

7. U.S. Environmental Protection Agency 1992.

8. *Flue-cured Tobacco Cooperative Stabilization Corp., the Council for Burley Tobacco, Inc., Universal Leaf Tobacco Company, Inc., Philip Morris, Inc., R. J. Reynolds Tobacco Co., and Gallins Vending Co. v. United States Environmental Protection Agency, and Carol Browner, Administrator, Environmental Protection Agency, Defendants.* 6:93CV00370. United States District Court for the

middle District of North Carolina, Winston-Salem Division. 4F. Supp. 2d 435; 1998 U.S. Dist. LEXIS 10986; 1998 OSHD (CCH) P31,614; 28 ELR 21445. July 17, 1998, Decided. July 17, 1998, Filed. Citations and footnotes omitted.

9. See *Flue-Cured Tobacco Cooperative Stabilization Corp. v. U.S. Environmental Protection Agency, et al.*, 4 F. Supp. 2d 435 (M.D.N.C. 1998) at 461–62.

10. Rather than employ multivariate controls, each study did, however, attempt to have a control group or utilize a cohort study approach.

11. This example is drawn from Robert J. Barro, "Send Regulations Up in Smoke," *Wall Street Journal*, June 3, 1994.

12. See U.S. Environmental Protection Agency 1994, exhibit 7-1.

13. The EPA estimates appear on p. 12 of U.S. EPA 1994, and the OSHA estimates appear on p. 16011 of the *Federal Register*, April 5, 1994. The OSHA figures pertain to the average number of lung cancers over the next 45 years, whereas the EPA estimates pertain to the current risk estimates.

14. To the extent that the improvements in tar are achieved through devices such as filters rather than changes in the composition of cigarettes, there would then be less than a 100 percent effect. If, however, the benefits of tar reduction are diminished for smokers who inhale low tar cigarettes more deeply, then there would be a comparable effect for ETS.

15. See the Centers for Disease Control, National Center for Environmental Health, "National Report on Human Exposure to Environmental Chemicals," March 21, 2001 (report available at www.cdc.gov/nceh/dls). That smoking bans do in fact reduce overall levels of smoking is documented in Evans, Farrelly, and Montgomery 1999.

16. Panel 2 in table 9 is not adjusted, since OSHA did not indicate its smoking restriction assumption underlying the risk estimates.

17. In particular, Steenland (1992) makes the following observations:

> While the lung cancer risk among never-smokers exposed to ETS is well established, a possible risk of heart disease due to ETS is more controversial (p. 94). . . . Environmental tobacco smoke is difficult to measure directly (p. 94). . . . The relative contribution of ETS exposure at work to total exposure is not well known (p. 94). . . . The principal weaknesses in the epidemiologic evidence to date have been the indirect methods of assessing exposure (via spousal smoking) and the lack of data on exposures to ETS outside the home (p. 95). . . . Also, there may be risk factors for heart disease, and it is difficult to control well for all of them. Another problem with the epidemiologic data is the seemingly large effect that ETS has on heart disease compared with the effect of mainstream smoking (p. 95). . . . They showed no excess of lung cancer, and cross-sectional smoking data revealed smoking was unlikely to explain the excess heart disease risk (p. 96). . . . A number of assumptions are involved in estimating the heart disease mortality due to ETS, adding an unfortunate level of uncertainty. The most important assumption is that the relative risks for ETS and heart disease, derived from the epidemiologic evidence, are reasonably accurate. The epidemiologic results may be questioned, given the inherent uncertainties of any epidemiologic study (p. 98). . . . Considerable uncertainty is involved in extrapolating from the epidemiologic data, which consider the relative risks for never-smokers living with smokers to estimating relative risks for those exposed to ETS (anywhere) vs. those truly not exposed (anywhere) (p. 98).

18. These data are drawn from the following three articles on risk beliefs in Spain: Antonanzas et al. 2000, Rovira et al. 2000, and Viscusi et al. 2000.

19. Ibid.

20. Ibid.

21. See Gallup Organization, Stanford University, and the University of Southern California 1999a.

22. *Industrial Union Department, AFL-CIO v. American Petroleum Institute,* 448 US 607 (1980).

23. See the Gallup Organization, "A Survey of California's Law for a Smoke Free Workplace (AB 13): Attitudes after the First Year of Implementation," March 1996.

24. Richard C. Paddock, "Non-Smoker Warning Signs Due Up Saturday," *Los Angeles Times,* March 31, 1989, pp. 3 and 26.

25. For empirical evidence see Viscusi 1988a, 1992b.

26. See Field Research Corporation, "A Survey of California Bar Patrons about Smoking Policies and Smoke-Free Bars," March 1998, tables 7 and 8.

27. See California Department of Health Services, Tobacco Control Section, *Catalog of Tobacco Education Materials,* spring-summer 1998. Also see Tobacco Education Clearinghouse of California, *1999 Catalogue of Tobacco Cessation Materials.*

28. A summary of the extensive efforts by a large number of California health departments and health organizations appears in Tobacco Education Clearinghouse of California, *Tobacco Education Resource Directory, A Description of Projects Funded by the California Department of Health Services,* 1992–1993 edition, among other sources.

29. See the California Department of Health Services, Tobacco Control Section, "What Californians Believe about Environmental Tobacco Smoke: A Summary of Findings," June 1996. Also see California Department of Health Services, Tobacco Control Section, "What Californians Believe about Environmental Tobacco Smoke A Summary of Findings," August 1995.

30. Gallup Organization, Stanford University, and the University of Southern California 1999a, 43, 50.

31. Ibid., 45.

32. Ibid.

33. Ibid., 50.

34. See *Norma R. Broin et al. v. Philip Morris, Inc., et al.,* No. 91-49738, Fla. Cir., Dade Co., 11th Dist.

35. For further background see "Dissident Flight Attendants Object to Secondhand Smoke Settlement," *Washington Post,* January 27, 1998, p. A7.

36. Ibid.

37. Ibid. Also see Milo Geyelin, "Airline Staffs Object to Deal in Smoke Case," *Wall Street Journal,* January 7, 1998, p. B9.

38. The settlement was affirmed by the Dade County circuit judge and by the Florida appellate court. See "Judge Rejects Opposition to Broin Settlement," *Mealey's Litigation Report: Tobacco,* vol. 11, no. 20, February 19, 1998; and "Court Affirms Settlement in Broin Class Action; Lets 8 Objectors Intervene," *Mealey's Litigation Report: Tobacco,* vol. 12, no. 23, April 1, 1997.

39. Otsuka et al. 2001.

Chapter Seven

1. *Federal Cigarette Labeling and Advertising Act of 1965,* Public Law 89-92, §4, 79 Stat. 282, 283 (amended 1970).

2. *Public Health Cigarette Smoking Act of 1969,* Public Law 91-222, §4, 84 Stat. 87-88 (effective July 1, 1970) (amended 1984).

3. *Comprehensive Smoking Education Act,* Public Law 98-474, §4, 98 Stat. 2200, 2201–02 (1984). Codified as 15 U.S.C. §1333 (a) (1) (1994).

4. These requirements were extended in 1959 by the Nematocide, Plant Regulator, Defoliant, and Descriant Amendment of 1959.

5. *Federal Register* 25, no. 59 (March 25, 1960), Title 21, Part 131, pp. 2516–24.

6. I discuss the details of this analysis in Viscusi 1992a.

7. The Alcoholic Beverage Labeling Act was passed in 1988. I testified before the U.S. Senate on this bill in 1988. The warnings initially proposed attempted to mimic the rotating cigarette warnings. However, because some draft warnings did not appear warranted, Congress instead chose to require the two most salient warnings to be on all containers rather than rotating the warnings.

8. For a listing of these reports see Viscusi 1992b, 29–30. Many also appear in the references in this book under U.S. Department of Health, Education, and Welfare and the U.S. Department of Health and Human Services.

9. Viscusi 1992b, 35–36.

10. This survey question U.S. Gallup 54-532 Q12a, administered from June 12, 1954, to June 17, 1954, is compiled in the Roper Center for Public Opinion Research database.

11. Statement of Surgeon General LeRoy Burney, "False and Misleading Advertising (Filter-Tip Cigarettes)," *Hearings of the U.S. House of Representatives, Legal and Monetary Affairs Subcommittee of the Committee on Government Operations*, 85th Cong., 1st sess., July 23, 1957, p. 139.

12. Gallup Poll, "Cigaret Smoking and Cancer," July 21, 1957.

13. More specifically, he observed: "More than three out of four adults questioned, or 77 per cent, said they had heard or read about the report, a phenomenal figure in polling annals." This excerpt is from the nationally syndicated article by George Gallup, director of the American Institute of Public Opinion, "Cigarettes Linked to Cancer? Public Thinks So," which appeared nationally on July 20, 1957, in the Syracuse, NY, *Evening Bulletin,* the Cleveland, OH, *Plain Dealer,* and other newspapers.

14. "Full Text of AMA Letter of Testimony to FTC," *Journal of the American Medical Association* 188 (1): 31 (April 6, 1964).

15. See keynote address by William H. Stewart, "Influencing Smoking Behavior," *World Conference on Smoking and Health*, sponsored by the National Interagency Council on Smoking and Health, September 1967 (New York: National Interagency Council on Smoking and Health), p. 119.

16. Nancy Sharp, "Is End Near for Smoking?" *Syracuse Herald-American*, November 3, 1968, p. 20.

17. Viscusi 1992b, 37. The full text of the ad is reproduced on p. 38.

18. Unfortunately, these filters also contained asbestos, which posed its own risks.

19. "Cigarette Health Scare: What Will the Trade Do?" *Business Week*, December 5, 1953, p. 60.

20. These Gallup poll results are documented in Viscusi 1992b, 49–50.

21. See the U.S. Bureau of Alcohol, Tobacco, and Firearms, *Final Report of the Research Study of Public Opinion Concerning Warning Labels on Containers of Alcoholic Beverages*, December 1988, vol. 1, table 2.

22. Gaba and Viscusi 1998.

23. For a fuller critique see Levy and Marimont 1998.

24. The entire text of the 1985 survey appears in Viscusi 1992b, app. A, 153–57.

25. Note that the character of what respondents were told was symmetric and should not produce any bias (e.g., "Have you heard . . . Cigarette smoking is dangerous to a person's health . . . Cigarette smoking is not bad for a person's health," etc.).

26. See Viscusi and Zeckhauser 2000.

27. These calculations are described in Viscusi 1992b, 69–70, 85.

28. See Viscusi and Magat 1987 and Magat and Viscusi 1992.

29. See, for example, Cosmides and Tooby 1996 for exploration of these issues.

30. Viscusi 1992b, 76–80.

31. Ibid., 77.

32. As in the case of the national survey undertaken in 1985, the survey research firm used for the survey was Audits and Surveys, located in New York.

33. My estimates take into account the number of smoking-related deaths cited by the U.S. surgeon general and the size of the U.S. smoking population. See Viscusi 1992b. Estimates for heavy smokers are within my estimated risk range. The 1989 report of the U.S. surgeon general (U.S. Department of Health and Human Services 1989a, 206) indicated that one out of three heavy smokers would die prematurely before the age of eighty-five because of smoking-related diseases. Researchers at the National Cancer Institute found that "as many as one-third of heavy smokers age 35 will die before age 85 of diseases caused by their smoking." See Mattson, Pollack, and Cullen 1987, 425. Heavy smokers are consequently at the upper end of my estimated mortality range, which is quite consistent with my findings.

34. See Malarcher et al. 2000 for the 19 percent estimate and discussion of the flaws in the surgeon general's estimates.

35. See Sterling et al. 1993 for the 40 percent estimate.

36. Estimates of smoking mortality rates as high as half have been found in a study of British doctors, but this study did not include multivariate controls. Somewhat curiously, the authors' article on the smoking risks of doctors reported in Doll et al. 1994b is followed immediately by the article on the hazards of the drinking habits of these doctors in Doll et al. 1994a, where it is reported that many doctors consumed over twenty-one drinks per week. Yet, the independent influence of these and other risk factors is never examined.

37. For example, see Viscusi 1992b, 69, table 4-2 for comparable 1985 data.

38. Viscusi 1992b, 80.

39. The recent report by the Institute of Medicine (2001, 1–2) cited results indicating a 6.6 year average reduction in life expectancy for smokers. An earlier report by the U.S. surgeon general (U.S. Department of Health and Human Services 1989a, 206) indicated that a-pack-a-day smokers at age thirty shorten their lives by six to eight years.

40. These figures, discussed above, are from Viscusi 1992b.

41. Slovic 1998, 2000.

42. See Viscusi 1992b.

43. In his deposition in the Joe Camel litigation, Slovic answered the question as follows: "Q. How much, in fact, is a little bit of harm? A. I don't have the answer to that. You have to ask a physiologist who studies effects of smoking." Deposition of Paul Slovic in Re: RJ Reynolds 8-16-98 cr. 69876 United States of America before the Federal Trade Commission in the Matter of Docket Number 9285: R. J. Reynolds Tobacco Company, a corporation, Washington, D.C.; Friday, August 16, 1998, p. 236.

44. Schoenbaum 1997.

45. Comparison of the assessed life expectancy results in Hamermesh and Hamermesh 1983 with my findings based on questions that provide normal life expectancy information suggests that this omission alone could account for apparent underestimation of the risk. In Viscusi 1992b I develop this comparison in further detail.

46. There are other serious shortcomings of the Schoenbaum 1997 tests as well. For example, his true survival probability reference point is substantially miscalculated due to a mathematical error. See Viscusi and Hakes (forthcoming) for a detailed review.

47. Deposition of Jon Hanson, October 13, 1998, *Superior Court of the State of Washington for King County vs. American Tobacco Co., Inc. et al.*, no. 96-2-15056-8SEA, p. 106.

48. Question wording varied a bit by year. The 1990 survey on July 18 (Question I.D.: U.S. Gallup 071890.R08) used the wording "Do you think smoking is or is not harmful to your health?" However, the survey in June 1987 (see GALLUP.87LUNG.R3) asked: "Is smoking harmful to your health?" The 1993 results are from The Gallup Organization report, "Smoking Prevalence, Beliefs, and Activities by Gender and Other Demographic Indicators," prepared by Rosita Thomas and Max Larsen, May 1993.

49. Viscusi 1992b, 100.

50. Rethans 1979.

51. Weinstein 1987.

52. Viscusi and Magat 1987.

53. Ayanian and Cleary 1999.

54. *International Brotherhood of Teamsters, Local 734 Health and Welfare Fund v. Philip Morris, Inc.*, 196 F. 3d 818 (7th Cir. 1999).

55. Many of the comparative questions offered the respondent five different gradations of responses rather than three, such as much better, somewhat better, about the same, somewhat worse, or much worse. Even with five gradations rather than three, 37 percent of the sample assessed their health as being about the same as others, and 42 percent described their relative income when growing up as the same as average.

56. Benthin et al. 1993.

57. U.S. Department of Health, Education, and Welfare 1964.

58. U.S. Department of Health and Human Services 1988.

59. Barry Meier, "Philip Morris Official Calls Nicotine a Drug, But Not as Defined in Federal Law," *New York Times*, March 3, 2000, p. A17.

60. According to the surgeon general (U.S. Department of Health and Human Services 1988, p. iv):

> The central element among all forms of drug addiction is that the user's behavior is largely controlled by a psychoactive substance (i.e., a substance that produces transient alterations in mood that are primarily mediated by effects in the brain). There is often compulsive use of the drug despite damage to the individual or to society, and drug-seeking behavior can take precedence over other important priorities. The drug is "reinforcing"—that is, the pharmacologic activity of the drug is sufficiently rewarding to maintain self-administration. "Tolerance" is another aspect of drug addiction whereby a given dose of a drug produces less effect or increasing doses are required to achieve a specified intensity of response. Physical dependence on the drug can also occur, and is characterized by a withdrawal syndrome that usually accompanies drug abstinence. After cessation of drug use, there is a strong tendency to relapse.

61. The decline in nicotine levels of cigarettes is documented on p. 88 of the U.S. Department of Health and Human Services 1989a.

62. Becker, Grossman, and Murphy 1996.

63. See Hersch 1998 for further discussion of smoking beliefs of teenagers and the population more generally.

64. See U.S. Department of Health and Human Services 1990.

65. Centers for Disease Control and Prevention, Tobacco Information and Prevention Source, "Current Smoking Status among Adults, 1965–1995," at http://www.cdc.gov/tobacco/research_data/adults_prev/tab_3.htm.

66. See Hersch and Viscusi 1990; Hersch and Pickton 1995; Hersch and Viscusi 1998; and Viscusi and Hersch 2001.

67. Viscusi and Chesson 2000.

68. This unresponsiveness is not, however, an assumption or a property of the rational addiction models.

69. For a detailed review, see Viscusi 1992b, 101–9, and Hersch 2000.

70. See Lewit, Coate, and Grossman 1981 and Wasserman et al. 1991.

71. The classic compendium of demand elasticities is Houthakker and Taylor 1970, table 4.2.

72. Longo et al. 1996; Toni Thomas, "Readers Forum," *Courier Journal*, February 1, 1991, p. 10A.

73. See Evans, Farrelly, and Montgomery 1999 for a thorough econometric examination of workplace bans. The U.S. Department of Health and Human Services (2000) provides a detailed review of the effects of smoking restrictions on smoking behavior.

74. See note 65 above.

75. Centers for Disease Control, Office on Smoking and Health, National Center for Chronic Disease Prevention and Health Promotion, "Cigarette Smoking among Adults—United States, 1995," *Morbidity and Mortality Weekly Report* 46 (51): 1217–20 (December 26, 1997).

76. In Viscusi 1979, I present evidence on workers' intentions to quit.

77. Kozlowski, Herman, and Frecker 1980.

78. For details, see the COMMIT Research Group 1995a, 1995b.

79. The authors report univariate results for intervention status and multivariate results for the effect of all variables other than intervention status, which was included in the estimation but not reported. Upon replicating the analysis, I found that the smoking intervention variable did not have a significant effect. Even with this attempt to hide what were clearly disappointing results, the net implications of the findings they chose to present failed to indicate a significant beneficial effect.

Chapter Eight

1. One exception is the detailed analysis of youth smoking trends and price effects which appears in Gruber 2000.

2. Monitoring the Future (2000), Trends on Cigarette Smoking, table 1; accessed at http://monitoringthefuture.org/data/00data.html#2000data-cigs; Substance Abuse and Mental Health Services Administration (SAMHSA) (1997), Office of Applied Studies, 1997 National Household Survey on Drug Abuse, table 2.8: Trends in Percentage Reporting Alcohol and Tobacco Use in Past Month by Age Group, 1979–1997; SAMHSA (1999), Office of Applied Studies, 1999 National Household Survey on Drug Abuse, table 4.2: Percentage Reporting Past Month Use of Illicit Drugs, Alcohol, and Tobacco among Persons Aged 12 to 17: 1994–1999 PAPI. SAMHSA studies accessed at www.samhsa.gov/oas.

3. Monitoring the Future (2000), loc. cit.

4. See Hersch 1998 for discussion of state regulations.

5. Ibid., 1150.

6. See Gallup Organization, Stanford University, and the University of Southern California 1999b.

7. See Stuart Elliot, "Joe Camel, A Giant in Tobacco Marketing Is Dead at 23," *New York Times*, July 11, 1997, p. D1.

8. Ibid.

9. David Segal, "Joe Camel Fired: Cigarette Ads Were Accused of Luring Youth," *Washington Post*, July 11, 1997, A1.

10. Statement of Senator Edward M. Kennedy on the death of Joe Camel (July 11, 1997) http://www.senate.gov/~kennedy/statements/970711camelrip.html/.

11. See Fischer et al. 1991.

12. Data for 1993 are from the industry's survey conducted by Audits and Surveys.

13. Data for 1993 are from Audits and Surveys, while data for 1998 are from the 1998 Monitoring the Future survey (see http://monitoringthefuture.org/data/cigbrands.html).

14. The results by Slovic (2001), discussed in chapter 7, found an even greater relative overestimation of lung cancer risks by youths than I did in the 1985 survey data.

15. Monitoring the Future (2000), Drugs and Alcohol, Trends in Attitudes, table 9, at http://monitoringthefuture.org/data/00data/htm#2000data-drugs.

16. See U.S. Department of Health and Human Services, Youth and Tobacco, *Preventing Tobacco Use among Young People, A Report of the Surgeon General* (Rockville, MD: U.S. Department of Health and Human Services, 1994), table 18, p. 83.

17. See, in particular, Benthin, Slovic, and Severson 1993.

18. See Clayton, Scutchfield, and Wyatt 2000 and Peterson et al. 2000.

19. A survey of these studies appears in Viscusi 1992b, 102–5.

20. The first such estimate indicating youth responsiveness is from Lewit, Coate, and Grossman 1981.

21. See Gruber and Zinman 2000.

22. One study that questions whether there is any differential responsiveness of youths to prices is that by Wasserman et al. 1991.

23. Detailed evidence using both quantity and discrete choice information appears in research by Hersch (2000). The price elasticity efforts differ by gender and family income level, and for some groups there is no sensitivity. I have also found a failure of tax rates or price differences across states to affect the probability of smoking, using the 1997 national survey data discussed earlier in chapter 7.

24. See DiFranza and Tye 1990.

25. See Cummings, Pechacek, and Shopland 1994.

26. See "Controversy Brewing over Budget Cuts Made to Florida's Youth Anti-Smoking Campaign," National Public Radio, *Morning Edition,* December 16, 1999.

27. See Mary Ellen Klas, "House Panel Moves to End Teen Smoking Effort," *Palm Beach Post*, March 16, 1999, p. 1A.

28. See David Cox, "Layoffs Hit Fight against Smoking; Budget Cuts Hurt Teens' Campaign," *Orlando Sentinel*, June 3, 1999, p. D1.

29. See V. Dion Haynes, "In California Anti-Cigarette Ads Designed to Scare," *Chicago Tribune*, April 7, 1997, p. 1.

30. Monitoring the Future (2000), Trends on Cigarette Smoking, table 4, http://monitoringthefuture.org/data/00data.html#2000data-cigs.

31. Carey Goldberg, "Study Details Smoking Fad among Youth," *New York Times*, September 17, 1999, p. A2.

Chapter Nine

1. In Code of Federal Regulations: 29 CFR 1910.23 (d) (1I-v).

2. 49 CFR 571.208 (54.1).

3. 16 CFR 1616.65 (3).

4. U.S. Department of Commerce, *Statistical Abstract of the United States* (Washington, DC: U.S. Government Printing Office, 1997), p. 145.

5. As the article by Joni Hersch (1998) indicates, even age restrictions on cigarette purchases may not be very effective.

6. The degree to which tar levels are correlated with the riskiness of cigarettes remains

a matter of dispute. Lower-tar cigarettes appear to reduce the lung cancer risks, but not many of the other hazards of smoking. See the report of the surgeon general, U.S. Department of Health and Human Services 1989a.

7. Laura Klepacki, "Low-Tar Brands 'Light' Up Cigarette Category," *Supermarket News*, January 28, 1991, p. 21: "Health warnings and antismoking campaigns have caused some smokers to cut back. But many, rather than quit, are switching to low- and very-low-tar cigarettes."

8. The "Tar Derby" is discussed in Viscusi 1992b, 39–40. For a more detailed discussion, see Calfee 1985, and Ringold and Calfee 1989.

9. Calfee 1985.

10. Ibid.

11. One possibility is that the surgeon general did not support low-tar cigarettes, see Viscusi 1992b, 40; and Calfee 1985, 45.

12. Ibid.

13. Best Value Brands have 13 mg tar, Players Brands have 23 mg of tar, and Commander Brands have 22 mg of tar. Source: Federal Trade Commission, "'Tar,' Nicotine, and Carbon Monoxide of the Smoke of 1294 Varieties of Domestic Cigarettes for the Year 1998," July 7, 2000, FTC file #992 3169, http://www.ftc.gov/opa/2000/07/t&n2000.htm.

14. One such possibility would be plain cigarette packaging in which color on packages and distinctive lettering would be replaced by "tombstone advertising" in which only the brand name was indicated in black and white.

15. The data discussed below are drawn from p. 314 of the report of the U.S. surgeon general, U.S. Department of Health and Human Services 1989a, with additional discussion appearing on p. 665.

16. See Viscusi 1992b; Mulholland 1991.

17. See Mulholland 1991.

18. The FTC has recently proposed analyzing cigarette smoke for tar and nicotine levels using a test that simulates intakes for those smokers who take more and deeper drags from their cigarettes. See "New Tobacco Advertising" (CNN-FN broadcast, September 10, 1997), available in LEXIS, NEWS library, CURNEWS File.

19. The FDA procedures for the testing of new pharmaceutical products are discussed in 21 CFR §§312, 1993. See, especially, §§312.21(a), 312.21(b), and 312.21(c).

20. Russo et al. 1986.

21. Federal Trade Commission, "'Tar,' Nicotine, and Carbon Monoxide of the Smoke of 1206 Varieties of Domestic Cigarettes for the Year 1994," July 15, 1997, http://www.ftc.gov/os/1997/9707/, FTC file #962 3099.

22. National Cancer Institute 1996:

> To find the tar levels a machine does the following:
> 1. Smoke cigarettes to a 23 mm. butt length, or to the length of the filter and overwrap plus 3 mm. if in excess of 23 mm.; 2. Base results on a test of 100 cigarettes per brand, or type; 3. Cigarettes to be tested will be selected on a random basis, as opposed to "weigh selection"; 4. Determine particulate matter on a "dry" basis employing the gas chromatograph method published by C. H. Sloan and B. J. Sublett in Tobacco Science 9, page 70, 1965, as modified by F. J. Schultz' and A. W. Spears' report published in Tobacco Vol. 162, No. 24, page 32, dated June 17, 1966, to determine the moisture content; 5. Determine and report the "tar" yield after subtracting moisture and alkaloids (as nicotine) from particulate matter; 6. Report "tar" yield to the nearest whole milligram and nicotine yield to the nearest 1/10 milligram (32 Fed. Reg. 11,178 (1967)).

The Cambridge Testing method is also used to measure the carbon monoxide and nicotine yield of cigarettes. The 1980 FTC announcement contained specifications regarding a new testing methodology to determine the carbon monoxide (CO) and nicotine yield of cigarettes. These specifications are the following:

1. Determine CO concentration using a 20-port sequential smoking machine described by H. C. Pillsbury and G. Merfeld at the 32nd Tobacco Chemists Research Conference, October 1978; 2. The concentration of CO will be reported as milligrams per cigarette; 3. The present method for "tar" and nicotine determination will be modified to use the method described in an article entitled, "Gas Chromatographic Determination of Nicotine Contained on Cambridge Filter Pads," by John R. Wagner, et al., as presented at the annual meeting of the Association of Official Analytical Chemists, October 1978 (45 Fed. Reg. 46,483 (1980)).

23. The FTC released a proposal in 1997 to change the way that the tar, nicotine, and carbon monoxide are measured by the above method. "FTC Proposes New Method for Testing Amounts of Tar, Nicotine and Carbon Monoxide in Cigarettes," press release September 9, 1997, http://www.ftc.gov/opa/1997/9709/.

24. National Cancer Institute 1996.

25. *Bureau of National Affairs Product Liability Daily,* "Tobacco: Massachusetts Proposes New Rules Requiring Makers to List Toxic Ingredients," September 11, 1998.

26. "1st Circuit Affirms Injunction against 1997 Mass. Law on Cigarette Ingredients," *Mealey's Litigation Report: Tobacco,* vol. 12, no. 14 (November 19, 1998). *Bureau of National Affairs Product Liability Daily,* September 11, 1999, p. 1.

27. Associated Press, "No Additives Does Not Mean Safer Cigarette," *Denver Rocky Mountain News,* March 5, 1999, p. 51A.

28. FTC File #9923025, press release March 3, 1999, p. 1, http://www.ftc.gov/opa/1999/9903/.

29. The specified insert described below appeared in the February 2000 issue of *Car and Driver* magazine.

30. Federal Trade Commission, "'Tar,' Nicotine, and Carbon Monoxide for 1994."

31. This ad text appeared in *Boston Magazine,* August 1999, p. 281. For more information, see www.bwtarnic.com.

32. For a detailed discussion of health, safety, and environmental regulations, see Viscusi 1992a, and Breyer 1993.

33. Joanne Lipman, "Tobacco Concerns Are Hopeful about 'De-nicotined,'" *Wall Street Journal,* March 28, 1991, p. B8.

34. AP Wire, "Coalition Wants 'De-Nic' Cigarettes Classified as a Drug," *Orlando Sentinel Tribune,* April 8, 1991, p. 43.

35. Barnaby Fecler, "A Safer Smoke or Just Another Smoke Screen?" *New York Times,* April 12, 1996.

36. Doug Levy and Melanie Wells, "RJR Retools Low-smoke Eclipse," *USA Today,* September 18, 1997, p. 2B.

37. The general properties of the Premier cigarette are discussed in Viscusi 1992b, 147–48, and are explored thoroughly in R. J. Reynolds Tobacco Company 1988.

38. Barry Meier, "False Starts and Failures Thwart Quest for Safe Cigarettes," *New York Times,* July 3, 1997, p. A16.

39. See Viscusi 1992b, 147–48.

40. See R. J. Reynolds Tobacco Company 1988.

41. For a detailed analysis of the risks associated with cigarettes, see ibid.

42. 21 CFR 101.14.

43. R. J. Reynolds, Premier warning label (1988).

44. Risks of tobacco smoke are particularly linked to the cancer hazards of smoking. The Premier cigarette would largely eliminate these risks. See R. J. Reynolds Tobacco Company 1988.

45. "Philip Morris Announces Development of Cigarette Paper Less Likely to Burn Fabric," *Product Safety Liability Reporter*, vol. 28, no. 2, p. 43.

46. Gordon Fairclough, "Here's a New Cigarette Pitch: More Puffs per Pack," *Wall Street Journal*, February 15, 2000, p. B1.

47. U.S. Dept of Health and Human Services 1989a.

48. Glenn Collins, "What Smoke? New Device Keeps Cigarettes in a Box," *New York Times*, October 23, 1997, p. A1.

49. Ibid.

50. Suen Hwang, "Latest Move to Make a Safer Smoke Uses Special Tobacco," *Wall Street Journal*, April 29, 1999. Some companies have developed innovative products such as a nicotine-free cigarette and cigarettes with lower levels of nitrosamines. How they can market these is unclear. See Gordon Fairclough, "Vector Producers Nicotine-Free Cigarette Using Genetically Modified Tobacco," *Wall Street Journal*, January 16, 2001, p. A2. Also see idem, "The Race to Produce a 'Safer' Cigarette Shifts to High Gear," *Wall Street Journal*, February 13, 2001, p. A1.

51. See R. J. Reynolds Tobacco Company 1988, pp. ix–x.

52. Ibid., p. xii.

53. Ibid., p. xiii.

54. Ibid.

55. For example, these studies did not ascertain the long-term health risks from prolonged exposure to the product.

56. It could be, for example, that the government could develop an overall index of the risk of heart disease or other major consequences of smoking. Thus, it might be possible to develop a list of health outcomes of cigarettes, including possible addiction, and to rate the riskiness of different cigarettes with respect to these hazards. In the above listing, giving carbon monoxide levels indicates a chemical exposure but not the risk of a health outcome.

57. See Viscusi and Magat 1987, and Magat and Viscusi 1992. The results of these studies are reported in Viscusi 1998b.

58. See Magat and Viscusi 1992.

59. See ibid., 14, 88–92, 103, 185–56.

60. See, e.g., Magat and Viscusi 1992, Viscusi and Magat 1987.

61. Surgeon General C. Everett Koop popularized the idea of a smoke-free future; U.S. Department of Health and Human Services 1989a, p. vii.

62. See Viscusi 1992a, 285, 288.

Chapter Ten

1. "Setback for Anti-Tobacco Suite in Canada," *New York Times*, February 22, 2000, section 6, p. 10 (Reuters byline).

2. Barry Meier, "Jury Finds That Cigarettes Caused Smokers' Diseases: Huge Punitive Award Likely to Follow," *New York Times*, April 8, 2000, p. A7.

3. Transcript of conference call with Richard Scruggs, hosted by Prudential Securities, moderator Barbara Dreyfuss, November 5, 1999; "National Class Action Lawsuit Filed against the Nation's Largest HMO, Charging RICO, ERISA Violations" (available on PR

Newswire in LEXIS); and Adam Bryant, "Who's Afraid of Dickie Scruggs?" *Newsweek*, December 6, 1999, p. 46.

4. Transcript of conference call, pp. 18–19.

5. Ibid.

6. See Adam Bryant, "Who's Afraid?" p. 46.

7. Transcript of conference call, p. 16.

REFERENCES

Adler, R., and D. Pittle. 1984. "Cajolery or Command: Are Education Campaigns an Adequate Substitute for Regulation?" *Yale Journal on Regulation* 2:159–94.

American Law Institute. 1965. *Restatement of the Law (Second) of Torts*. St. Paul: American Law Institute Publishers.

Ames, Bruce N., and Lois S. Gold. 1993. "Environmental Pollution and Cancer: Some Misconceptions." In *Phantom Risk*, edited by K. R. Foster, D. E. Bernstein, and P. W. Huber, 153–81. Cambridge, MA: MIT Press.

Antonanzas, F., W. K. Viscusi, J. Rovira, F. J. Brana, F. Portillo, and I. Carvalho. 2000. "Smoking Risks in Spain: Part I—Risks to the Smoker." *Journal of Risk and Uncertainty* 21 (2/3): 161–86.

Atkinson, A. B., and J. L. Skegg. 1973. "Anti-Smoking Publicity and the Demand for Tobacco in the U.K." *Manchester School of Economics and Social Studies* 41 (3): 265–82.

Ayanian, J. Z., and P. D. Cleary. 1999. "Perceived Risks of Heart Disease and Cancer among Cigarette Smokers." *Journal of the American Medical Association* 281 (11): 1019–21.

Barendregt, J. J., L. Bonneux, and P. J. Vandermaas. 1997. "The Health Care Costs of Smoking." *New England Journal of Medicine* 337:1052–57.

Becker, G. S., M. Grossman, and K. M. Murphy. 1996. "An Empirical Analysis of Cigarette Addiction." *American Economic Review* 84:396–418.

Becker, G. S., and K. M. Murphy. 1988. "A Theory of Rational Addiction." *Journal of Political Economy* 96:675–700.

Benthin, A., P. Slovic, and H. Severson. 1993. "A Psychometric Study of Adolescent Risk Perception." *Journal of Adolescence* 16:153–68.

Bishop, J. A., and J. H. Yoo. 1985. "Health Scare: Excise Taxes and Advertising Ban in the Cigarette Demand and Supply." *Southern Economic Journal* 52 (2): 402–11.

Breyer, Stephen. 1993. *Breaking the Vicious Circle: Toward Effective Risk Regulation*. Cambridge, MA: Harvard University Press.

Brownson, R. C., M. C. Alavanja, E. T. Hock, and T. S. Loy. 1992. "Passive Smoking and Lung Cancer in Nonsmoking Women." *American Journal of Public Health* 82 (11): 1525–30.

Bulow, J., and P. Klemperer. 1998. "The Tobacco Deal." *Brookings Papers on Economic Activity: Microeconomics 1998*, 323–94.

Calfee, J. E. 1985. "Cigarette Advertising, Health Information, and Regulation before 1970." FTC Working Paper 134. Washington, DC: Federal Trade Commission.

———. 1986. "The Ghost of Cigarette Advertising Past." *Regulation* 10 (6): 35–45.

California Environmental Protection Agency, Office of Environmental Health Hazard Assessment. 1997. *Health Effects of Exposure to Environmental Tobacco Smoke, Final Report.* Also published in *Tobacco Control* 6 (4): 346–53.

Centers for Disease Control and Prevention. U.S. Department of Health and Human Services. 1993. "Cigarette Smoking—Attributable Mortality and Years of Potential Life Lost—United States, 1990." *Morbidity and Mortality Weekly Report* 42 (33): 645–49.

———. 1994. "Cigarette Smoking among Adults—United States, 1992, and Changes in the Definition of Current Cigarette Smoking." *Morbidity and Mortality Weekly Report* 43 (19): 342–46.

———. *See also* U.S. Department of Health and Human Services.

Chaloupka, F. 1991. "Rational Addictive Behavior and Cigarette Smoking." *Journal of Political Economy* 49 (4): 722–42.

Clayton, R. R., F. D. Scutchfield, and S. W. Wyatt. 2000. "Hutchinson Smoking Prevention Project: A New Gold Standard in Prevention Science Requires Transdisciplinary Thinking." *Journal of the National Cancer Institute* 92 (24): 1964–65.

COMMIT Research Group. 1995a. "Community Intervention Trial for Smoking Cessation (COMMIT): I. Cohort Results from a Four-Year Community Intervention." *American Journal of Public Health* 85 (2): 183–92.

———. 1995b. "Community Intervention Trial for Smoking Cessation (COMMIT): II. Changes in Adult Cigarette Smoking Prevalence." *American Journal of Public Health* 85 (2): 193–200.

Cosmides, L., and J. Tooby. 1996. "Are Humans Good Intuitive Statisticians After All? Rethinking Some Conclusions from the Literature on Judgment under Uncertainty." *Cognition* 58 (1): 1–73.

Crist, P. G., and J. M. Majoras. 1987. "The 'New' Wave in Smoking and Health Litigation: Is Anything Really So New?" *Tennessee Law Review* 54:551–602.

Cummings, K. M., T. Pechacek, and D. Shopland. 1994. "The Illegal Sale of Cigarettes to U.S. Minors: Estimates by State." *American Journal of Public Health* 84 (2): 300–302.

Cutler, D., J. Gruber, R. S. Hartman, M. B. Landrum, J. Newhouse, and M. B. Rosenthal. 2000. "The Economic Impact of the Tobacco Settlement." NBER Working Paper No. W7760. Cambridge, MA: National Bureau of Economic Research.

Cutler, D. M., A. M. Epstein, R. G. Frank, R. Hartman, C. King III, J. P. Newhouse, M. B. Rosenthal, and E. R. Vigdor. 2000. "How Good a Deal Was the Tobacco Settlement? Assessing Payments to Massachusetts." *Journal of Risk and Uncertainty* 21 (2/3): 235–61.

DeCicca, P., D. Kenkel, and A. Mathios. 2000. "Racial Differences in the Determinants of Smoking Onset." *Journal of Risk and Uncertainty* 21 (2/3): 311–40.

DiFranza, J. R., and J. B. Tye. 1990. "Who Profits from Tobacco Sales to Children?" *Journal of the American Medical Association* 263 (20): 2784–87.

Doll, R., R. Peto, K. Wheatley, and R. Gray. 1994a. "Mortality in Relation to Consumption of Alcohol: Thirteen Years' Observations on Male British Doctors." *British Medical Journal* 309 (6959): 911–18.

Doll, R., R. Peto, K. Wheatley, R. Gray, and I. Sutherland. 1994b. "Mortality in Relation to Smoking: Forty Years' Observations on Male British Doctors." *British Medical Journal* 309 (6959): 901–11.

Eiser, J. R. 1983. "Smoking, Addiction, and Decision-Making." *International Review of Applied Psychology* 32:11–28.

Eiser, J. R., and J. VanDer Plight. 1986. "Smoking Cessation and Smokers' Perceptions of Their Addiction." *Journal of Social and Clinical Psychology* 4:60–70.

Elland, G., F. Johnstone, R. Prescott, W. Ji-Xian, and M. Jian-Hua. 1996. "Smoking during

Pregnancy: The Dose Dependence of Birthweight Deficits." *British Journal of Obstetrics and Gynaecology* 103 (8): 806–13.

Evans, W. N., M. C. Farrelly, and E. Montgomery. 1999. "Do Workplace Smoking Bans Reduce Smoking?" *American Economic Review* 89 (5): 729–47.

Evans, W. N., J. S. Ringel, and D. Stech. 1999. "Tobacco Taxes and Public Policy to Discourage Smoking." In *Tax Policy and the Economy 13*, edited by James Poterba, 1–55. Cambridge, MA: MIT Press.

Fischer, P. M., M. P. Schwartz, J. W. Richards, A. O. Goldstein, and T. H. Rojas. 1991. "Brand Logo Recognition by Children Aged Three to Six Years." *Journal of the American Medical Association* 266 (22): 3145–48.

Fischhoff, B., S. Lichtenstein, P. Slovic, S. L. Derby, and R. L. Keeney. 1981. *Acceptable Risk.* Cambridge: Cambridge University Press.

Fischhoff, B., and D. MacGregor. 1983. "Judged Lethality: How Much People Seem to Know Depends on How Much They Are Asked." *Risk Analysis* 3 (4): 229–36.

Fox, Brion J., J. M. Lightwood, and S. A. Glantz. 1998. "A Public Health Analysis of the Proposed Resolution of Tobacco Litigation." Report available at http://galen.library.ucsf.edu/tobacco/ustl/.

Fullerton, D., and D. L. Rogers. 1993. *Who Bears the Lifetime Tax Burden?* Washington, DC: Brookings Institution.

Gaba, A., and W. K. Viscusi. 1998. "Differences in Subjective Risk Thresholds: Worker Groups as an Example." *Management Science* 44 (6): 801–11.

Gallup Organization, Stanford University, and the University of Southern California. 1999a. *Final Report: Independent Evaluation of the California Tobacco Control Prevention and Education Program: Wave 1 Data, 1996–1997.* Report prepared for the State of California Department of Health Services, Tobacco Control Section.

———. 1999b. *Final Report: Independent Evaluation of the California Tobacco Control, Prevention, and Education Program: Wave 2 Data 1998, Wave 1 and Wave 2 Data Comparisons, 1996–1998.* Report prepared for the State of California Department of Health Services, Tobacco Control Section.

Gravelle, J., and D. Zimmerman. 1994. "Cigarette Taxes to Fund Health Care Reform: An Economic Analysis." Washington, DC: Congressional Research Service.

Gruber, J. 2000. "Youth Smoking in the U.S.: Prices and Policies." NBER Working Paper No. W7506. Cambridge, MA: National Bureau of Economic Research.

Gruber, J., and J. Zinman. 2000. "Youth Smoking in the U.S.: Evidence and Implications." NBER Working Paper No. W7780. Cambridge, MA: National Bureau of Economic Research.

Hadden, S. 1986. *Read the Label: Reducing Risk by Providing Information.* Boulder, CO: Westview Press.

Hamermesh, D. S., and F. W. Hamermesh. 1983. "Does Perception of Life Expectancy Reflect Health Knowledge?" *American Journal of Public Health* 73 (8): 911–14.

Hamilton, J. 1972. "The Demand for Cigarettes: Advertising, the Health Scare, and the Cigarette Advertising Ban." *Review of Economics and Statistics* 54:401–11.

Hammond, E. C., and D. Horn. 1954. "The Relationship between Human Smoking Habits and Death Rates: A Follow-Up Study of 187,766 Men." *Journal of the American Medical Association* 155:1316–28.

Hanson, J., and D. A. Kysar. 1999. "Taking Behavioralism Seriously: Some Evidence of Market Manipulation." *Harvard Law Review* 112 (7): 1420–1572.

Hanson, J., and K. Logue. 1998. "The Costs of Cigarettes: The Economic Case for Ex Post Incentive-Based Regulation." *Yale Law Journal* 107 (5): 1163–1362.

Harris, J. E. 1980. "Taxing Tar and Nicotine." *American Economic Review* 70:300–311.

Hastie, R., D. Schkade, and J. W. Payne. 1999. "Juror Judgments in Civil Cases: Effects of Plaintiff's Requests and Plaintiff's Identity on Punitive Damage Awards." *Law and Human Behavior* 23 (4): 445–70.

Hersch, J. 1998. "Teen Smoking Behavior and the Regulatory Environment." *Duke Law Journal* 47 (6): 1143–70.

———. 2000. "Gender, Income Levels, and the Demand for Cigarettes." *Journal of Risk and Uncertainty* 21 (2/3): 263–82.

Hersch, J., and T. S. Pickton. 1995. "Risk Taking Activities and Heterogeneity of Job-Risk Tradeoffs." *Journal of Risk and Uncertainty* 11 (3): 205–17.

Hersch, J., and W. K. Viscusi. 1990. "Cigarette Smoking, Seatbelt Use, and Differences in Wage-Risk Tradeoffs." *Journal of Human Resources* 25 (2): 202–27.

———. 1998. "Smoking and Other Risky Behaviors." *Journal of Drug Issues* 28 (3): 645–61.

Houthakker, H., and L. D. Taylor. 1970. *Consumer Demand in the United States: Analyses and Projections.* 2d ed. Cambridge, MA: Harvard University Press.

Huber, G. L., R. E. Brockie, and V. K. Mahajan. 1993. "Smoke and Mirrors: The EPA's Flawed Study of Environmental Tobacco Smoke and Lung Cancer." *Regulation* 3:44–54.

Institute of Medicine. 2001. *Clearing the Smoke.* Washington, DC: Institute of Medicine.

Insurance Information Institute. 1998. *The Fact Book 1999: Property/Casualty Insurance Facts.* New York: Insurance Information Institute.

International Agency for Research on Cancer. 1985. *Tobacco: A Major International Health Hazard.* New York: Oxford University Press.

Ippolito, P. M. 1987. "The Value of Life Saving: Lessons from the Cigarette Market." In *Risk Assessment and Management,* edited by L. B. Lave, 439–52. New York: Plenum Press.

Ippolito, P. M., and R. A. Ippolito. 1984. "Measuring the Value of Life Saving from Consumer Reactions to New Information." *Journal of Public Economics* 25:53–81.

Ippolito, R. A., R. D. Murphy, and D. Sant. 1979. *Staff Report on Consumer Responses to Cigarette Health Information.* Washington, DC: Federal Trade Commission.

Janerich, D. T., W. D. Thompson, L. R. Varela, P. Greenwald, S. Chorost, C. Tucci, M. B. Zaman, M. R. Melamed, M. Kiely, and M. F. McKneally. 1990. "Lung Cancer and Exposure to Tobacco Smoke in the Household." *New England Journal of Medicine* 323:632–36.

Jenks, R. 1992. "Attitudes, Perceptions, and Risk-Taking Behaviors of Smokers, Ex-smokers, and Nonsmokers." *Journal of Social Psychology* 132 (5): 569–75.

Johnson, T. R. 1978. "Additional Evidence on the Effects of Alternative Taxes on Cigarette Prices." *Journal of Political Economy* 86 (2): 325–28.

Keeler, T. E., T. Hu, and P. G. Barnett. 1991. "Taxation, Regulation, and Addiction: A Demand Function for Cigarettes Based on Time-Series Evidence." University of California, Berkeley, Department of Economics, Working Paper 91-173.

Kenkel, D. S. 1991. "Health Behavior, Health Knowledge, and Schooling." *Journal of Political Economy* 95 (2): 287–305.

Kessler, D. 2001. *A Question of Intent.* New York: Public Affairs.

Kozlowski, L. T., C. P. Herman, and R. C. Frecker. 1980. "What Researchers Make of What Cigarette Smokers Say: Filtering Smokers' Hot Air." *Lancet,* March 29, 699–700.

Leu, R. E. 1984. "Anti-Smoking Publicity, Taxation, and the Demand for Cigarettes." *Journal of Health Economics* 3 (1): 101–16.

Levy, R., and R. Marimont. 1998. "Lies, Damned Lies and 400,000 Smoking Related Deaths." *Regulation* 21 (4): 24–29.

Lewit, E. M., and D. Coate. 1982. "The Potential for Using Excise Taxes to Reduce Smoking." *Journal of Health Economics* 1 (2): 121–45.

Lewit, E. M., D. Coate, and M. Grossman. 1981. "The Effects of Government Regulation on Teenage Smoking." *Journal of Law and Economics* 24 (3): 545–69.

Lichtenstein, S., P. Slovic, B. Fischhoff, M. Layman, and B. Combs. 1978. "Judged Frequency of Lethal Events." *Journal of Experimental Psychology: Human Learning and Memory* 4:551–78.

Liu, J., and C. Hsieh. 1995. "Risk Perception and Smoking Behavior: Empirical Evidence from Taiwan." *Journal of Risk and Uncertainty* 11 (2): 139–57.

Longo, D., R. C. Brownson, J. C. Johnson, J. E. Hewett, R. L. Kruse, T. E. Novotny, R. A. Logan. 1996. "Hospital Smoking Bans and Employee Smoking Behavior Results of a National Survey." *Journal of the American Medical Association* 275:1252–57.

Magat, W. A., and W. K. Viscusi. 1992. *Informational Approaches to Regulation*. Cambridge, MA: MIT Press.

Malarcher, A. M., J. Schulman, L. A. Epstein, M. J. Thun, P. Mowery, B. Pierce, L. Escobedo, and G. A. Giovino. 2000. "Methodological Issues in Estimating Smoking-Attributable Mortality in the United States." *American Journal of Epidemiology* 152 (6): 573–84.

Manning, W. G., E. B. Keeler, J. P. Newhouse, E. M. Sloss, and J. Wasserman. 1989. "Taxes of Sin: Do Smokers and Drinkers Pay Their Way?" *Journal of the American Medical Association* 26 (11): 1604–9.

———. 1991. *The Costs of Poor Health Habits*. Cambridge, MA: Harvard University Press.

Marsh, A. 1985. "Smoking and Illness: What Smokers Really Believe." *Health Trends* 17:7–12.

Mattson, M. E., E. Pollack, and J. Cullen. 1987. "What Are the Odds That Smoking Will Kill You?" *American Journal of Public Health* 77 (4): 425–30.

McAuliffe, R. 1988. "The FTC and the Effectiveness of Cigarette Advertising Regulations." *Journal of Public Policy and Marketing* 7:49–64.

Merrill, R. A. 1998. "The FDA May Not Regulate Tobacco Products as 'Drugs' or as 'Medical Devices.'" *Duke Law Journal* 47:1071–94.

Monitoring the Future. 2000. 2000 Data from In-School Surveys of 8th, 10th, and 12th Grade Students. Accessible at http://monitoringthefuture.org/data/00data.html #2000data.

Moore, M. J., and C. W. Zhu. 2000. "Passive Smoking and Health Care: Health Perceptions Myth vs. Health Care Reality." *Journal of Risk and Uncertainty* 21 (2/3): 283–310.

Mulholland, J. 1991, "Policy Issues Concerning the Promotion of Less Hazardous Cigarettes." Bureau of Economics, FTC Working Paper. Washington, DC: Federal Trade Commission.

National Cancer Institute. 1996. *The FTC Cigarette Test Method for Determining the Tar, Nicotine, and Carbon Monoxide Yields of U.S. Cigarettes. Report of the NCI Expert Committee.* Smoking and Tobacco Control Monograph 7. NIH Publication no. 96-4028. Bethesda: NCI.

National Research Council Committee on Passive Smoking. 1986. *Environmental Tobacco Smoke: Measuring Exposures and Assessing Health Effects*. Washington, DC: National Academy Press.

Oster, G., G. A. Colditz, and N. L. Kelly. 1984. *The Economic Costs of Smoking and Benefits of Quitting*. Lexington, MA: D. C. Heath and Company.

Otsuka, R., H. Watanabe, K. Hirata, K. Tokai, T. Muro, M. Yoshiyama, K. Takevchi, and J. Yoshikawa. 2001. "Acute Effects of Passive Smoking on the Coronary Circulation in Healthy Young Adults." *Journal of the American Medical Association* 286 (4): 436–31.

Overholt, R. H., W. Neptune, and M. Ashraf. 1975. "Primary Cancer of the Lung." *Annals of Thoracic Surgery* 20:511–19.

Peterson, A. V., K. Kealy, S. Mann, P. Marek, and I. Sarason. 2000. "Hutchinson Smoking Prevention Project: Long-Term Randomized Trial in School-Based Tobacco Use Prevention—Results on Smoking." *Journal of the American National Cancer Institute* 92 (24): 1979–91.

Rethans, A. 1979. *An Investigation of Consumer Perceptions of Product Hazards.* Doctoral dissertation, University of Oregon, Eugene.

Ringold, D. J., and J. E. Calfee. 1989. "The Informational Content of Cigarette Advertising: 1926–1986." *Journal of Public Policy and Management* 8:1–23.

R. J. Reynolds Tobacco Company. 1988. *Chemical and Biological Studies on New Cigarette Prototypes that Heat Instead of Burn Tobacco.* Winston-Salem, NC: R. J. Reynolds Tobacco Co.

Rovira, J., W. K. Viscusi, F. Antonanzas, F. J. Brana, F. Portillo, and I. Carvalho. 2000. "Smoking Risks in Spain: Part II—Environmental Tobacco Smoke Externalities." *Journal of Risk and Uncertainty* 21 (2/3): 187–212.

Russo, J. 1989. "An Optimal Cigarette Tax." Doctoral dissertation, Northwestern University.

Russo, J. E., R. Staelin, C. A. Nolan, G. J. Russell, and B. L. Metcalf. 1986. "Nutrition Information in the Supermarket." *Journal of Consumer Behavior* 13 (48): 48–70.

SAMHSA (Substance Abuse and Mental Health Services Administration), Office of Applied Studies. 1997. Table 17: Percentages Reporting Past Month Use of Cigarettes, by Age Group, Race/Ethnicity, and Sex 1979–1997. 1997 National Household Survey on Drug Abuse, http://www.health.org:80/govstudy/BKD275/97tab.htm#E10E68 (accessed 09/21/01).

Schelling, T. C. 1984. *Choice and Consequence.* Cambridge, MA: Harvard University Press.

———. 1986. "Economics and Cigarettes." *Preventive Medicine* 15:549–60.

Schmalensee, R. 1972. *The Economics of Advertising.* Amsterdam: North-Holland.

Schneider, F. W., and L. A. Vanmastrig. 1974. "Adolescent Preadolescent Differences in Beliefs and Attitudes about Cigarette Smoking." *Journal of Psychology* 87:71–81.

Schneider, L., B. Klein, and K. Murphy. 1981. "Governmental Regulation of Cigarette Health Information." *Journal of Law and Economics* 24 (3): 575–612.

Schoenbaum, M. 1997. "Do Smokers Underestimate the Mortality Effects of Smoking? Evidence from the Health and Retirement Survey." *American Journal of Public Health* 87 (5): 755–59.

Schwartz, A. 1989. "Views of Addiction and the Duty to Warn." *Virginia Law Review* 75:509–60.

Schwartz, G. 1999. "Tobacco, Liability, and Viscusi." *Cumberland Law Review* 29 (3): 555–68.

———. 2000. "Cigarette Litigation's Offspring: Assessing Tort Issues Related to Guns, Alcohol, and Other Controversial Products in Light of the Tobacco Wars." *Pepperdine Law Review* 27 (4): 751–57.

Shopland, D. R., H. J. Eyre, and T. F. Pechacek. 1991. "Smoking-Attributable Cancer Mortality in 1991: Is Lung Cancer Now the Leading Cause of Death among Smokers in the United States?" *Journal of National Cancer Institute* 83 (16): 1142–48.

Shoven, J. B., J. O. Sundberg, and J. P. Bunker. 1989. "The Social Security Cost of Smoking." In *The Economics of Aging,* edited by D. A. Wise, 231–51. Chicago: University of Chicago Press.

Slovic, P. 1998. "Do Adolescent Smokers Know the Risks?" *Duke Law Journal* 47 (6): 1133–41.

———. 2000. "What Does It Mean to Know A Cumulative Risk? Adolescents' Perceptions of Short-term and Long-term Consequences of Smoking." *Journal of Behavioral Decision Making* 13 (2): 259–66.

————. 2001. "Cigarette Smokers: Rational Actors or Rational Fools?" In *Smoking: Risk, Perception, and Policy,* edited by P. Slovic, 97–124. Thousand Oaks, CA: Sage Publications.

Steenland, K. 1992. "Passive Smoking and the Risk of Heart Disease." *Journal of the American Medical Association* 267:94–99.

Steenland, K., M. Thun, and C. Lally. 1996. "Environmental Tobacco Smoke and Coronary Heart Disease in the American Cancer Society CPA-II Cohort." *Healthcare Journal* 94 (4): 622–28.

Sterling, T. D., W. L. Rosenbaum, and J. J. Weinkam. 1993. "Risk Attribution and Tobacco-Related Deaths." *American Journal of Epidemiology* 138 (2): 128–39.

Stockwell, H. G., A. L. Goldman, G. H. Lyman, C. I. Noss, A. W. Armstrong, P. A. Pinkham, E. C. Candelora, and M. R. Brusa. 1992. "Environmental Tobacco Smoke and Lung Cancer Risk in Nonsmoking Women." *Journal of the National Cancer Institute* 84 (18): 1417–22.

Stratton, K., P. Shetty, R. Wallace, and S. Bondurant, eds. 2001. *Clearing the Smoke: The Science Base for Tobacco Harm Reduction.* Washington, DC: National Academy Press.

Sullivan, D. 1985. "Testing Hypotheses about Firm Behavior in the Cigarette Industry." *Journal of Political Economy* 93 (3): 586–98.

Sumner, D. A., and J. Alston. 1984. "Effects of the Tobacco Program: An Analysis of Deregulation." *American Enterprise Institute Occasional Paper 1-71.*

Sunstein, C., D. Kahneman, and D. Schkade. 1998. "Assessing Punitive Damages." *Yale Law Journal* 107 (7): 2071–53.

Sunstein, C. R. 1998. "Is Tobacco a Drug? Administrative Agencies as Common Law Courts." *Duke Law Journal* 47:1013–69.

Svenson, O. 1979. "Are We All among the Better Drivers?" Unpublished manuscript. Department of Psychology, University of Stockholm.

Tate, C. 1989. "In the 1800's, Antismoking Was a Burning Issue." *Smithsonian* 20 (4): 107–9.

Tobacco Institute. 1993. *The Tax Burden on Tobacco,* Vol. 28. Washington, DC: Tobacco Institute.

————. 1998. *The Tax Burden on Tobacco,* Vol. 33. Washington, DC: Tobacco Institute.

Tollison, R. D., and R. E. Wagner. 1988. *Smoking and the State: Social Costs, Rent Seeking, and Public Policy.* Lexington, MA: D. C. Heath and Company.

Tsumara, Ted. 1987. *Health and Safety for You.* New York: McGraw Hill.

Tversky, A., and D. Koehler. 1994. "Support Theory: A Nonextensional Representation of Subjective Probability." *Psychological Review* 101 (4): 547–67.

U.S. Department of Health and Human Services. 1979. *Smoking and Health, A Report of the Surgeon General.* Washington, DC: U.S. Government Printing Office.

————. 1980. *The Health Consequences of Smoking for Women, A Report of the Surgeon General.* Washington, DC: U.S. Government Printing Office.

————. 1981. *The Health Consequences of Smoking: The Changing Cigarette, A Report of the Surgeon General.* Washington, DC: U.S. Government Printing Office.

————. 1982. *The Health Consequences of Smoking: Cancer, A Report of the Surgeon General.* Washington, DC: U.S. Government Printing Office.

————. 1983. *The Health Consequences of Smoking: Cardiovascular Disease, A Report of the Surgeon General.* Washington, DC: U.S. Government Printing Office.

————. 1984. *The Health Consequences of Smoking: Chronic Obstructive Lung Disease, A Report of the Surgeon General.* Washington, DC: U.S. Government Printing Office.

————. 1985. *The Health Consequences of Smoking: Cancer and Chronic Lung Disease in the Workplace, A Report of the Surgeon General.* Washington, DC: U.S. Government Printing Office.

————. 1986. *The Health Consequences of Involuntary Smoking, A Report of the Surgeon General.* Washington, DC: U.S. Government Printing Office.

————. 1988. *The Health Consequences of Smoking: Nicotine Addiction, A Report of the Surgeon General.* Washington, DC: U.S. Government Printing Office.

————. 1989a. *Reducing the Health Consequences of Smoking: Twenty-five Years of Progress, A Report of the Surgeon General.* Washington, DC: U.S. Government Printing Office.

————. 1989b. *Smoking, Tobacco and Health: A Factbook.* Washington, DC: U.S. Government Printing Office.

————. 1990. *The Health Benefits of Smoking Cessation, A Report of the Surgeon General.* Washington, DC: U.S. Government Printing Office.

————. 1992. *Health United States, 1991.* Washington, DC: U.S. Government Printing Office.

————. 1993. *Annual Statistical Supplement of the Social Security Bulletin, 1993.* Washington, DC: U.S. Government Printing Office.

————. 2000. *Reducing Tobacco Use, A Report of the Surgeon General.* Washington, DC: U.S. Government Printing Office.

U.S. Department of Health and Human Services. National Cancer Institute. 1991. *Strategies to Control Tobacco Use in the United States.* Rockville, MD: U.S. Department of Health and Human Services.

U.S. Department of Health and Human Services. Public Health Service. Centers for Disease Control. 1990. *Smoking and Health: A National Status Report,* 2d edition. DHHS Publication No. (CDC) 87-8396 (revised 2/90).

————. *See also* Centers for Disease Control.

U.S. Department of Health and Human Services. Public Health Service. National Institutes of Health. 1993. *Major Local Tobacco Control Ordinances in the United States,* Smoking and Tobacco Control Monograph 3, U.S. NIH publication No. 93-3532, May 1993.

U.S. Department of Health, Education, and Welfare. 1964. *Smoking and Health: Report of the Advisory Committee to the Surgeon General of the Public Health Service.* Princeton: Van Nostrand.

————. 1967. *The Health Consequences of Smoking: A Public Health Service Review, A Report of the Surgeon General.* Washington, DC: U.S. Government Printing Office.

————. 1968. *Supplement to the 1967 Public Health Service Review, A Report of the Surgeon General.* Washington, DC: U.S. Government Printing Office.

————. 1969. *Supplement to the 1967 Public Health Service Review, A Report of the Surgeon General.* Washington, DC: U.S. Government Printing Office.

————. 1971. *The Health Consequences of Smoking, A Report of the Surgeon General.* Washington, DC: U.S. Government Printing Office.

————. 1972. *The Health Consequences of Smoking, A Report of the Surgeon General.* Washington, DC: U.S. Government Printing Office.

————. 1973. *The Health Consequences of Smoking, A Report of the Surgeon General.* Washington, DC: U.S. Government Printing Office.

————. 1974. *The Health Consequences of Smoking, A Report of the Surgeon General.* Washington, DC: U.S. Government Printing Office.

————. 1975. *The Health Consequences of Smoking, A Report of the Surgeon General.* Washington, DC: U.S. Government Printing Office.

————. 1976. *The Health Consequences of Smoking: Selected Chapters from the 1971–1975 Reports, A Report of the Surgeon General.* Washington, DC: U.S. Government Printing Office.

————. 1978. *The Health Consequences of Smoking, 1977–1978, A Report of the Surgeon General*. Washington, DC: U.S. Government Printing Office.

————. 1979. *Smoking and Health: The Health Consequences of Smoking, The Behavioral Aspects of Smoking, Education and Prevention, A Report of the Surgeon General*. Washington, DC: U.S. Government Printing Office.

U.S. Department of Health, Education, and Welfare. National Institute of Education. 1979. *Teenage Smoking: Immediate and Long-term Patterns*. Washington, DC: U.S. Government Printing Office.

U.S. Environmental Protection Agency. Indoor Air Division. Office of Radiation and Indoor Air. 1994. *The Costs and Benefits of Smoking Restrictions: An Assessment of the Smoke-Free Environment Act of 1993 (H.R.3434)*. Washington, DC: U.S. Environmental Protection Agency.

U.S. Environmental Protection Agency. Office of Health and Environmental Assessment. Office of Research and Development. 1992. *Respiratory Health Effects of Passive Smoking: Lung Cancer and Other Disorders*. EPA / 600 / 6-90 / 006F. Washington, DC: U.S. Environmental Protection Agency.

U.S. Federal Trade Commission. 1981. *Staff Report on the Cigarette Advertising Investigation*. Washington, DC: Federal Trade Commission.

————. 1992. *Federal Trade Commission Report to Congress for 1990 Pursuant to the Federal Cigarette Labeling and Advertising Act*. Washington, DC: Federal Trade Commission.

Vernon, J., N. W. Rives, and T. H. Naylor. 1969. "An Econometric Model of the Tobacco Industry." *Review of Economics and Statistics* 61:149–58.

Viscusi, W. K. 1979. *Employment Hazards: An Investigation of Market Performance*. Cambridge, MA: Harvard University Press.

————. 1988a. "Predicting the Effect of Food Cancer Risk Warnings on Consumers." *Food Drug Cosmetic Law Journal* 43 (2): 283–307.

————. 1988b. "Consumer Processing of Hazard Warning Information." *Journal of Risk and Uncertainty* 1 (2): 201–32.

————. 1990. "Do Smokers Underestimate Risks?" *Journal of Political Economy* 98 (6): 1253–69.

————. 1991a. "Age Variations in Risk Perceptions and Smoking Decisions." *Review of Economics and Statistics* 73:577–88.

————. 1991b. *Reforming Products Liability*. Cambridge, MA: Harvard University Press.

————. 1992a. *Fatal Tradeoffs: Public and Private Responsibilities for Risk*. New York: Oxford University Press.

————. 1992b. *Smoking: Making the Risky Decision*. New York: Oxford University Press.

————. 1993. "The Value of Risks to Life and Health." *Journal of Economic Literature* 31:1912–46.

————. 1994. "Cigarette Warnings: The Perils of the Cipollone Decision." *Supreme Court Economic Review* 3:239–75.

————. 1995a. "Cigarette Taxation and the Social Consequences of Smoking." In *Tax Policy and the Economy*, edited by J. Poterba, 51–101. Cambridge: MIT Press.

————. 1995b. "Secondhand Smoke: Facts and Fantasy." *Regulation* 18 (3): 42–49.

————. 1997a. "Alarmist Decisions with Divergent Risk Information." *The Economic Journal* 107 (445): 1657–70.

————. 1997b. "From Cash Crop to Cash Cow: How Tobacco Profits the States." *Regulation* 20 (3): 27–32.

————. 1998a. "Constructive Cigarette Regulation." *Duke Law Journal* 47 (6): 1095–1131.

————. 1998b. *Rational Risk Policy.* Oxford: Oxford University Press.

————. 1998c. "Smoke and Mirrors: Understanding the New Scheme for Cigarette Regulation." *Brookings Review* 16 (1): 14–19.

————. 1999a. "A Postmortem on the Cigarette Settlement." Rushton Distinguished Lecture, *Cumberland Law Review* 29 (3): 523–53.

————. 1999b. "Public Perception of Smoking Risks." In *Valuing the Cost of Smoking: Assessment Methods, Risk Perception and Policy Options,* edited by Claude Jeanrenaud and Nils Soguel, 151–64. Norwell, MA: Kluwer Academic Publishers.

————. 1999c. "The Governmental Composition of the Insurance Costs of Smoking." *Journal of Law and Economics* 42 (2): 575–609.

————. 2000. "The Perils of Qualitative Smoking Risk Measures." *Journal of Behavioral Decision Making* 13 (2): 267–71.

Viscusi, W. K., I. Carvalho, F. Antonanzas, J. Rovira, Francisco J. Brana, and F. Portillo. 2000. "Smoking Risks in Spain: Part III—Determinants of Smoking Behavior." *Journal of Risk and Uncertainty* 21 (2/3): 213–34.

Viscusi, W. K., and H. Chesson. 2000. "The Heterogeneity of Time-Risk Tradeoffs." *Journal of Behavioral Decision Making* 13 (2/Apr-Jun): 251–58.

Viscusi, W. K., and J. Hakes. Forthcoming. "Risk Ratings That Do Not Measure Probabilities." *Journal of Risk Research.*

Viscusi, W. K., and J. Hersch. 1990. "Cigarette Smoking, Seatbelt Use, and Differences in Wage-Risk Trade-Offs." *Journal of Human Resources* 25 (2): 202–27.

————. 1998. "Smoking and Other Risky Behaviors." *Journal of Drug Issues* 28 (3): 645–61.

————. 2001. "Cigarette Smokers As Job Risk Takers." *Review of Economics and Statistics* 83 (2): 269–80.

Viscusi, W. K., and W. A. Magat. 1987. *Learning about Risk: Consumer and Worker Responses to Hazard Information.* Cambridge, MA: Harvard University Press.

Viscusi, W. K., W. A. Magat, and J. Huber. 1991. "Communication of Ambiguous Risk Information." *Theory and Decision* 31 (2/3): 159–73.

Viscusi, W. K., and R. J. Zeckhauser. 2000. "The Denominator Blindness Effect: Accident Frequencies and the Misjudgment of Recklessness." Working Paper, Harvard Law School.

Warner, K. E. 1977. "The Effects of the Anti-Smoking Campaign on Cigarette Consumption." *American Journal of Public Health* 67 (7): 645–50.

————. 1981. "Cigarette Smoking in the 1970's: The Impact of the Antismoking Campaign." *Science* 211 (4483): 729–31.

————. 1989. "Effects of the Antismoking Campaign: An Update." *American Journal of Public Health* 79 (2): 144–51.

Wasserman, J., W. G. Manning, J. P. Newhouse, and J. D. Winkler. 1991. "The Effects of Excise Taxes and Regulations on Cigarette Smoking." *Journal of Health Economics* 10 (1): 43–64.

Weinstein, N. P. 1987. "Unrealistic Optimism about Susceptibility to Health Problems: Conclusions from a Community-Wide Sample. *Journal of Behavioral Medicine* 10 (5): 441–60.

Wells, A. J. 1988. "An Estimate of Adult Mortality in the United States from Passive Smoking." *Environmental International* 14:249–65.

INDEX

Accord cigarettes, 210
addiction risk perceptions
  addiction characteristics, 167, 236n60
  addiction vs. habituation, 166–67
  behavior characteristics of smokers vs.
    nonsmokers, 168–70, 169t
  compensation for risk taking, 170
  demand elasticity for cigarettes and,
    171–72
  difficulty in interpreting a stated desire
    to quit, 173–74, 237n79
  rational addiction concept, 168
  smokers' awareness of future harms, 171
  smokers' knowledge of addictive as-
    pects of smoking, 168
  smokers' response to smoking restric-
    tions, 172
  transaction costs for behavior changes,
    167–68. See also risk beliefs
additives controversy, 204–6
advertising of cigarettes
  anticompetitive nature of restrictions,
    38–40
  bans in proposed federal settlement, 23,
    25
  competitive advertising on safety di-
    mension, 141
  danger of reducing brand identity, 198,
    239n14
  federal accusations of racketeering, 85–
    86
  industry bans, 179, 198
  low-tar ads, results of, 197–98
  need for credibility in antismoking cam-
    paigns, 192

  restrictions in proposed federal settle-
    ment, 23
  restrictions on advertising to youths,
    179–80
  risk perceptions' role, 141–42
AFL-CIO v. American Petroleum Institute, 122
Alabama
  settlement allocation plans, 58
  share of settlement funds, 48
Alcoholic Beverage Labeling Act (1988),
    234n7
American Cancer Society, 115
antismoking campaigns and programs,
    130–32, 189–90, 191
  antismoking groups' response to
    nicotine-free brands, 207–8
  need for credibility, 192
Apostolou, Bonnie, 10, 224n18
asbestos, 3
assumption-of-risk defense, 16
attorneys. See plaintiffs' attorneys

bans on smoking. See smoking bans' eco-
    nomic effects
Becnel, Daniel E., Jr., 5, 223n10
Best Value Brands, 239n13
bidis, 192
Blasingame, F., 140
Bliley, Tom, 27
Boeken, Richard, 10, 11, 45
Bravo cigarettes, 208
Breyer, Stephen, 20
Broughton, Martin, 28–29
Brown and Williamson / American
    Brands, 39, 39f, 40, 211

Brownson, R. C., 106
Bunker, J. P., 72
Burney, LeRoy, 140

California
  antismoking campaigns, 130–32
  antismoking program, 190
  bans on smoking, 129
  Proposition 65, 129
  Proposition 99, 130, 190
  public awareness of ETS risks, 132
  settlement allocation plans, 57–58
  warning signs requirement, 130
Cambridge Testing Method, 202–3
Camel cigarettes, 7, 183–84
Carlton cigarettes, 206
Cellucci, Paul, 53
Center for Indoor Air Research, 38
Chamber of Commerce, 4
Chapter 234 (Massachusetts), 204
Chesson, Harrell, 171
Child Protection and Toy Safety Act
  (1969), 139
chlorinated water risks, 122–23
cigarette litigation
  basis in financial costs to states, 4
  case awards, 45, 226n10
  federal settlement (see proposed federal
    settlement)
  flight attendants' ETS damage case,
    133–34
  industry successes, 3, 10
  legal protections from warning labels,
    137
  plaintiffs' attorneys, 4–5
  plaintiff wins, 9–11
  populism and, 5
  state lawsuits settlement (see state law-
    suits settlement)
cigarette taxes
  to discourage consumption, 24
  exclusion from state costs estimates,
    88–89
  federal and state revenues from, 63
  imposed by litigation, 7–8
  increase proposals (1994), 60
  as litigation substitute, 34–37, 226n1
  as percentage of retail price, 64
  regressivity of, 64

relative to purchase amount, 63, 229n3
shifted to smokers under proposed settlement, 18–19, 225n7
Clinton, President Bill
  lack of support for settlement, 26–27,
    32
  tax increase proposals, 60
Coase, Ronald, 123
Cochran, Johnnie, 5
Colorado, 57
Commander Brands, 239n13
Community Intervention Trial for Smoking Cessation (COMMIT), 174
Congressional Research Service, 72
Connecticut, 58
Conrad, Kent, 28
contingency fees, 49–50
cost estimation of smoking
  components of estimates, 74
  contradictory treatment of tar market-
    ing, 69
  demographic and risk characteristics of
    smokers, 70–71
  discounting of costs, 69–70, 72, 74
  environmental damage costs, 75
  external costs, 71–72
  gross medical cost to states, 18
  implications of estimation, 77–78
  incremental costs, isolation of, 67
  life expectancy effects, consideration of,
    67–68
  net financial costs, calculation of, 74
  net financial gain, conclusions about,
    75–77
  riskiness of today's cigarettes, 71
  temporal character of cost effects, 76
  total net costs, 72, 73t, 74
  See also financial costs to federal gov-
    ernment; financial costs to society;
    financial costs to states
Council for Tobacco Research, 38
Czechoslovakia, 76

*Dawn Apostolou, Administratrix of the Es-
  tate of Bonnie Apostolou v. The American Tobacco Company, et al.,* 224n18
death credit, 68, 87
DeCicca, P., 188
discount rate, 72, 74

Doral cigarettes, 209
Duke cigarettes, 198

Easterbrook, Frank, 164
Eclipse cigarettes, 195, 208–10, 241n44
economic costs of cigarettes. *See* financial
    costs to federal government; finan-
    cial costs to society; financial costs to
    states
education on smoking
    risk perceptions by education level,
        150, 151–52t
    risks of smoking, 131–32
    state settlement provisions, 42
    See also risk beliefs
Environmental Protection Agency (EPA)
    and ETS. *See* EPA study of ETS
environmental tobacco smoke (ETS)
    California policy effort (*see* California)
    cost of damage from, 75
    device to reduce, 210
    extent of public no-smoking policies,
        101, 231n1
    heart disease risks (*see* heart disease
        risks from ETS)
    key policy issues, 101–2
    litigation, 133–34
    losses due to smoking bans, 125, 126t,
        127t, 128–29
    lung cancer risks (*see* lung cancer risks
        from ETS)
    popular support for restrictions, 102
    private behavior's role in limiting ETS
        exposure, 132
    public perceptions of risks (*see* public
        perceptions of smoking's risks)
    regulation proposal (*see* OSHA pro-
        posal for regulation of ETS)
    reliability of estimates of health conse-
        quences, 103–4
    risk estimation considerations, 104–5
    smoking restrictions, considerations of,
        134–35
    voluntary restrictions on workplace
        smoking, 124
EPA study of ETS
    court critique of analysis, 108–9
    neglected risk aspects, 109–10, 232n10
    vs. OSHA assessments, 110, 232n13

risk assessment of ETS, 103, 104
statistical significance of studies, 105,
    107, 231n6
study results, 105–8, 106t
understatement of current ETS protec-
    tions, 110
ETS. *See* environmental tobacco smoke
excise tax. *See* cigarette taxes
externalities, smoking, 34, 95, 96–97t, 97,
    124

FDA. *See* Food and Drug Administration
Federal Caustic Poison Act (1927), 137
Federal Food, Drug, and Cosmetic Act
    (1938), 137
Federal Hazardous Substance Labeling
    Act (1960), 138
Federal Insecticide, Fungicide, and Ro-
    denticide Act (1947), 138
federal tobacco settlement. *See* proposed
    federal settlement
Federal Trade Commission (FTC), 65
    cigarette ratings tests, 202, 239–40n22
    industry agreement to ban ads, 198
filter cigarettes, 198–200, 202
financial costs to federal government
    allegations of industry wrongful be-
        havior, 84
    average state and federal estimates, 92,
        93, 94t
    federal share of state payments, 81–82
    industry motivation for a settlement,
        99
    net financial gain from cigarettes, 98–
        99
    racketeering accusations regarding
        low-tar cigarettes, 85–86
financial costs to society
    cigarette tax profile (*see* cigarette taxes)
    due to adverse effect on individual
        health, 34
    estimating (*see* cost estimation of smok-
        ing)
    inefficiencies in cost analysis, 61–62
    political reasons for imposing taxes,
        61
    self-financing conclusion, 72
    tar levels and cigarette safety, 65–67
    tax increase proposals (1994), 60

financial costs to states
  allegations of industry wrongful behavior, 83–84
  average state and federal estimates, 93, 94t, 95
  cost calculations, 89–90, 231n21
  cost components, consideration of, 81
  differences across states, 97–98
  excise tax exclusion, 88–89
  federal share of payment, 81–82
  focus on cost vs. smokers' health, 68
  income and insurance, per pack basis, 93
  industry motivation for a settlement, 99
  life expectancy assumptions, 82–83, 83f, 230n7
  medical care costs, per pack basis, 90, 91t, 92
  net economic damage issue, 88
  pension costs, per pack basis, 92–93
  procedure used to estimate, 90, 231n24
  reaction to negative cost estimate, 86–87
  retroactive liability laws, 80
  risk awareness issues as basis, 80
  scenarios considered, 90, 91t
  self-financing conclusion, 97, 98
  smoking externalities, 95, 96–97t, 97
  states filing suits, 230n1
flight attendants' ETS damage case, 133–34
Florida
  antismoking program, 189–90
  attorneys' payoffs, 51, 52
  retroactive liability laws, 80
  settlement allocation plans, 57
  state settlement, 37, 226n2
Flue-Cured Tobacco Cooperative Stabilization Corp. v. U.S. Environmental Protection Agency, et al., 108, 231n8, 232n9
Food and Drug Administration et al. v. Brown and Williamson Tobacco Corporation et al., 225n8
Food and Drug Administration (FDA)
  overview rights in proposed settlement, 23
  potential role in testing cigarettes, 201, 239n18
  question on regulating cigarettes as a drug, 20–21
  role in establishing guidelines, 212, 241n55
"A Frank Statement to Smokers," 86
FTC. *See* Federal Trade Commission

Gallup, George, 140, 234n13
Gallup polls, 142–43, 163, 236n48
General Motors, 11
Gingrich, Newt, 29
Goldstone, Steven F., 29
Gravelle, J., 72
Great Tar Derby, 197–98
Gregoire, Christine, 48, 49
gun industry, 8, 58, 219

Hammond, Cuyler, 141
Hanson, Jon, 161, 162, 166
Harshbarger, Scott, 35
Hawaii, 54
Health and Retirement Study, 161
Health and Safety for You (textbook), 131
health care system, 8, 58, 219
Health (textbook), 131
heart disease risks from ETS
  mortalities from heart disease per year, 114–15
  mortality estimates, inside the home, 117, 117t
  mortality estimates, outside the home, 115, 116t, 117
  social costs of passive smoking, 117–18, 118t
  uncertainty regarding an ETS connection, 115, 232n17
Henley, Patricia, 9, 11
Hersch, Joni, 70, 168, 170, 171, 180–81, 187
Horn, Daniel, 141
hospitals and no-smoking policies, 101, 231n1
Howard A. Engle, M.D., et al., Plaintiffs, v. R.J. Reynolds Tobacco, et al., Defendants, 224n21
Hsieh, C., 156
Humphrey, Skip, 35

Illinois
  attorneys' payoffs, 54
  settlement allocation plans, 57

Industrial Union Department, AFL-CIO v. American Petroleum Institute, 233n22
information, regulation of about cigarettes
  cigarette consumption adjusted for tar level, 196–97, 197f, 238–39n6
  filter cigarettes, adoption trends, 198–99, 199f
  government role in establishing risk ratings, 200
  industry low-tar ads, results of, 197–98
  potential danger of regulating cigarettes, 198
International Brotherhood of Teamsters, Local 734 Health and Welfare Fund v. Philip Morris, Inc., 236n54
Iowa
  attorneys' payoffs, 54
  share of settlement funds, 49
Iowa Supreme Court, 16

Jeffords, James, 28
Jenks, R., 163
Joe Camel, 7, 183–84
juries
  motivation for large awards, 11, 218
  possible influence of resolution of suits, 41
  questionable ability to make fair awards, 10, 11

Kansas, 54
Kenkel, D., 188
Kennedy, Ted, 27, 60
Kent cigarettes, 197
Kentucky
  extent of public no-smoking policies, 231n1
  share of settlement funds, 49
Kessler, David, 13, 30
Koop, C. Everett, 30
Kysar, D. A., 166

Laminack, John, 4
lead paint, 8, 58, 219
life expectancy effects in cost estimates
  consideration of, 67–68
  financial costs to states, 82–83, 83f, 230n7

public perceptions of smoking's risks, 121
  risk beliefs, 160–62, 235nn45, 46
litigation vs. taxes
  advantage of a tax over legal action, 34–35
  consumer responsibility for externalities, 34
  industry motivation for a settlement, 36
  penalty approach, 37
  political motivations for litigation, 35
  tax structure, impact on consumers, 36, 226n1
Liu, J., 156
Logue, K., 161, 166
Lorillard Tobacco Company, 39, 39f, 40
Los Angeles, California, 57–58
Lott, Trent, 27
Louisiana, 54
low-tar cigarettes. *See* tar levels
lung cancer risks from ETS, EPA studies
  court critique of analysis, 108–9
  neglected risk aspects, 109–10, 232n10
  vs. OSHA assessments, 110, 232n13
  statistical significance of studies, 105, 107, 231n6
  study results, 105–8, 106t
  understatement of current ETS protections, 110
lung cancer risks from ETS, estimates by dollar value
  inside-the-home risk estimates, 114, 114t
  outside-the-home risk estimates, 113, 113t

Magat, Wesley, 163
mainstream smoke, 131
Manning, W. G., 72, 74
market economy
  consumers' smoking choices and, 1–2
  recognition of consumer choice, 213
  stock market's reaction to litigation awards, 9–10, 224n16
marketing of cigarettes. *See* advertising of cigarettes
Marlboro cigarettes, 183, 184, 198, 201, 203t, 206
Maryland, 80

Massachusetts, 53, 204
Master Settlement Agreement, 7, 11
  advertising limitations, 38–39
  general provisions, 38
  individual state settlements, 37, 226n2
  litigation shielding for industry, 40–41
  magnitude of settlement, 44–45
  new entrant penalties, 40
  original participating manufacturers,
    40
  payment structure, 41–42, 43t, 44, 44t
  possible influence on juror attitudes, 41
  potential influence on case awards, 45
  See also state lawsuits settlement
Mathios, A., 188
McCain, John, 28, 29, 30, 35
Medicaid costs
  included in financial costs to states, 81
  original focus of suits, 58
  state and federal share of costs, 90
medical costs of smoking
  calculations for state settlements, 46–
    47t, 47–49
  gross costs to states, 18
  per pack costs to states, 90, 91t, 92
  smokers' life expectancy assumptions,
    82–83, 83f, 230n7
Merit cigarettes, 85
Merrill, Richard, 20
Michigan, 57
Minnesota
  allegations of industry wrongful be-
    havior, 83–84
  attorneys' payoffs, 54
  state settlement, 37, 226n2
Mississippi
  attorneys' payoffs, 51, 53
  cost calculations, 90
  reaction to negative cost estimates, 87
  state settlement, 37, 226n2
Missouri, 58
Mitchell, George, 60
Monitoring the Future, 186, 190
Moore, Mike, 17, 35, 53–54, 58, 114, 121
Morales, Dan, 54
Murr, Marc, 54

National Bureau of Economic Research,
  60, 77

Ness, Motley, Loadholt, Richardson, and
  Poole, 52, 53, 54
The Netherlands, 76
Newport cigarettes, 184
New York
  net financial gain from cigarettes, 98
  taxes in health-care reform bill, 61
nicotine
  argument over regulation as a drug, 20
  included in rating system, 206–7
  levels in cigarettes, 167
  response to nicotine-free brands, 207–8
Norma R. Broin et al. v. Philip Morris, Inc., et
  al., 233n34
North Carolina, 49
North Dakota, 58

Occupational Safety and Health Act
  (1970), 139
Occupational Safety and Health Administration. See OSHA proposal for regulation of ETS
O'Connor, Sandra Day, 20
Ohio Ironworkers Union, 226n5
Oklahoma, 57
on-product warnings, 2. See also warnings
  on cigarette labels
optimism bias, 162, 163–64, 186–87
O'Quinn, John, 4
Oregon, 57
OSHA proposal for regulation of ETS
  claim of net cost savings, 129
  level of risk claimed, 123
  market bargains for externalities, 124
  range of cost estimates, 128
  risk assessment of ETS, 103, 104
  risk level implications for smoking
    bans, 123
  stated justification for, 122

paternalism, 2–3, 223n2
payment structure of state settlement
  for education outlays, 42
  for enforcement efforts, 42
  payment schedule, 42, 43t, 44, 44t
  price per pack tax equivalent, 41
personal injury litigation, 3
Philip Morris
  advertising bans, 179

advertising restrictions, consequences of, 38

financial impact study, 76

lost litigation, 9, 224n22

market share, 39, 39f

participation in proposed settlement, 40

racketeering accusation by government, 85

stock performance, 36

Piuze, Michael, 10

plaintiffs' attorneys

annual payout cap, 51

compensation reform need, 220

contingency fee basis, 49–50

disproportionalities in fees awarded, 51

fee award in flight attendants' ETS damage case, 133–34

fee proposal in federal settlement, 23, 25

fees from state settlement, 4, 9, 17

lead class action attorneys, 4–5

legal teams' multiple payoffs, 54

padding of legal efforts, 51–52

payoffs vs. lawyers' efforts, 52–53

"reasonable time and fee" agreement, 50

risk premium vs. prospects of success, 52

separation from state settlements, 50–51

speculations about backroom dealings, 53–54

Players Brands, 239n13

Premier cigarettes, 195, 208–10, 211–12, 241n44

press coverage, 77–78

product liability litigation, 3

proposed federal settlement

advertising bans, 23, 25

attorney fee considerations, 29

Congressional changes, 27, 28

demise of, 30

disregard for standard regulatory practices, 7

factors contributing to failure, 31–32

immunity provisions, elimination of, 28, 29

industry liability restrictions, 25

industry rejection of congressional proposals, 28–29

lack of active White House support, 26, 27–28, 32

litigation used to impose taxes, 7–8

new set of rotating warnings, 21–22

parties involved, 17

plaintiffs' attorneys' fees, 9

policies for lower-risk cigarettes, 23

political stakes, 19–20

product liability criteria applied, 16

Proposed Resolution, 15, 17

regulating cigarettes as a drug, 20–21

sales volume linkage, 18

state claims of economic loss, 16

states' use of money received, 8–9

tax shift to smokers, 18–19, 225n7

timing of payments, 17–18, 19

tobacco sales restrictions, 23

underage smoking emphasis, 29–30

underage smoking reduction measures, 23, 24

warning label shortcomings, 22–23

See also state lawsuits settlement

Proposition 65, California, 129

Proposition 99, California, 130, 190

Pryor, William, 48

public perceptions of smoking's risks. See risk beliefs

Qualifying Statutes, 40

Radon Research Act, 108

Raleigh, Sir Walter, 223n1

RAND Corporation, 72

rating system proposal

additives controversy, 204–6

comparative risk ratings use, 201–2, 202t, 203t

informational strategy, components of, 203

label information, 204–5

proposal overview, 195

tar and nicotine significance, 206–7

rational addiction concept, 168

regressivity of cigarette taxes, 64

regulatory policies

established process for creating, 8

forms of, 12

regulatory policies (*continued*)
  need for consumer welfare focus, 13–14
Rhode Island, 219
Ricci, Linda, 30
Rice, Joseph F., 5
Richard Boeken v. Philip Morris, International House of Pancakes, 223n3, 224n19
Riordan, Richard, 58
risk beliefs
  about addiction (*see* addiction risk perceptions)
  disparity between believed and actual risks, 119–21
  dissemination of information on risks, 139–40
  estimated life expectancy loss due to smoking, 121
  example from Spain, 119–20
  extent of public belief in harmful effects, 142
  extent of public knowledge of risk, 140–41, 234n13
  Gallup poll responses, 162–63, 236n48
  misconceptions of mortality probabilities, 120
  optimism bias, 162, 163–64
  poll data changes over time, 142–43, 143f
  public awareness in polls, 143
  quantitative risk perception values for life expectancy, 160–62, 235nn45, 46
  rebuttal to criticisms of studies, 157–58
  rise in awareness of risks, 132
  role of cigarette advertising, 141–42
  Slovic's lung cancer risk survey design, 159–60
  state of current knowledge, 174–75
  survey use (*see* smoking risk beliefs surveys)
  warnings on labels (*see* warnings on cigarette labels). *See also* risks of smoking
riskless rates, 70
risks of smoking
  continuance of smoking despite information, 86
  cost estimates, accuracy of, 6

education on smoking, 131–32
heart disease and (*see* heart disease risks from ETS)
low-birthweight babies, 72, 229n17
lung cancer and (*see* lung cancer risks from ETS)
mainstream vs. sidestream smoke, 131
public policy and, 6–7
secondhand smoke and, 6
smokers' knowledge of, 1, 6, 10, 223n1, 228n54
tar levels, 65
warning signs, required in California, 130
See also addiction risk perceptions; risk beliefs
R. J. Reynolds Tobacco Company
  lack of advertising bans, 179
  market share, 39, 39f
  participation in proposed settlement, 40
  Premier cigarettes, 208
  racketeering accusation by government, 85
Rodham, Hugh, 17

safer cigarettes, promotion of
  goal of informed consumer risk taking, 195–96
  government's allegations of safety suppression by industry, 214
  government's current approach, 214
  government's role in establishing guidelines, 212, 241n55
  industry efforts (*see* tobacco industry's safer cigarettes efforts)
  need for support for technological advancement, 195
  need to study hazard warning design, 212–13
  product alteration precedents, 194
  rating system (*see* rating system proposal)
  recognition of consumer choice, 213
  regulation through information (*see* information, regulation of about cigarettes)
  smokers' behavior response to information about health hazards, 200

Safer Smokes, 208
Schoenbaum, M., 161, 235n46
Schwartz, A., 224n14
Scruggs, Richard (Dickie), 5, 53–54, 219, 224n11
seat belt use, 22, 169–70
secondhand smoke
    cost estimates, 117–18, 118t
    risks of smoking and, 6
settlements. *See* proposed federal settlement; state lawsuits settlement
Shoven, J. B., 72
sidestream smoke, 131
sin taxes, 61
Slovic, Paul
    lung cancer risk survey design, 159–60, 235n43
    risk perception studies criticized, 157–59
    survey design influences on responses, 165
smokers
    addiction beliefs (*see* addiction risk perceptions)
    demographic and risk characteristics, 61, 70–71
    percent of American adults, 63
    risk beliefs about smoking (*see* risk beliefs)
    true risk of smoking (*see* risks of smoking)
    See also youth smoking
smoking bans' economic effects
    lost consumers' surplus, 125, 126t
    lost producers' surplus, 125, 126t, 128
    lost tax revenue, 127t, 128
    OSHA claim of net cost savings, 129
    OSHA's range of cost estimates, 128
smoking cessation clinics, 173–74
smoking externalities, 34, 95, 96–97t, 97, 124
smoking prevention programs, 187
smoking risk beliefs survey, critique of
    importance of baseline life expectancy values, 162
    quantitative risk perception value for life expectancy, 160–62, 235nn45, 46
    Slovic's lung cancer risk survey design, 159–60

smoking risk beliefs surveys
    classes of risk and surveys analyzed, 144
    controls, use of, 148–49, 235n6
    critique of other survey approaches (*see* smoking risk beliefs survey, critique of)
    data used, 143–44
    design's influence on responses, 164–66, 236n55
    groups who have heard about risks, 150, 152, 153t, 154
    indications of universal understanding of risks, 149, 149t
    methodology, 145, 235n25
    perceived risks vs. scientific estimates, 155–57, 156–57f
    probabilistic terms, use of, 145–46
    rebuttal to criticisms of studies, 157–58
    respondents' estimates of life expectancy loss, 147–48t, 154–55, 155t, 235n39
    respondents' overestimation of risks, 149–50
    responses relating risk perception, 146, 147–48t, 235n33
    risk perceptions by education level, 150, 151–52t
social costs of smoking. *See* financial costs to society
Social Security in cost estimates of cigarettes, 92–93
Spain
    perceived risk of lung cancer from smoking, 156
    public perceptions of ETS risks, 119–21
state lawsuits settlement
    attorneys' payoffs (*see* plaintiffs' attorneys)
    contradictory treatment of tar marketing, 69
    financial costs to states (*see* financial costs to states)
    influence on other litigation, 219
    judicial process issues, 59
    legal questions, 58
    litigation consequences for industry, 217–18
    litigation vs. taxes, 34–37, 226n1

state lawsuits settlement (*continued*)
    overview, 215–16
    political motivations for litigation, 35, 45
    resolution of suits (*see* Master Settle-
        ment Agreement)
    states' allocation plans, 55–57
    states' shares of funds, 45, 46–47t, 47–49
    See also proposed federal settlement
State v. Philip Morris, Inc., 225n4
Steenland, K., 115, 232n17
Stewart, William H., 140–41
Stockwell, H. G., 106
Sundberg, J. O., 72
Sunstein, Cass, 20
*Superior Court of the State of Washington for
    King County v. American Tobacco Co.,
    Inc. et al.,* 236n47
Supreme Court, U.S., 122
surgeon general
    opposition to safer cigarette policies,
        198
    smoking risk beliefs survey, 148–49,
        235n6
surveys. *See* smoking risk beliefs surveys

Taiwan, 156
tar levels
    behavioral response to low-tar ciga-
        rettes, 66–67
    cigarette consumption adjusted for,
        196–97, 197f, 238–39n6
    cost impact of adjustments in, 74–75
    definition by FTC, 65
    differences between brands, 201, 202t,
        203t
    in ETS risk assessment analysis, 112,
        112t, 232n14
    in generic brands, 198, 239n13
    low-tar cigarettes, marketing and rack-
        eteering accusations, 85–86
    in rating system, 206–7
    safety assumptions about reduction in
        tar, 23, 65
    testing of cigarettes, 202, 239–40n22
taxes. *See* cigarette taxes
teen smokers. *See* youth smoking
Texas
    attorneys' payoffs, 51, 52
    state settlement, 37, 226n2

tobacco industry
    allegations of wrongful behavior, 84
    competitive advertising on safety of
        cigarettes, 141
    depiction as evil, 4
    liability restrictions in proposed settle-
        ment, 25
    litigation consequences, 217–18
    litigation successes, pre-1990s, 3
    market shares, 39, 39f
    motivation for a settlement, 99
    racketeering accusations regarding
        low-tar cigarettes, 85–86
    safer cigarettes, promotion of (*see* to-
        bacco industry's safer cigarettes ef-
        forts)
    settlement deal with states, 4, 223n4
    settlement payment structure, 41–42,
        43t, 44, 44t
    trust fund payments, 11, 224n22
tobacco industry's safer cigarettes efforts
    antismoking groups' response to nico-
        tine-free brands, 207–8
    independent assessment of Premier,
        211–12
    low-nitrosamine leaves, 211, 241n50
    nonburning cigarettes, 208–10, 241n44
    puff-activated lighter, 210
Tobacco Institute, 38, 226n3
tobacco tax. *See* cigarette taxes
True cigarettes, 85
TRUTH Campaign, 189

underage smoking. *See* youth smoking
Urban II, Pope, 223n1
U.S.A. v. Philip Morris et al., 230nn1, 9

Vantage cigarettes, 85
Virginia
    net financial gain from cigarettes, 98
    share of settlement funds, 49

warnings on cigarette labels
    changes in wording, 137, 138t
    impetus for other product warnings,
        139, 234n7
    industry liability and, 226n10
    key issues for warnings efforts, 136–37
    needed objective of, 137

non-cigarette acute hazards warnings, 137–38, 234n4
in proposed federal settlement, 21–22
shortcomings, 22–23
signs requirement in California, 130
Washington state, 48–49
water risks. *See* chlorinated water risks
West Virginia, 58
Whitely, Leslie, 226n10
William Barnes et al. v. The American To-
bacco Company, Inc, et al., 223n10
Williams, Jesse, 10, 11
Williams, Stephen, 80
Winston cigarettes, 204, 205–6

youth smoking
alternative cigarette products, consideration of, 193
cigarette sources as reported by youths, 182–83
Joe Camel ads' impact on, 184–85
Joe Camel's rise and fall, 183–84
legal smoking age per state, 179, 180t

number of cigarettes sold to youths, 188–89
optimistic bias analysis, 186–87
parental influence, importance of, 187, 192
penalties for selling to, 23
policy proposal components, 191–93
restrictions' effectiveness, 181
restrictions on advertising to youths, 179–80
smoking prevention programs, effectiveness of, 187
state antismoking campaigns' impact, 189–90, 191
tax effects on, 24
teens' awareness of smoking's risks, 185–86
teens' disapproval of smoking, 190–91
teens' price sensitivity, 19, 188, 238n23
trends in, 176–78, 178t

Zhu, C. W., 114, 121
Zimmerman, D., 72